LATIN AMERICA'S ECONOMY

LATIN AMERICA'S ECONOMY:
DIVERSITY, TRENDS, AND CONFLICTS

Eliana Cardoso
Ann Helwege

The MIT Press
Cambridge, Massachusetts
London, England

This book was set in Trump Mediæval by The MIT Press and was printed and bound in the United States of America.

Library of Congress Cataloging-in-Publication Data

Cardoso, Eliana A.
    Latin America's economy: diversity, trends, and conflicts / Eliana Cardoso and Ann Helwege.
        P.   cm.
    Includes bibliographical references and index.
    ISBN 0-262-03186-8
    1. Latin America—Economic conditions.   I. Helwege, Ann.
    II. Title.
    HC125.C337   1992
    330.98—dc20   91-24787
                                                              CIP

To Gabriela, Olivia, and Simon

CONTENTS

DETAILED CONTENTS

FIGURES

TABLES

ACKNOWLEDGMENTS

We thank the many scholars who send us recent research on Latin America. This generous flow of information keeps us up-to-date and aware of new work in the field.

We also appreciate the encouragement of our colleagues and friends in Latin America, in Cambridge, Mass., at Tufts University, and at other universities in the United States. To those who have straightened our misconceptions, edited drafts, and taken on extra work to free our time, we extend our deepest thanks.

To our parents, husbands, and kids, we owe the laughter that has made this project fun to complete.

LATIN AMERICA'S ECONOMY

Chapter 1

THE ECONOMIC LANDSCAPE

The goal of this book is to lay out the major issues that confront Latin American countries. We focus on broad patterns of development. Like an intricate *huipil* woven by the Mayans, the most interesting elements of Latin America's development lie in its details, the combination of specific problems facing individual countries. We hope this overview inspires a closer look at the region.

1 DIVERSITY

A popular poster in the United States presents a New Yorker's map of the world: Fifth Avenue and Broadway loom large against the Hudson, while the 3000 miles that lie between it and the West Coast are lilliputian. It is easy to imagine a gringo's comparable map of Latin America: Mexico bulges forth and Colombia is sketched in as a supplier of cocaine, but Chile's 2000-mile coastline ranks no more space than the beach at Cancun. After eight years of U.S. funding of a war in Nicaragua, most Americans still could not locate it. And President Ronald Reagan, when visiting Brazil in 1982, toasted the Bolivians.

The map in figure 1.1 is worth studying before embarking on a discussion of monetary policy or trade protectionism in specific countries. Latin America's land area is more than twice the size of the United States, including Alaska. The region holds 430 million people in twenty countries, with populations ranging from 2.4 million (Panama) to 147 million (Brazil). Diversity partly reflects the region's sheer size. In Chichicastenango, Guatemala, the local people wear handloomed clothing bearing the traditional pattern of

Figure 1.1
Latin America

their home town. Women work backstrap looms between tending fields and cooking meals. In Buenos Aires, Argentina, women race between supermarkets, nursery schools, their offices, and their psychoanalysts. Half of the population of Guatemala cannot read and write; Argentina's illiteracy is less than 5 percent. Both countries face debt crises, inflation, and unemployment, yet the differences in their economic bases are so profound as to make a mockery of efforts to address their problems in the same breath.

Table 1.1 presents basic data on population, land area, and country share in Latin America's output. Brazil, Mexico, and Argentina account for more than two-thirds of regional output. As a result, regional averages reflect events in these three countries rather than what is happening in most others. In fact, events in Brazil alone strongly color the images portrayed by averages unfit to capture Latin America's diversity.

Ethnic composition plays a key role in explaining contrasts within the region. Bolivia, Ecuador, Peru, and Guatemala have very large indigenous populations that have never been incorporated into social structures dominated by people of European descent. Poverty is concentrated among these people, especially among those in the countryside. Blacks, who account for nearly half of the population in Brazil and more than a quarter of that in Colombia, also fall in the bottom deciles of the income distribution. Relative equality in Argentina, Uruguay, and Costa Rica is attributable as much to a lack of racial division as to laudable policies.

Nature has unevenly endowed the region. In a poor, densely populated country like El Salvador, the challenge is to pacify a struggle caused by too many people fighting over too little land. In contrast, the local joke in Argentina, where fertilizer use is among the lowest in the world, is that "Argentines undo during the day what God fixes at night."

The Andes begin in Colombia and run the entire western coast of South America. Within the narrow boundaries of Ecuador and Peru lie three different climatic conditions: hot coastal lowlands appropriate for growing sugar and bananas; the cold sierra where potatoes and other indigenous crops are virtually suspended from the mountainsides; and a portion of the Amazon jungle, where landless migrants flow to squeeze one or two years of fertility from the land using slash-and-burn agriculture. Mexico shares similar

Table 1.1
Population, land area, and share in regional GDP, Latin American
countries, 1989

	Population 1989 (millions)	Land area (thousands of sq. kilometers)	Share of regional GDP[a] 1980–1989 (percent)
Argentina	31.9	2,767	11.9
Bolivia	7.1	1,099	0.7
Brazil	147.4	8,512	38.7
Chile	13.0	757	3.4
Colombia	31.2	1,139	4.9
Costa Rica	2.9	51	0.5
Cuba	10.0	111	
Dominican Republic	7.0	49	0.6
Ecuador	10.3	248	1.5
El Salvador	5.1	21	0.7
Guatemala	8.9	109	0.9
Haiti	6.4	28	0.3
Honduras	5.0	112	0.5
Mexico	86.7	1,958	21.0
Nicaragua	3.7	130	0.4
Panama	2.4	77	0.6
Paraguay	4.2	407	0.7
Peru	21.8	1,285	4.1
Uruguay	3.1	177	1.1
Venezuela	19.2	912	7.4
Latin America	427.3	19,949	100.0

a. Regional GDP excluding Cuba.
Sources: Inter-American Development Bank, *Economic and Social Progress in Latin America*, (Washington, D.C.: Inter-American Development Bank 1990); World Bank, *World Development Report* (Washington, D.C.: World Bank, 1990).

extremes. Climatic diversity has not proved a particularly good hedge against climatic shock and market trends. Instead, too little of the land is easily cultivated to support growing populations.

Minerals are unevenly distributed and account for an assortment of export profiles. Chile is the region's leading nonfuel mineral producer (copper), followed by Peru (copper), Brazil (bauxite and iron), and Mexico (copper, lead, zinc, and silver). Venezuela and Mexico alone account for 85 percent of the region's known oil reserves. Oil shocks of the past two decades have been a boon for them, but they nonetheless fell into the same debt trap that snared oil import-dependent Brazil.

In short, a vast range of cultural and physical differences distinguish the countries that lie between Tijuana and Punta Arenas. What holds these disparate countries together in the concept of Latin America? History has bound these nations together in important ways. The twenty countries of Latin America are traditionally united by language, religion, culture, bureaucratic outlook, and timing of postindependence experience based on nineteenth-century liberalism. Most Latin Americans speak Spanish, except Brazilians, who speak Portuguese, and Haitians, who speak French, but there are also some 800 local languages. Haiti is included among Latin American countries not because of its Latin-based French language but because of its interaction with the Dominican Republic, which it ruled between 1822 and 1844. Former non-Spanish colonies of the Caribbean and South America are excluded because they have had little interaction in the events of Latin America. Puerto Rico is excluded because it has never been independent, belonging to Spain until 1898 and then to the United States.

Colonization by the Spanish and Portuguese left a common cultural and economic legacy. Cycles of commodity booms and busts skewed development, while mercantilist policies thwarted economic diversification.[1] Spain and Portugal were slow to industrialize, and Latin America remained on the periphery as the Industrial Revolution took off. When independence came in the nineteenth century, Latin American countries had neither a strong industrial base nor secure markets for their primary product exports. In contrast, the United States, which was colonized a century later, benefited from its early ties with England's dynamic industrial market and emerged in the nineteenth century as an industrial powerhouse in its own right.

In the twentieth century, Latin American countries have pursued similar economic policies. Import substituting industrialization policies were adopted in the 1930s in an effort to break dependence on primary exports. Although the limitations of this strategy were apparent by the late 1950s, the trade barriers associated with this strategy still have not been completely dismantled. In the meantime, nearly every country in the region borrowed beyond its capacity to pay and declared itself broke in the debt crisis of the 1980s. Even Colombia, which managed its money conservatively, suffered from guilt by association: once bankers defined Latin America as a bad risk, Colombia could borrow no more easily than its neighbors.

Basic Indicators

Table 1.2 shows average incomes, infant mortality, and literacy rates for Latin American countries. Precise comparisons of these and other indicators should be avoided because definitions, exchange rate conversions, and the completeness of surveys vary across countries. Still, average income per capita varies among the market economies by roughly a factor of six. The infant mortality rate in Chile is just double that of the United States, but a Bolivian baby is ten times as likely as an American to die within its first year. Skewed income distribution leads to vastly different life-styles—not only within the region but also within countries. The wealthy neighborhoods of Quito, Ecuador, sport Mercedes and satellite dishes, while rural women in the same country walk hours to collect water.

Underlying the differences among Latin American countries are important variations in economic structure. More than 40 percent of the labor force works in agriculture in Bolivia, Guatemala, Honduras, Nicaragua, and Paraguay. In the near term, programs for economic development in these countries must focus on issues of agricultural modernization, land reform, and delivery of social services to the rural poor. In the highly urbanized economies—Argentina, Uruguay, Chile, Venezuela, and Mexico—teenagers who

Table 1.2
Basic economic and social indicators, Latin American countries, 1989

	GDP per capita (dollars)[a]	Urban population (percentage of total population)	Infant mortality (per thousand live births)	Adult illiteracy (percentage)
Argentina	2,700	81	32	4.5
Bolivia	760	51	110	25.8
Brazil	2,300	74	63	22.3
Chile	2,500	84	20	5.6
Colombia	1,400	72	46	11.9
Costa Rica	1,700	51	18	6.4
Cuba	n.a.	74	12	4[b]
Dominican Republic	800	62	65	22.7
Ecuador	1,300	56	63	17.6
El Salvador	1,000	49	59	27.9
Guatemala	900	35	59	45.0
Haiti	300	27	117	62.4
Honduras	900	43	69	40.5
Mexico	2,000	71	47	9.7
Nicaragua	700	60	62	13.0
Panama	1,900	51	23	11.8
Paraguay	1,500	41	42	11.8
Peru	1,300	70	88	13.0
Uruguay	2,900	89	27	4.6
Venezuela	3,000	79	36	13.1

a. Preliminary.
b. 1985.
Sources: Inter-American Development Bank, *Economic and Social Progress in Latin America*; World Bank, *World Development Report 1990*; United Nations, *Human Development Report 1990* (New York: United Nations, 1991).

swallow flaming swords drenched in gasoline for tips make plain the need for more industrial jobs. Policymakers in these settings face distinctly different challenges and vastly different sets of resources.

2   REGIONAL TRENDS

Latin America's population multiplied from 150 million in 1950 to 430 million people in 1990. Real gross domestic product (GDP) per capita more than doubled between 1950 and 1980, as a result of an expanding world economy, strong demand for primary products, and industrialization.[2] During the three decades following World War II, the growth rate of employment exceeded that of the working-age population in most countries. Growth was characterized by a marked transformation of the production structure. As many Latin American countries diversified their exports, the proportion of manufactured intermediate and final goods in exports increased. Latin America evolved from a rural to a predominantly urban society, experiencing dramatic changes in occupational and social mobility. The urban population increased from 50 percent in 1950 to 66 percent in 1980. The face of Latin America changed with shifting demographic patterns and rising GDP. The number of television sets per thousand population increased from 14 in 1960 to 106 in 1980. Private cars invaded the streets. In Brazil, for instance, the number of private cars per thousand increased from fewer than 8 in 1960 to more than 50 in 1980. Cities grew immensely (table 1.3).

After the first oil shock in 1973, the world economy slowed, but Latin America kept growing, tapping a massive supply of foreign capital at negative real interest rates. Social spending and investments in sanitation, water, health, and education brought substantial progress in terms of life expectancy, literacy, and infant mortality. Infant mortality dropped from 107 deaths per thousand in 1960 to 69 in 1980, a decline of 36 percent. In human terms, this represents a major gain for parents—mostly poor—who would have watched their children die.

Prospects for accelerating this progress dimmed with the second oil shock in 1979. During the following years, real interest rates increased dramatically as industrialized countries began a major effort to stop inflation. Demand for Latin American exports plunged. Starting in 1982, the supply of foreign capital dried up, and Latin

Table 1.3
Population in major cities, Latin America, 1985-1990 (millions)

	Population	
Major cities	1985	1990[a]
Mexico City (Mexico)	16.65	19.37
São Paulo (Brazil)	15.54	18.42
Buenos Aires (Argentina)	10.76	11.58
Rio de Janeiro (Brazil)	10.14	11.12
Lima (Peru)	5.44	6.50
Bogotá (Colombia)	4.74	5.59
Santiago (Chile)	4.23	4.70
Caracas (Venezuela)	3.51	3.96

a. Projected.
Source: United Nations, *Prospects of World Urbanization* (New York: United Nations, 1989).

America began to transfer approximately 4 percent of its GDP abroad. Interest payments on the debt became an enormous drain on export earnings and savings. Income and investment declined, inflation accelerated, and real wages fell. By 1989, per capita GDP had fallen below its 1980 level in all Latin American countries except Brazil, Chile, Colombia, and the Dominican Republic.

The 1980s stands in sharp contrast to the preceding three decades (table 1.4). Latin America's setback in this decade compares dismally with the surging performance of the Asian countries. Led by the four newly industrializing countries (NICs) of South Korea, Hong Kong, Singapore, and Taiwan but extending to many others, Asia sprinted ahead in the 1980s at an average annual per capita growth in excess of 5 percent. This difference is widely interpreted as proving the errors of the import substitution strategy favored by Latin America during much of the postwar period. That strategy relied on two pillars: industrialization through governmental intervention and barriers to trade.

Critics of this strategy contend that statist economic policy attitudes have persisted in Latin America since the 1930s and that the liberal international order created by Organization for Economic Cooperation and Development (OECD) member countries has influenced policy in Asia but left Latin America virtually untouched

Table 1.4
Per capita gross domestic output and growth rates, Latin American
countries, 1950–1989

	GDP per capita (1975 dollars)		Growth rate of GDP per capita (percentage per year)	
	1950	1980	1950–1980	1981–1989[a]
Brazil	637	2,152	4.2	0.0
Mexico	1,055	2,547	3.0	-1.0
Argentina	1,877	3,209	1.8	-2.6
Colombia	949	1,882	2.3	1.5
Venezuela	1,811	3,310	1.5	-2.8
Peru	953	1,746	2.1	-2.7
Chile	1,416	2,372	1.8	1.1
Uruguay	2,184	3,269	1.4	-0.8
Ecuador	638	1,556	3.1	-0.1
Guatemala	842	1,422	1.8	-2.0
Dominican Republic	719	1,564	2.6	0.2
Bolivia	762	1,114	1.3	-2.9
El Salvador	612	899	1.3	-1.9
Paraguay	885	1,753	2.4	0.0
Costa Rica	819	2,170	3.3	-0.7
Panama	928	2,157	2.9	-1.9
Nicaragua	683	1,324	2.3	-3.7
Honduras	680	1,031	1.4	-1.3
Haiti	363[b]	439	0.7	-2.1
Latin America[c]			2.7	-0.8

Note: Countries ordered by average share in regional GDP between 1950 and 1985.
a. Preliminary.
b. 1960.
c. Latin America except Cuba.
Sources: Robert Summers and Alan Heston, "Improved International Comparisons of
Real Product and Its Composition: 1950–1980," *Review of Income and Wealth* 30
(June 1984): 207–262; and ECLAC, *Preliminary Overview of the Latin American
Economy* (New York: United Nations, 1989).

until recently. Many current distortions are policy induced, and thus, far from inevitable, they are created by irrational *dirigisme*.

No doubt, in small countries, import substitution policies (based on quantitative restrictions, differentiated tariffs, and a lack of commitment to competitive exchange rates) have led to disaster. Even large countries have suffered from extended overvaluation.[3] Nonetheless, the criticism of import substitution policies fails to consider that, during the 1950s, most Latin American countries moved toward an import substitution strategy because it seemed to fit their needs. After the Great Depression of the 1930s and the disruption of World War II, the international economy did not appear to be a propitious engine of growth.

Import substitution industrialization (ISI) played a successful role in fomenting Latin America's high growth rates prior to the 1980s, but it erred by downplaying the market role. Protection led to overvalued exchange rates and, hence, to an eventual reduction in the export growth. Import substitution policies exaggerated industrial growth at the expense of agriculture. Moreover, relatively capital-intensive manufactures absorbed only a fraction of the increment in the labor force, placing pressure on government to serve as an employer of last resort. Finally, as the resources taxed away from primary exports failed to increase, subsidies to industrial investment and growing government responsibilities put new pressures on the budget. Monetization of the deficit led to persistent inflation.

The precariousness of the Latin American economies became fully apparent only in the early 1980s. In retrospect, countries of the region badly chose their adjustment style after 1973. They did not just blindly follow the original import substitution bias of the 1950s. Problems increased with their asymmetric opening to the world economy as they borrowed heavily but limited trade penetration. And new fiscal distortions reduced the room to maneuver. Growth in the late 1970s depended on bloated government deficits, which could no longer be easily financed in the 1980s.

Part of Latin America's misery in the 1980s originated in unfavorable external conditions, including the suspension of private loans and worsening terms of trade. Although these factors were important, they do not provide a complete picture of what went wrong. Many of the problems derived from domestic mistakes. Since

1982, Latin American countries have faced the choice between adjustment or accommodation, as debt repayment forced a massive reversal of resource transfers to the north. Chile and Mexico chose adjustment, suffered a deep recession, and reformed their economies. After 1984, Chile recovered fast as a result of a moderation of its laissez-faire strategy, an aggressively depreciating real exchange rate, and the revival of both public and private investment. Mexico's recovery is still in process.

Argentina and Brazil chose accommodation. By 1990, Argentina and Brazil's lack of adjustment had resulted in both inflation and recession. Financial instability has hurt investment and the prospects for future growth, especially in Argentina. The rapid acceleration of inflation in Argentina and Brazil to annual levels over 1,000 percent in the late 1980s cannot be directly attributed to the debt crisis. At different points in time, their governments have run moratoriums on external debt service and have allowed the real exchange rate to appreciate. In both countries, the acceleration of inflation resulted from the lack of domestic adjustment and the consequent flight from money. The extreme financial instability in Brazil and Argentina at the end of the 1980s offers a sharp contrast with the recently mastered stability in Chile and Mexico.

Chile's poor economic performance during the 1950s and 1960s derived in good measure from the combination of growing protection and state intervention as a development strategy. As prices lost their role as a guide to investment, fiscal and credit subsidies increased, and with them, distortions and inefficiencies multiplied. At the same time, budget deficits, inflation, and payments crises perennially appeared. Inward-looking growth led to overdiversification of production for a small domestic market and concentration of exports in a few primary activities like copper. After gross errors in the direction of excessive liberalization and political repression, reforms have finally overcome past mistakes and the megainflation of the mid-1970s. Since about 1985, a pragmatic exchange rate policy, more moderate interest rates, and selective government intervention have supported a recovery driven by export growth and the revival of foreign investment. The transition to democracy without capital flight indicates that Chile might finally be on a stable development path.

The same cannot yet be said of Mexico. In the aftermath of major economic reforms in the 1980s, Mexico still seems far from Chile's success. Between 1983 and 1990, remarkable reforms took place on the fiscal and trade fronts. Yet despite all these reforms and five years of falling income per capita, the orthodox program did not succeed in stopping inflation. A new program introduced in 1988, the *Pacto Social*, used a fixed exchange rate supported by price controls and a wage freeze to halt inflation. As a result of the *Pacto*, monthly inflation rates dropped from an average of about 15 percent in January 1988 to only 1 percent for the second half of the year. Of additional help was Mexico's 1989 agreement with commercial bank creditors on a multiyear financing package and two alternative debt-exchange options. Capital, having flown abroad for years, began to return to Mexico. The picture is not perfect yet. Although expectations have improved, fed by modernization and by the prospect of free trade with the United States, investment has not increased sufficiently to generate sustainable growth.

3 FIVE ISSUES

The challenge of development is a complex tangle of interrelated problems. Five issues stand out: stalled industrialization, balance of payments crises, inflation, poverty, and inequality.

Stalled Industrialization and Trade Policy

Only Paraguay among all Latin American countries relies on agriculture to produce more than a quarter of GDP. By comparison, agriculture accounts for more than a third of GDP in nearly all African countries. For Latin America as a whole, agriculture contributes only 10 percent of GDP, while industry accounts for 37 percent (table 1.5).

Exchange rate policies, tariffs, quotas, and government subsidies have favored industry over agriculture. Yet most industry in Latin America is uncompetitive in world markets. Few countries have successfully broken the bonds of their dependency on primary exports. Mexico and Brazil manufacture roughly half of their exports. Elsewhere, progress has been limited; manufactured exports are predominantly processed primary goods, such as roasted coffee

Table 1.5
Composition of output, by sector of origin, Latin America and the
Caribbean, 1961–1989

	Percent of output, 1989	Growth rates for each sector		
		1961–1970	1971–1980	1981–1989
Agriculture	9.8	3.6	3.3	2.0
Industry	37.2	5.9	6.1	0.6
Mining	3.8			
Manufacturing	25.4			
Construction	5.9			
Electricity	2.1			
Services	48.0	5.5	6.2	1.4
Finance	13.9			
Commerce	15.5			
Transportation	6.2			
Government	5.4			
Other	7.0			
Residual[a]	5.0			
Total GDP	100.0	5.4	5.9	1.1

a. Differences between total GDP and output by sector of origin occur because nine
countries calculate the components of value added at factor costs, whereas GDP is
calculated at market prices.
Source: Inter-American Development Bank, *Economic and Social Progress in Latin
America.*

and spun cotton. Most countries in the region remain heavily
dependent on primary commodity exports (table 1.6). In some cases,
this represents a significant exposure to volatility in the price of one
commodity; Venezuela (oil), Bolivia (natural gas), and El Salvador
(coffee) have linked their fates to a single commodity. Elsewhere,
there has been considerable diversification within the primary
export sector. Chile, for example, has reduced its dependence on
copper exports from approximately three-quarters of all exports in

Table 1.6
Major export commodities, Latin American countries, 1985

	Commodity	Percentage of export earnings
Argentina	Wheat	13.5
	Corn	9.1
Bolivia	Natural gas	59.8
	Tin	29.9
Brazil	Coffee	9.2
	Soybeans and products	9.9
Chile	Copper	46.1
Colombia	Coffee	50.2
	Fuel oil	11.5
Costa Rica	Coffee	32.2
	Bananas	22.1
Dominican Republic	Sugar	25.9
	Ferronickel	16.4
	Dore	15.5
	Coffee and cocoa	16.6
Ecuador	Crude petroleum	62.8
	Bananas	7.6
El Salvador	Coffee	66.9
Guatemala	Coffee	42.5
	Cotton	6.8
Haiti	Coffee	26.0
	Bauxite	8.6
Honduras	Bananas	31.1
	Coffee	22.7
Mexico	Petroleum	66.6
Nicaragua	Cotton	34.1
	Coffee	30.4
Panama	Bananas	23.3
	Shrimp	17.8
Paraguay	Cotton	48.9
	Soybeans	33.2
Peru	Petroleum (crude and products)	21.8
	Copper	15.6
	Zinc	9.1
Uruguay	Wool	19.2
	Meat	13.8
Venezuela	Petroleum	84.3

Source: James Wilkie, ed., *Statistical Abstract of Latin America*, vol. 27 (Los Angeles: UCLA Latin American Center Publications, 1989).

the 1960s to less than half in the 1980s, mainly by expanding agricultural exports.

Whereas several Asian countries have taken off in the past two decades by vigorously exporting labor-intensive goods, this model has not yet found a home within Latin America. Chapter 4 discusses ISI strategies pursued between 1940 and 1980. Governments played an active role in establishing steel, auto, pharmaceutical, airline, and even computer industries in the region. The hope was that growth in these sectors would spill over into related industries by generating demand for inputs, improving skills, and establishing the infrastructure necessary for industrialization.

Instead, ISI policies created industrial sectors heavily dependent on imported inputs and exclusive access to domestic markets. Subsidized interest rates created a bias favoring capital-intensive methods. Monopolistic control over domestic markets and overvaluation limited incentives to become competitive in world markets. Protection of local industry led to poor quality and high prices. At the same time, policies intended to support industrialization penalized agricultural exporters.

Under neoconservative programs, which began in the 1970s, trade was liberalized, labor repressed, and money creation tightened. Recessions and political instability evolved as side effects of this bitter medicine. With the debt crisis of the 1980s, the role of the state as a major investor in industrialization has diminished sharply. Most governments are too bankrupt to maintain essential infrastructure, much less to finance construction of factories. High interest rates, negative growth, and financial uncertainty have also depressed private investment.

Despite trade liberalization, export growth slowed from 5.8 percent per year in the 1960s to 3.1 percent in the 1980s, a trend that opens the question of whether Latin America's natural resource base can support its growing population. With population set to double over the next forty years, can the land generate that much more output? Do seams of precious minerals lie beneath the ground, awaiting discovery? How fast can agriculture grow? In the past three decades, some of the gain in agricultural output came from an expansion of the area cultivated. The consequences are an environmental disaster. If deforestation is to slow down, better yields need to be achieved through commercialization. Yet rapid commercialization of agriculture may run counter to land reform efforts aimed at overcoming rural poverty. The fact that the Far East NICs achieved rapid growth through manufacturing is not lost on Latin Americans.

The task remains to identify a path of growth that provides opportunities for all Latin Americans. Development involves faster creation of industrial jobs. Latin America is now predominantly urban, and the limited capacity of the rural sector to generate more jobs is reflected in a continuing exodus to the cities. Latin Americans have not lost sight of the goal that lay behind thirty years of ISI: the establishment of industry that will provide workers with modern skills and offer them the opportunity to earn a decent living.

Debt Crises

Low interest rates and excess liquidity in world credit markets made borrowing easy in the 1970s. Governments ran huge deficits to finance projects that had little or no payoff in higher productivity. Overvalued exchange rates were sustainable because of the steady inflow of borrowed dollars; little progress was made toward export expansion. At the end of 1990, Latin America's external debt amounted to $425 billion. Servicing this debt required diverting as much as 40 percent of export earnings to foreign creditors. In a region that depends heavily on imported fertilizers, fuel, and industrial components, diversion of foreign exchange to service debt has brought about an economic collapse comparable to the Great Depression.

Did not Latin Americans foresee the difficulty of repaying these loans? Compared to an individual, countries typically have more leeway to rollover debt—or they did until 1982. A sudden run-up in international interest rates, the collapse of important Latin American export markets, and increasingly apparent fiscal irresponsibility led to a massive withdrawal of credit to Latin America. Governments could no longer finance their activities with foreign loans. In fact, they now needed to raise revenue both to finance current operations and to repay the debt. Once the credit crunch began, nearly everyone anticipated the resulting debacle; the wealthy quickly shifted their assets to Miami, exacerbating the crisis. (Debt crises, their solution, and new debt agreements are the subject of chapter 5.)

Inflation

Latin America has long had a reputation for galloping inflation, but until the 1980s this mainly derived from a small number of incidents in which inflation topped 100 percent. Argentina, Chile, Brazil, Bolivia, and Uruguay experienced high inflation in the 1950s and 1960s, while the remainder of the region had very low rates of inflation.

Today, 100 percent inflation per year is considered low in Latin America. Argentina, Bolivia, Brazil, Peru, and Nicaragua have experienced rates of inflation of more than 2,000 percent. This new breed of inflation runs faster, partly because the modern sector of the economy responds quickly to external shocks and policy errors by shifting assets abroad electronically. The poor are left behind in the dust.

Chapters 6 and 7 discuss inflation and stabilization. Attempts at stabilization fall into two broad categories: orthodoxy and heterodoxy. Orthodoxy assumes that inflation is caused by excessive money creation—which is itself the result of government deficits. The remedy is a sharp cut in government spending and credit creation, with higher interest rates and a tight lid on wages. Failures of orthodoxy in the region are ascribed by monetarists to the inability of governments to stick to the program and to make the required cuts.

Heterodoxy, popular in the mid-1980s, sought an alternative solution. Based on the premise that inflation is largely the result of self-fulfilling expectations, heterodoxy has used price controls to slow inflation's inertial momentum. Although heterodoxy calls for better trade policies and fiscal balance, it seeks to avoid a reduction in output, on the grounds that is in itself destabilizing. Heterodox programs in Peru, Argentina, and Brazil never succeeded in achieving fiscal discipline, and all failed. Only Mexico's more moderate application of heterodoxy's call for an incomes policy worked.

In their desperate search for inflation's cure, Latin American countries seem willing to try any new medicine that comes on the market. Old populism, the subject of chapter 8, reappears from time to time under new guises. Between 1985 and 1989 President Alan Garcia of Peru helped to create the chaos faced by President Alberto Fujimori, in 1990. Fujimori eliminated price controls, and inflation soared to 400 percent for the month of August while wages were tightly controlled. The result was a surge in demand at soup kitchens, which lacked food to fill the extra stomachs. Like many experimental medicines, stabilization programs have potent side effects.

Poverty and Inequality

Although all Latin American countries (except Haiti) now fall into the class of middle-income developing countries, the average Guatemalan had a per capita income in 1990 of just $2.50 per day. Given that the bottom 20 percent of the population receives just 5.5 percent of national income, it is hard to fathom how poor Guatemalans survive on an average of 70 cents a day. In fact, many do not. The infant mortality rates in table 1.1 attest to the poverty in Latin America.

Chapter 9 discusses poverty and income distribution. Hondurans, Guatemalans, and Peruvians must deal with the fact that a third or more of their countrymen cannot afford even a minimally adequate diet, much less pay for shelter and other needs. This extreme destitution is less common in the countries with higher per capita income. Very few Uruguayans and Argentines suffer poverty at this level. Nonetheless, an estimated 13 percent of Venezuelans and 22 percent of Mexicans could not afford a basic food basket in 1986, although these are among the wealthier nations in the region.

Unequal income distribution is the proximate cause of extensive poverty in Latin America. The income share of the top 20 percent of the population is estimated to be at least fifteen times that of the poorest 20 percent in eight countries in the region. Because of high average incomes in the region, the elimination of indigence could be accomplished by transfers to the poor. Implementing direct transfer programs is difficult, but it has also proved difficult for Latin Americans to shift their budget priorities to the poor. The military not only absorbs scarce resources but occasionally stands in the way of political change that would give the poor more power.

The international aid community has taken the approach that growth is the most important strategy for overcoming poverty. Brazil's rapid growth between 1964 and 1975 is often cited as a model of expanding income for all classes. A closer look at these data raises the question of whether growth could have been achieved while distributing a larger share of the pie to the poor. In the current context, there is no growth to support trickle down. Unless Latin American economies get a jump-start in the next decade, redistribution is essential to overcome poverty.

Land Reform

Because poverty rates are especially high in Latin America's rural areas, one looks to land reform as a solution to poverty. In Brazil, less than 10 percent of agricultural holdings contain 77 percent of the country's farmland. The situation is even more extreme in Paraguay: just 1 percent of landholdings encompass 80 percent of agricultural land.

Several countries have tried to solve the problem of landlessness by expanding into the frontier. Ambitious projects in this direction, like Brazil's National Integration Program, which led to construction of the Transamazon highway, have been an environmental debacle. The forest is burned off to support a few years of crop cultivation in marginally fertile soil. Once its nutrients are spent, this fragile land can at best support low-density cattle grazing. Large ranchers ultimately control the land, the forest is destroyed, and peasants remain unable to support themselves.

The price of genuine land reform is often a trade-off between higher rural consumption and production for urban or export markets. Ideally, land reform would enable peasants to operate with the same yields and marketing efficiency as commercial farmers. Many land reform programs have attempted to integrate peasants into the modernization of agriculture through access to better extension services, credit for irrigation and new seed strains, and the establishment of cooperatives to take advantage of economies of scale. In practice, land reform has stopped far short of this vision. Yet costs have also generally been less than expected. In both Mexico and Bolivia, land reform has yielded considerable improvements in rural standards of living, with relatively small costs in output.

Before we address specific issues of land reform experiences in Latin America (chapter 10), we have a lot of ground to cover. We start with the historical background of Latin America.

FURTHER READING

Economic Commission for Latin America and the Caribbean. *Preliminary Overview of the Economy*. ECLAC, Santiago, Chile,1991.

Hirschman, A. "The Political Economy of Latin American Development: Seven Exercises in Retrospection," *Latin American Research Review* 3 (1987).

Sheahan, J. *Patterns of Development in Latin America: Poverty, Repression, and Economic Strategy.* Princeton, N.J.: Princeton University Press, 1987.

Chapter 2

HISTORICAL ROOTS

Half a millennium after Columbus's landing, can the study of Latin America's colonial history possibly be relevant to understanding its current problems? After all, we would not feel compelled to cover the Renaissance in a book about modern European economies. But what is distinctive about Latin America's history is the recurrence of patterns of growth and crisis and the continuity of problems such as extremely unequal income distribution throughout the past 500 years.

Beginning with gold, commodity booms have attracted eager fortune seekers and sparked optimism about the region's future. These booms have not been sustainable, ultimately giving way to slumps. Nor have the booms—with their single product focus—succeeded in overcoming the longstanding problems of a backward agricultural sector and slow industrial growth. Indigenous people have remained at the bottom of the class structure and have borne much of the burden of this slow development. Standards of living have improved dramatically over time, of course, but the region remains underdeveloped.

Western Europe was already relatively rich before the Industrial Revolution. Centuries of gradual accumulation, based on investment and the appropriation of foreign resources and labor, scientific precocity, and organizational and financial superiority explain Europe's advantage. By the end of the 1800s, the United States was catching up with Europe, but Latin America lagged well behind. Why is it that a region rich in natural resources failed to match the development of other areas that were no more developed than Latin America in 1500? There is no simple answer to this question. As a matter of fact, the income gap has increased. In 1820, U.S. product per head was more than twice that of Brazil and Mexico (table 2.1). Just before World War I, the product per head of the United States was almost nine times larger than the product per head in Brazil and Mexico. Argentina was at European income levels in 1900 but then slowed while the United States continued its rapid growth. Per capita income growth in advanced countries exceeded per capita growth in Latin America until the early 1970s, and thus the per capita income gap between industrialized countries and Latin American countries increased (table 2.2).

This chapter summarizes the most important aspects of Latin America's economies from discovery to the Great Depression. Box 2.1 contains a brief chronology.

1   SPANISH COLONIES

Because of the near total destruction of indigenous economic life during the conquest and the marginalization of what remained, our historical background to Latin America's present economic structure begins with the arrival of Cortés in Mexico and Pizarro in Peru. By 1533, both the Aztecs and the Incas had been conquered. The success of a small number of Spaniards in defeating somewhere between 90 million and 120 million native Americans is attributed

---

Box 2.1
A brief chronology: Latin America before the Great Depression

Period		Comment
Colonial years	1500–1700	Colonial plunder, mineral extraction
	1700–1810	Hacienda production
Wars of independence	1810–1824	
Export-led growth	1825–1870	Entry into the world economy
	1870–1914	Golden years
	1915–1930	Stalled progress

Table 2.1
GDP per capita, selected countries, 1820–1950 (1965 U.S. factor cost)

Country	1820	1870	1913	1950
Argentina		420	804	1,013
Brazil	97	101	169	309
Mexico	112	110	143	282
United Kingdom	312	668	1,025	1,439
United States	276	567	1,344	2,384

Source: Angus Maddison, "A Comparison of levels of GDP per Capita in Developed and Developing Countries, 1970–1980," *Journal of Economic History* 43 (March 1983): 27–42.

Table 2.2
Growth of GDP per capita, selected countries, 1820-1980 (percentage)

Country	1820–1870	1870–1913	1913–1950	1950–1973	1973–1980
Argentina		1.5	0.6	2.2	0.1
Brazil	0.1	1.2	1.6	4.3	5.0
Colombia			1.3	2.3	3.1
Mexico	0.0	0.8	1.7	3.1	2.4
Peru			2.2	2.7	-0.7
Arithmetic average	0.05	1.17	1.48	2.92	1.98
Advanced country average[a]	1.1	1.4	1.2	3.8	1.8

a. Sixteen advanced countries.
Source: Ibid.

to superior weapons, internal strife among the Native Americans, and the sheer surprise and confusion caused by the foreigners' arrival. Once under Spanish control, the indigenous population declined drastically. Colonial culture appropriated roads and irrigation systems but decimated indigenous civilizations.

The immediate discovery of gold dominated Spanish America's early colonial development. Conquistadors arrived seeking wealth to repatriate to Spain. With the blessing of the Spanish crown, they were granted control over huge tracts of land (*encomiendas*), as well as the right to use indigenous labor on the land in exchange for a share of the output (the *repartida*). Far from trying to colonize the area, the early arrivals maintained their roots in Spain, using forays into the New World to leverage their social status and wealth at home. Their lack of interest in colonizing the region is often blamed for the slow development of nonmining industries, but the allure of gold no doubt would have drawn the efforts of even the most committed immigrants toward mining.[1]

The Spanish monarch set about encouraging the movement of gold and silver to Spain immediately after its discovery. To some extent this happened naturally in the early years, as natives of Spain wanted to ship their wealth home. The predominance of mercantilist ideas—based on the belief that a country's wealth and prosperity increase with the amount of gold and silver in its coffers—drove the crown to emphasize mineral development.

In addition to direct confiscation of bullion under the *encomienda* system, the crown accumulated gold and silver through trade with the colonists. It discouraged any manufacturing and agriculture in the New World that might compete with production in Spain, although the long delays and cost involved in buying goods from Spain spurred some development. In order to perpetuate its trade surplus with the colonies, Spain monopolized trade routes to and from the colonies, authorizing annual fleets to carry goods from the homeland. Not only did Spain forbid the colonists to trade with other European countries, it denied them rights to ship between ports in Spanish America, preventing the development of stronger economic independence in the region as a whole. Smuggling was widespread, but mercantilist restrictions succeeded in dampening output and trade.

An immense amount of gold already worked by native Americans provided the first riches. Having confiscated this, the conquistadors moved on to alluvial gold, following Native Americans to their sources. Alluvial gold quickly became scarce, and by the mid-1500s, silver mining took over as the main economic activity. The greater investment and scale of operations required for silver mining helped to establish a more permanent Spanish presence in the area.

The discovery of a mercury amalgamation technique in 1554 made extraction of poor-grade silver ore profitable, providing an incentive for greatly expanding mining activities. Native Americans provided labor under the *encomienda* system, which entitled the *encomendero* to output from the Native Americans in his ward. To prevent outright slavery, the crown shifted to the *mita* system, which secured communal land for the Native Americans and protected the integrity of indigenous communities. Nonetheless, by obliging the communities to provide labor in the mines, where arduous work and poor safety conditions prevailed, the *mita* system perpetuated the demise of the local population.

Two centers of silver production emerged: Potosí in the Andes and the Zacatecas, Pachuca, and Sonora mines in Mexico. Economic activity elsewhere in Spanish America was dominated by the needs of the silver-mining regions. Argentina supplied draft animals and basic crafted goods, while some agricultural goods needed in the Andean mines came from northern Chile. Activity in the Spanish Caribbean centered on servicing fleets transporting ore from Mexico to Spain. Farther beyond the silver mining centers, economic activity was modest; Colombia's export of emeralds was an exception. Conquistadors explored Central America, southern Chile, and Argentina, but the development of these areas did not take off until much later.

By the mid-seventeenth century, silver production slackened in Spanish America, particularly in the Andean mines. High-grade veins of ore were spent, and extraction efforts yielded increasingly less output. The explosion of activity that followed the conquest, including the construction of ornate cities to secure the role of the church and crown, began to sag. *Encomenderos* had to renegotiate the *repartida* owed to the Spanish crown to account for lower mineral output. In some areas, mines closed altogether, and agriculture took over as the mainstay of the economy.[2]

Several commodity booms affected individual countries between the mid-seventeenth and mid-eighteenth centuries, especially as the demand for sugar, cocoa, tobacco, hides, cotton, and indigo grew in Europe. Venezuela, for example, flourished in the early 1700s as a major exporter of cocoa, Havana grew with its tobacco production, and Buenos Aires became successful as a supplier of hides. In contrast to Andean producers, Mexico managed to maintain a steady output of silver throughout its colonial experience, avoiding a profound collapse. Nonetheless, if we can generalize about the region as a whole, the mid-seventeenth century marks the end of exuberant economic expansion under the Spanish crown.

Spain's control over trade with the colonies began to erode with the emergence of Britain and France as major powers. The British defeat of the Spanish Armada in 1588 was the most obvious sign of Spain's demise. With it, Britain gained increasing access to trade with Latin America. The Spanish crown did not formally cede control over trade until the eighteenth and nineteenth centuries, but illicit trade became increasingly possible as the Spanish were unable to defend their control over American ports. This problem was exacerbated by the 1713 Treaty of Utrecht (a product of the War of the Spanish Succession), which gave control over slave trade to the British. With a legitimate excuse to enter ports, British ships were able to increase the flow of contraband. After the Decree of Free Trade in 1778, which allowed colonies to trade among themselves and more ports in Spain, the crown retained only vestigial power to monitor trade in the colonies.

More important than Spain's loss of control over shipping lanes was its failure to match Britain's industrial growth as the Industrial Revolution began. Spain was increasingly unable to provide the goods sought by the colonists or to provide them at competitive prices. The strength of Britain's industrial capacity provided incentives for smuggling, but even many of the goods traded through Spain were in fact made in Britain.

By the early eighteenth century, the traditional centers of economic activity in Spanish America were increasingly isolated from the international economy. Silver exports were not easily replaced by agricultural exports. Spain's economy had collapsed with its military power and could not provide an adequate market for the colonies' output. Other European countries protected their domestic farmers and imported from their own colonies the raw materials that could not be supplied domestically. Haciendas, noted for their self-sufficiency, took a central role in Latin America's economy. With few products to sell abroad, landowners had little incentive to produce for the market, though most were well versed in the mechanics of capitalism and sought opportunities to earn cash.

2   A PORTUGUESE COLONY

While growth rates were slowing in Spanish America, the Brazilian economy was just beginning to develop momentum by the mid-eighteenth century. The Portuguese held claim to the northeastern coast of modern Brazil under the Treaty of Tordesillas of 1494. This treaty between Spain and Portugal divided the unexplored New World along a line drawn 370 leagues west of the Cape Verde Islands. (This lines lies just to the west of modern São Paulo.) Inland territorial expansion took off in the seventeenth century.

The Portuguese began their exploration of Brazil at the same time that the Spaniards entered Peru and Mexico, but they found no obvious deposits of gold and silver to stimulate colonization. The indigenous population was more scattered than in Spanish America and had not developed an interest in precious metals. With no Native Americans to identify their location, the huge mineral deposits of Brazil were left untouched for nearly two centuries. Instead, development took place more gradually. Exports of brazilwood, used for dye, were the first basis of Portuguese economic activity. The dye's success in the textile industries of Europe attracted the French to Brazil, prompting the Portuguese crown to encourage colonization in the 1530s as a means of securing its claim to the territory.

On huge estates established under the crown's allocation of land, sugar became an important cash crop. Because the indigenous population was an inadequate source of labor for the sugar plantations, massive imports of African slaves began in the late 1500s. This labor enabled Brazil to become the world's largest producer of sugar by the mid-1600s, and the economy vaulted into prosperity. Its lucrative position proved short-lived, however. After unsuccessfully invading Brazil to control its sugar wealth in 1624, the Dutch set up their own plantations in the Caribbean. The competition created by these plantations, and others established by the British and

French, eroded Brazil's market power. Sugar prices tumbled by the end of the 1600s, and Brazil lost access to important European markets.

Just as the Brazilian economy was slipping into recession with the loss of its sugar revenues, gold was discovered in Minas Gerais in 1690. Prospecting yielded vast amounts of gold through 1760. Compounding this gold rush was the discovery of diamonds in 1729. Revenues from the two minerals generated an era of spectacular opulence that lasted into the second half of the eighteenth century. Portugal took a sudden interest in its Brazilian colony, increasing its control of trade and taxing output, much as the Spanish had done earlier in their American colonies.

Prior to the discovery of gold, Portuguese mercantilist policies had a less restraining effect on Brazil than Spanish policies had elsewhere in Latin America. The failure to find precious metals had established agriculture as the early basis of Portuguese taxation of Brazil. Sugar and tobacco enriched the crown well before the discovery of gold, and the Portuguese crown took an active interest in promoting the development of other potentially successful crops. Furthermore, Portugal saw Brazilian economic diversification as a means of establishing a stronger colonial base to defend its claim to the territory. This is not to say that Portugal gave Brazil free rein in its development. The crown attempted to monopolize some export industries and prohibited activities that competed with Portuguese products. For example, wine production and blacksmith apprenticeships were forbidden. Trade was also confined to Portuguese ports, except that direct slave trade with Africa was permitted. Nonetheless, policies that seemed similar in proclamation to Spanish edicts were weaker in practice. The importance of slave trade to the success of the sugar industry made it difficult for the crown to control ships plying the southern Atlantic. Because the Portuguese empire was more far-flung than that of the Spanish and its naval strength weaker, contraband flourished.

With the discovery of gold and diamonds, Portugal tightened its grip on Brazil. The crown controlled trade into and out of the mining areas of Brazil, confiscating enough gold to finance several decades of government spending in Lisbon. In 1785, it went so far as to prohibit all manufacturing in Brazil in an attempt to turn relative prices in Portugal's favor, at least as an entrepôt for shipping British industrial goods to Brazil. While these policies can be interpreted as a resurgence of the mercantilist fascination with bullion in Portugal, they more likely reflect the ease of taxing Brazil's mineral output through monopsonistic pricing. By this time, it was apparent that Brazil's agricultural production was an important part of the flow of wealth from Portugal's cash cow, and thus the crown made no efforts to limit this sector. Mercantilism had given way to colonial domination of a more diversified economy.

However tightly Portugal tried to control Brazil in the eighteenth century, its power to monopolize trade in the colony was substantially reduced by the 1703 Treaty of Methuen, which granted the British access to Portugal and its colonies in exchange for favorable treatment of Portuguese wine in the British market. The combination of this formal arrangement and the rapidly rising demand for manufactured goods during the Brazilian gold rush meant that England was deeply involved in trade with Brazil throughout the eighteenth century. Access to British manufactured goods contained Brazil discontent over Portuguese control, but it also marked a shift away from colonial ties to more independent trade relations.

3   MERCANTILISM, MONOCULTURE, DUTCH DISEASE

The impact of colonial domination during the mineral booms of Spanish and Portuguese America merits closer attention, for mercantilist policies of the two crowns are often blamed for slow development in the region. In pursuit of bullion, European countries tried to increase their exports to other countries while reducing their imports, setting the accumulation of bullion as a goal in itself. This seemingly irrational attraction of royalty to gold and silver may be more understandable if one recalls that the importance of trade was rising in Europe during this period. As the economy shifted from feudalism to market-oriented relations, silver and gold represented the ability to buy goods from other regions. Whereas one could not always be sure of the marketability of the kingdom's products, gold and silver were highly liquid and provided a relatively secure asset. In dealing with its colonial territories, Spain's rationale for focusing on bullion is even more obvious: given a limited amount of labor and equipment to exploit the territory's wealth, mining was no

doubt the most profitable use of resources, particularly because of
the ease of taxing its output.

As an economic theory of development, mercantilism lost favor
by the mid-eighteenth century. In particular, once the fruits of the
Industrial Revolution became apparent, economists shifted their
interest to more productive assets and to the benefits of commerce.
The demise of mercantilism as a popular theory among economists
coincided with the waning of Spanish control over trade in its
American colonies, but policies that smacked of mercantilism
persisted for some time, as evidenced by Spain's refusal to relinquish
formal control over Latin American trade before independence. In
the case of Brazil, mercantilist policies were strengthened about the
same time that mercantilism was renounced by economists.

To what extent did mercantilist policies affect development?
Royal monopolies on essential goods reduced output and growth in
these industries, as did prohibition of industries competing with
output from the mother country. Limits on trade between the
colonies prevented Latin Americans from taking advantage of regional differences in resources, forcing inefficient local production
where the benefits of specialization might have been realized. (These
restraints on intraregional trade were, however, the most easily
circumvented.) Control over access to other European markets was
especially harmful, because there were many products that the
colonists could not easily sell to Spain and Portugal. Latin America's
mild climate was closer to that of the Iberian Peninsula than to that
of northern Europe; thus greater comparative advantages could have
been realized with an opening of trade. For example, hides from
Argentina had little market in Spain but were sought elsewhere in
Europe. Only with the erosion of Spanish control over trade was
Argentina able to realize the benefits of this industry. The colonies
might also have established a foothold in some markets such as that
for cotton, which was ultimately supplied to Britain by its own
colonies.

It is easy to overstate the importance of mercantilist policies in
dampening growth. In the initial years of the conquest, mercantilism may not have been as important in slowing industrial and
agricultural growth as the distorting nature of the mineral boom
itself. With an abundance of silver to be extracted, resources gravi-
tated toward the lucrative mining industry. Other activities were

forced to compete with the mines for scarce labor and capital. Costs were high, discouraging local production even in the absence of the crown's fiats. With gold and silver readily available, local producers would find it difficult to compete with cheap imports. This is a historically recurrent phenomenon referred to today as Dutch disease, a term derived from Holland's experience with natural gas. A similar concentration of resources occurred in the 1970s, when countries rich in oil found that their nonoil industries tended to decline as high wages and profits in the oil industry drew resources away from traditional activities. Cocoa production plummeted in Nigeria, industry collapsed in Britain and Norway, and Mexican agriculture stagnated as these once-diversified economies turned their efforts to oil production. Dutch disease not only struck Latin America during its colonial years but infected the region after independence, as a series of commodity booms occurred in the late nineteenth century. Long after mercantilist controls have ended, single-commodity bubbles still distort Latin America's growth.

Another factor compounding the effect of Dutch disease in Spanish America during the gold and silver boom may have been the weak domestic demand generated by early excavators. Many conquistadors viewed their stay in the New World as an opportunity to accumulate wealth for their return to Spain. Their savings rates were high, but investment and consumption in the colonies were nowhere near equal to the value of gold extracted. With the expansion of silver production, income distribution was so concentrated that the indigenous population did not provide a strong market for goods. Weak domestic demand provided few incentives for the establishment of industries.

It is also not clear that mercantilism is to blame for the slow development of agricultural exports once bullion production declined. Other constraints on trade were also operating. Most European countries were extremely protectionist until the late nineteenth century, particularly with regard to agricultural products. England was exceptional in its pursuit of raw materials from abroad, but even its farmers managed to secure protection until the early 1800s. Trade barriers had an especially dampening effect on the Southern Cone countries (Chile, Argentina, and Uruguay), whose economies might have grown through exports of wheat and other temperate climate grains. Semitropical and tropical commodities that did not compete with Northern European farmers were generally produced in British, French, and Dutch colonies. For example, Latin American colonies had trouble competing with North American cotton and Caribbean sugar in the British market. This was partly due to differences in transportation costs, but the British had good reasons to favor their own colonies in trade. Despite these impediments, the existence of extensive smuggling is prima facie evidence of demand for Latin American products outside Spain and Portugal. How much trade would have occurred in the absence of mercantilism, given import restrictions in other European markets, is hard to assess.

Control by the Portuguese crown did not have as important an impact on Brazilian development as Spanish control did elsewhere in Latin America. The early development of a fairly diverse agricultural base helped to stabilize the Brazilian economy. As in Spanish America, however, Dutch disease took its toll. The country was catapulted from boom to bust as individual commodities swept into and out of favor. Particularly at the peak of the upswings caused by sugar, gold, and diamonds, imbalanced distribution of resources hurt the country's long-run development. Yet throughout these booms, cattle ranching, tobacco, and cotton coexisted as important secondary industries. The sequential timing of Brazil's commodity booms also helped the country to avoid the prolonged slump that affected much of Spanish America in the eighteenth century. Although depressions were interspersed throughout its history, the country did not experience the economic disintegration that affected Spanish America.

4   AGRICULTURAL DEVELOPMENT

Mercantilist policies and the pull of resources toward mining dampened incentives for agricultural development, particularly in Spanish America. Although the crown's policies were directed at the accumulation of gold and silver, these policies had a profound and lasting impact on the structure of agriculture. The *encomienda* system, by which the crown granted the right to labor and tribute from indigenous communities in exchange for a portion of its output, resulted in highly concentrated control over huge tracts of land. The indigenous population was deprived of its land not so much for the sake of controlling the land itself, which was often not used, but to force the indigenous population to provide labor in the mines. The *mita* system secured communal land for the Native Americans but only partially reversed a trend toward the partitioning of land into huge, underutilized tracts controlled by the Spaniards. The system in Brazil was not substantially different, although its effect on a more dispersed indigenous population was less severe. In their efforts to colonize Brazil, the Portuguese apportioned immense amounts of land (*capitanias hereditarias*) to those who would settle in the territory. The result was intense concentration of landholdings.

The land holdings granted by the crown evolved into large estates, the *latifundio* of the region. While creoles inherited this land, the indigenous and poor mestizo population crowded into the remaining land, working small plots of land in the *minifundio* sector. Typically the *minifundio* would not yield enough to sustain a family, and therefore *minifundistas* were forced to work on the large estates some days of the week to supplement their income. It was also not uncommon for the *latifundistas* to grant workers access to a small plot of land in exchange for a portion of its output, a system that resulted in some land in the *latifundio* sector being intensively farmed in the same manner as the *minifundio* land. Finally, communal lands granted to the Native Americans under the *mita* system took on intensive farming characteristics similar to that of the *minifundio* sector because of the small amount of cultivable land per person.

Whereas the *minifundista* engaged in subsistence farming, the *latifundista* sought crops with marketable value, a difference that reflects more knowledge about market networks, better access to capital, and a greater ability to take risks. As a rule, *latifundio* land was geared toward less labor-intensive uses, such as cattle ranching, while the *minifundistas* worked the soil to squeeze out the highest possible yield per acre, given their limited tools and credit. Even those *latifundistas* who used their land to produce labor-intensive crops like cotton came nowhere near the labor use per acre typical of a subsistence plot.

Because most rural peasants depended on large estates for work opportunities or access to land, the hacienda became a central feature of the Latin American rural landscape. Often stereotyped as feudal, haciendas functioned as fairly isolated economic communities. Many of the needs of the plantation were produced within its borders, particularly during years of depression in commodity markets, when little revenue was brought in by the sale of cash crops. Isolation was especially common in Spanish America during the century between the mid-1600s and mid-1700s, when few commodity booms replaced declining mineral activity, and again in the nineteenth century as political violence wracked the region following independence. Workers often labored under a system of debt peonage, carrying the fruits of their labor to the same owner who sold provisions to them on credit at prices high enough to rule out any possibility of emerging from debt.

The absence of money involved in labor relations and the exchange of access to land for a portion of its output are indeed similar to European feudal relations, but the parallels should not be overdrawn. While European vassals engaged in very little commerce because trade networks had not yet developed, the *latifundistas* were very much geared toward production for the world market. Cotton, tobacco, and cattle were generally the central focus of plantation activity. Production for internal consumption was a necessary mechanism for dealing with the physical isolation of the hacienda and the periodic crash of commodity markets. Nor were the political roots similar; the Latin American indigenous population strained under a system known to be the consequence of the conquest. Few *patrones* enjoyed the political legitimacy based on communal needs for protection common to European feudal lords.

This concentrated land structure has persisted into the twentieth century, with large estates increasingly shifting to purely commercial production based on wage labor. The low intensity of land use on large estates has been central to peasant demands for land reform. Not only is the system seen as inequitable, it also appears inefficient. Were land to be more evenly distributed, there would no doubt be a substantial improvement in standards of living among the rural poor. Yet land reform has rarely been undertaken wholeheartedly. Although this partly reflects the political strength of the landed elite compared to the peasantry, foot-dragging on agrarian reform is also motivated by a need to maintain the market-oriented output of the *latifundio* sector.

The colonial division of property had implications not only for the usage of land but for the political structure of the region as well. The *encomienda* system established a landed aristocracy that dominated political life for centuries and then shared power as industry displaced agriculture as the central economic activity. It established a sharp division between the haves and the have-nots, creating a class structure that is extremely bifurcated by comparison to other cultures. Problems of unequal income distribution and widespread rural poverty that face the region today are rooted in events of the sixteenth and seventeenth centuries. (We discuss the dilemmas posed by agrarian reform and the problems of income distribution in chapters 9 and 10.)

5   INDEPENDENCE AND ENTRY INTO THE WORLD ECONOMY

Spain's eroding control over its Latin American colonies finally came to an end with the success of independence movements in the 1820s. Several factors motivated the struggle for independence. First, Spain was unable to provide much in the way of support to justify the taxes and trade constraints that it imposed on its colonies. Second, American-born creoles, who exercised increasing economic power in the region, were denied governing positions as the crown put its trust only in the loyalty of Spanish-born *peninsulares*. This denial of rights to participate in government ran counter to the popular ideals of the Enlightenment movement. Third, particularly in Mexico, the indigenous communities demanded access to more land. Finally, France's control of the Spanish throne threw into question the legitimacy of the Spanish crown in both Spain and Latin America, providing a catalyst for successful revolution. Table 2.3 provides the data on independence wars.

Because of Portugal's interest in Brazil's mineral wealth, its ties with Brazil were much closer in the 1700s. Nonetheless, a set of forces similar to those operating in Spanish America prompted the independence of Brazil. Self-rule had become an important political ideal. The British had made substantial commercial inroads there following the Treaty of Methuen in 1703 (by which British wool and woolens were admitted into Portugal duty free and Portuguese wine into England at a greatly reduced rate). When the French army, assisted by the Spanish, took Lisbon in 1807, the royal family fled

Table 2.3
Political independence, Latin American countries

Countries	Independence As a result of war declared	Won	From	Independence As a result of special circumstances	From
Argentina	1810	1816	Spain		
Bolivia	1809	1825	Spain		
Brazil				1822	Portugal
Chile	1810	1818	Spain		
Colombia	1810	1818	Spain[a]		
Costa Rica		1821	Spain[b]		
Cuba		1898	Spain	1902	U.S.
Dominican Republic		1821	Spain	1844	Haiti[c]
Ecuador	1809	1822	Spain[a]		
El Salvador		1821	Spain[b]		
Guatemala		1821	Spain[b]		
Haiti	1791	1804	France		
Honduras		1821	Spain[b]		
Mexico	1810	1821	Spain		
Nicaragua		1821	Spain[b]		
Panama				1903	Colombia
Paraguay				1811	Spain
Peru	1821	1824	Spain		
Uruguay	1811	1814	Spain	1828	Brazil
Venezuela	1810	1821	Spain[a]		

a. Gran Colombia united Colombia, Ecuador, and Venezuela from 1819 to 1830. The breakup of Gran Colombia came by 1830.
b. Became part of Mexico in 1822–1823. From 1823 to 1841, the United Provinces of Central America united Costa Rica, El Salvador, Guatemala, Honduras, and Nicaragua. The breakup came by 1838, and attempts to restore the union were defeated by 1842.
c. Hispaniola or Santo Domingo (future Dominican Republic) was governed by Haiti between 1822 and 1844. Spain reoccupied from 1861 to 1865.

to Brazil, where it reasserted powers that the colonialists had come to enjoy. With the return of King John VI to Portugal in 1821, his son, Pedro I, recognized local pressure for sovereignty and declared independence in 1822, sparing the country from war.

In the aftermath of independence, most Latin American countries faced the task of reconstruction. Boundary disputes and internal conflicts between factions seeking power compounded the damage done by the wars of independence. Violence between 1830 and 1850 hurt economic growth as much as Spanish taxation and restrictions had before independence. These conflicts established the tradition of seizing governmental control through force; nowhere did a democracy establish itself. The worst violence occurred in the small Central American countries and in Colombia, where no group was able to assert its dominance for long. In these cases, instability lasted throughout most of the nineteenth century. Among the former Spanish colonies, Chile was best able to avoid debilitating internal conflict after independence, perhaps because it had never really flourished under Spanish rule and already enjoyed a fair degree of autonomy.

The violence associated with the first half of the nineteenth century had serious economic repercussions. As security became a problem, many landowners retreated to their estates; the isolation of the haciendas reached an extreme during this period. Even in the absence of Spanish restrictions, Latin American countries were in a disadvantageous position in the world economy. England continued to be the center of the Industrial Revolution, and its needs for raw materials were adequately and cheaply supplied by its own colonies. During the first half of the nineteenth century, prices of cotton, sugar, and other tropical commodities were especially low. This did not, however, prevent the British from selling their goods to Latin America. Debt financing became common, and the difficulties of raising foreign exchange led to recurrent debt crises (a subject we will discuss in chapter 4).

In the 1840s, Latin America began participating in world trade more extensively, for several reasons. By this time, England was dismantling its protection of domestic agricultural interests and was more receptive to imports of raw materials from abroad. This change especially benefited the temperate climate agricultural producers like Argentina and Uruguay. Tropical producers still had to contend with preferential treatment of British colonies, but transportation costs had dropped considerably with the invention of the steam engine, propeller, and metal hull. This made it possible to compete with products from the Caribbean and North America that had previously enjoyed cost advantages in transportation to European markets. Technological advances in transportation and mineral extraction also gave rise to new mining activity as it became cost-effective to ship nonprecious metals to industrial centers. Finally, rapid industrialization in the United States created growing demand for raw materials and tropical commodities in the Western Hemisphere itself. Latin America became an important supplier to this new market. In addition to this new demand for tropical commodities, the rapid expansion of the western United States created a demand for temperate climate products from Chile, which enjoyed a considerable cost advantage during the gold rush years.

By mid-century, a few commodities dominated the exports of Latin America: copper and wheat from Chile, tobacco from Colombia, hides and meat from Argentina, guano from Peru, sugar from Cuba, coffee from Brazil, and cacao from Venezuela. As before independence, very little manufacturing took place on the continent; without rapidly growing economies of scale through mechanization, nascent industries in Latin America could not easily undercut costs in Europe and the United States.

6   THE GOLDEN AGE: 1870–1914

The fifty years after the wars of independence—the period between 1820 and 1870—were disappointing in terms of economic growth even if export booms were not lacking. This period left a mosaic of capitalist and noncapitalist relations of production, ranging from slavery and debt peonage to sharecropping, tenant farming, wage labor, and small-scale commodity production. It also created the conditions for the more extensive developments of the 1870–1914 period. Table 2.4 shows population estimates between 1820 and 1930 and the acceleration of population growth rates after 1870.

The entire nineteenth century was marked by export expansion, with world trade in primary products growing more rapidly than the

Table 2.4
Population estimates, Latin American countries, 1820-1930 (millions)

Country	1820	1870	1900	1930
Argentina	.53	1.80	4.61	12.05
Bolivia			1.77	2.40
Brazil	4.54	9.80	17.98	33.57
Chile			2.96	4.37
Colombia	1.24	2.56	3.89	7.43
Costa Rica			.31	.50
Cuba			1.60	3.65
Dominican Republic			.60	1.26
Ecuador			1.30	1.94
El Salvador			.80	1.44
Guatemala			.89	1.76
Haiti			1.25	2.42
Honduras			.42	.95
Mexico	6.53	9.00	13.61	16.55
Nicaragua			.42	.68
Panama			.26	.47
Paraguay			.49	.88
Peru	1.60	2.59	3.00	5.65
Uruguay			.96	1.73
Venezuela			2.45	3.71
Latin America			59.56	102.82
United States	9.64	39.82	76.09	123.07

Sources: Maddison, "Comparison of Levels of GDP"; James Wilkie, ed., *Statistical Abstract of Latin America*, vol. 27 (Los Angeles: UCLA Latin American Center Publications, 1989).

world trade in manufactures until the last quarter of the century, when the two rates of growth were approximately the same, at 3 percent per year. After the turn of the century, trade in manufactures grew more rapidly.

The rate of growth of industrial output in the center determined the rate of increase in the demand for exports of the peripheral economies. As part of this process, Latin America became increasingly integrated. The last two decades of the nineteenth century witnessed a dramatic strengthening of Latin America's trade links with the rest of the world. Argentina especially grew as a supplier of wool, wheat, and hides. Nitrates became a booming export in Chile. Central America added bananas to its exports of coffee. Brazil enjoyed rapid growth in its sales of coffee and rubber. Mineral exporting countries benefited from the demand for minerals associated with investment activity in the industrialized countries. The discovery of coal-based dyes in 1856 destroyed Guatemala's main export, cochineal (which accounted for 80 percent of export earnings), but the country was fairly successful in shifting to produce cotton and coffee.

The growth of the Latin American external sectors was not a steady process. Periodic instability in the core economies would cut it off from time to time. The post-1873 crisis in the United States and Europe weakened export prices and induced a rescheduling of the foreign debt of Honduras, Costa Rica, the Dominican Republic, Paraguay, Bolivia, Guatemala, Uruguay, and Peru. Argentina, Chile, and Colombia were also affected. The external sector was not an unfaltering source of support: cotton, wool, and wheat prices declined from the late 1860s to the mid-1890s. Peru's guano boom, which financed government spending in the 1860s and permitted excessive foreign borrowing, collapsed in the late 1870s as a result of instability and the loss of nitrate fields to Chile in the War of the Pacific. The dependence of the country on guano was sorely felt as exports fell by at least half. The crisis in industrial countries in the mid-1890s coincided with panic in British financial houses, default by Argentina, and a dip in foreign lending. In Brazil, the threat of default in 1898 was brought about by continually falling coffee prices, which domestic financial instability aggravated. Mexico suffered from the 1907–1908 world recession.

Variations in prices and volumes aside, economic expansion remained overwhelmingly export led and therefore primarily induced by demand in the advanced economies. The Latin American economies reacted differently to external stimulus, and in 1914 the contrasts were sharper than fifty years before. Argentina benefited the most. In fact, the forty-five years between 1870 and 1914 constitute the glorious period of Argentine growth, notwithstanding the debt crisis of the early 1890s.[3] Growth derived from a combination of technological innovations and educational methods that were wholly novel. Domingo Sarmiento, who was president from 1868 to 1874, encouraged railway construction and free immigration, established a national system of popular education, and created new institutes of scientific investigation. In the 1870s and 1880s, English breeds of sheep imported by immigrant ranchers from the British Isles began to replace the poor native flocks and made wool Argentina's major export product. This stage was followed by the upgrading of cattle, the installation of cheap barbed-wire fencing and steel windmills, and the introduction of clover and alfalfa, which increased the carrying capacity of the Argentine cattle ranges, permitting meat exports to take the lead. At the same time, the construction of railroads, port facilities, and packing houses utilizing European engineering techniques transformed the Litoral of the Río de la Plata and the Pampa.

The key innovations at the end of the nineteenth century were the development of new methods of processing and shipping meat long distances under refrigeration. The discovery that beef could be chilled, rather than frozen, and shipped across the tropics to arrive in England in good condition opened up a vast new market, stimulating the construction of packing houses with refrigeration and refrigerated steamships. By 1905, Argentina had displaced the United States as the chief exporter of fresh beef and mutton to the British market (figure 2.1). The cereal phase of agricultural development dominated by wheat production followed. Development proceeded at fast rates (figure 2.2), soon to give place to renewed balance of payments problems.

As the Argentine example shows, the expansion of the late 1800s was the result of several factors. First, serious international conflicts were few. The most important was the War of the Pacific (1879–

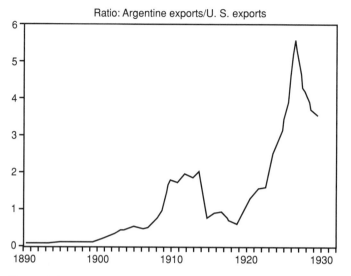

Figure 2.1
Argentine and U.S. beef exports, 1890–1930.
Source: B. R. Mitchell, *International Historical Statistics* (Detroit: Book Tower, 1983).

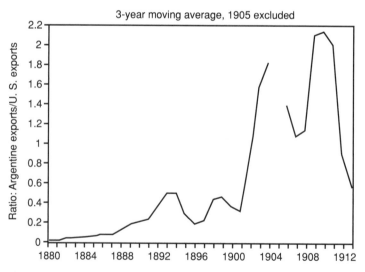

Figure 2.2
Argentine and U.S. wheat exports, 1880–1913.
Source: B. R. Mitchell, *International Historical Statistics* (Detroit: Book Tower, 1983).

1883) in which Bolivia lost access to the Pacific and Chile took over both Bolivia and Peru's major nitrate deposits.

Government authority became more stable. Domestic political stabilization in Argentina, Brazil, Chile, and Mexico formed the basis for prosperity. In Argentina, extreme internal conflicts, which had jostled the country until 1880, came to a halt with the imposition of successful oligarchic rule. In Brazil, the long rule of enlightened monarchy ended in 1888–1889 with the peaceful abolition of slavery and the inauguration of a republic. In Chile, the War of the Pacific and the 1891 civil war (terminating the Balmaceda administration) interrupted stability, but the Pacific War augmented the Chilean resource base. At the same time, landlords, merchants, and financiers joined forces to preside over a long wave of economic progress. In Mexico, an autocratic period of liberal rule, known as the *Reforma*, followed a half-century of incessant turmoil after independence. In 1876, the *Reforma* gave way to the *Porfiriato*, an authoritarian administration that enforced political stability and encouraged foreign investment until its fall in 1911.

If political stability played a major role in the economic development of the last decades of the 1800s, other factors were equally important. First, industrialization in Europe and the United States had intensified the demand for raw materials. Second, railroads made it possible to take advantage of undeveloped, fertile agricultural territory (particularly in Argentina), and refrigeration made it possible for the region to export meat and bananas. Third, capital markets had become much more sophisticated, so that much of the export expansion occurred as a result of foreign investment. The British were Latin America's most important foreign investors throughout the century, accounting for two-thirds of investment in Latin America by 1913, but U.S. firms took on an increasingly important role by the end of the nineteenth century. Massive resource transfers occurred through the mechanism of government borrowing, which financed a substantial improvement in the region's infrastructure. A long-term rise in trade taxes, chiefly from duties on imports, gave governments a more ample fiscal base. Growth of export earnings and the capacity to import eased the collection of resources for government-sponsored investment and current expenditure.

Table 2.5
Main exports and indexes of real purchasing power of exports, Latin American countries, 1913–1928

Country	Main exports (1923–1925)	Real purchasing power index		
		1913	1917–1918	1928
Venezuela	Copper, petroleum	100	37	281
Colombia	Coffee	100	54	276
Mexico	Petroleum, silver	100	178	251
Peru	Petroleum, cotton	100	106	198
Paraguay	Quebracho, timber	100	96	174
El Salvador	Coffee	100	82	167
Brazil	Coffee	100	48	158
Argentina	Wheat, maize	100	60	146
Guatemala	Coffee, bananas	100	34	139
Costa Rica	Coffee, bananas	100	52	118
Cuba	Sugar	100	118	118
Chile	Nitrates, copper	100	78	108
Nicaragua	Coffee, bananas	100	43	104
Uruguay	Meat, wool	100	87	100
Ecuador	Cocoa	100	48	93
Bolivia	Tin	100	95	82
Panama	Bananas	100	46	56

Source: Rosemary Thorp, "Economy, 1914–1929," in Leslie Bethel, ed., *Latin America Economy and Society*, 1870–1930 (New York: Cambridge University Press, 1989).

7   STALLED PROGRESS: 1914–1930

Although the rapid economic expansion between 1880 and 1910 was primarily based on export growth, Latin America began to industrialize during this period; processing plants for exports, textile factories, food packing plants, and factories for construction materials sprang up to accommodate new demand. Growing government bureaucracies, financial markets, and transportation services drew workers into the cities. The beginnings of urban labor movements in Latin America can be traced to this period.

The "Golden Age" of export-led growth broke down with World War I. Commodities markets became more unstable. The fall in nitrate prices provoked a severe export collapse in Chile. The coffee market continued to grow but only slowly. Meat exports, especially those of Uruguay, suffered from Britain's slow growth in the 1920s. In Central America food imports increased, generating new tension focused on foreign capital; in Costa Rica, the United Fruit Company worked less than 10 percent of the 274,000 hectares it controlled.

Table 2.5 shows Latin America's main exports in the 1920s, as well as the behavior of their purchasing power. Mexico appears as a success story despite the turmoil and destruction of the revolution. Oil played an important role in Mexico's performance, as it did in Venezuela and Peru. As the producer of 80 percent of the world's coffee, Brazil adopted a scheme for maintaining the price of coffee in 1906. The program kept prices high but failed to restrict Brazilian planting or the expansion of output from other countries. Colombia, for example, enjoyed strong coffee export earnings in the 1920s as a result of Brazil's self-imposed restriction on coffee sales. By 1929, Brazil was restraining exports to just half of its production. Coffee prices collapsed in 1930 but would have eventually done so even in the absence of the world depression.

The years between World War I and the Great Depression represent the key period in the transfer of British economic hegemony in Latin America to the United States. U.S. trade with Latin America increased significantly (figure 2.3). Between 1913 and 1929, while British investment in Latin America barely increased, U.S. investment soared (table 2.6). Minerals, oils, and public utilities drew the greatest amounts of investment. The role of banks became important. By 1926, there were sixty-one branches of U.S. banks in Latin America. Institutional change made the region more suitable to foreign investment; with the help of missions led by the U.S. financial advisor, Edwin Kemmerer, many Latin American economies strengthened their central banks and stabilized their exchange rates.

The outbreak of World War I brought a financial crisis of short duration to Latin America. By 1915 exports were rising strongly. Lack of access to imported goods induced some domestic production of substitutes. Celso Furtado, among other economists, favors the view that the war was a positive stimulus for industrial growth in Latin America.[4] The protective effect of the war encouraged small repair shops to broaden their activities, providing a basis for an incipient capital goods sector.

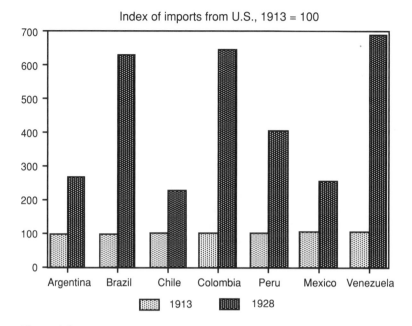

Figure 2.3
Index of imports from the United States, by selected countries, 1913–1928.
Source: B. R. Mitchell, *International Historical Statistics* (Detroit: Book Tower, 1983).

The 1920s were weakly protective but lacked a coherent industrial policy. Nonetheless, this period of delay helps explain why Latin America was able to recover relatively quickly from the 1930s crash. It formed the basis for a major reevaluation of economic policies that followed the sudden drop in export earnings after 1929.

8   THE 1930s

The Great Depression brought about a dramatic change in global economic conditions: a fall in economic activity in the industrialized countries, a fall in the value of world trade, high interest rates, appreciation of the dollar, and a fall in the real price of commodities.

Economic activity in Latin America had been dominated by international trade, while the money supply was determined by international reserves. Policymakers were unable to control the

Table 2.6
Stock of capital invested in South America by the United States and United Kingdom, 1913–1929 (millions of dollars)

Country	U.S. investments		U. K. investments		Ratio of U.S./U.K. investments (percentage)	
	1913	1929	1913	1929	1913	1929
Argentina	40	611	1861	2140	2.1	2.9
Bolivia	10	133	2	12	500.0	1,108.3
Brazil	50	476	1162	1414	4.3	33.7
Chile	15	396	332	390	4.5	101.5
Colombia	2	260	34	38	5.9	684.2
Ecuador	10	25	14	23	71.4	108.7
Paraguay	3	15	16	18	18.8	83.3
Peru	35	151	133	141	26.3	107.1
Uruguay	5	64	240	217	2.1	29.5
Venezuela	3	162	41	92	7.3	176.1
Total	173	2,293	3,835	4,485	4.5	51.1

Source: M. Winkler, *Investments of U.S. Capital in Latin America* (Boston: World Peace Foundation, 1929).

sharp deflationary impact of both the adverse demand shock caused by the depression and the ensuing capital flight.

The consequences of the crisis varied with each country's integration into the international system and the nature of its exports. In the case of tropical products, given the inelasticity of supply of perishable crops, the decline in demand provoked a large fall in prices. In the case of mineral products, the industrial slump in the importing countries led to the collapse of production in the exporting countries. Chile was among the hardest hit in Latin America. The countries in the least vulnerable position were those that exported commodities with annual crop cycles, such as Argentina, and specialized in temperate zone food products, with low income elasticities and better organized markets. Brazil's relatively rapid recovery stemmed from an early suspension of debt repayment and strong government intervention to prop up the income of coffee producers (table 2.7).

Table 2.7
Indexes of real output per capita, selected countries,1929–1933

Year	Argentina	Brazil	Chile	Mexico	Peru
1929	100.0	100.0	100.0	100.0	100.0
1930	93.5	93.6	92.0	91.2	87.2
1931	84.9	89.0	68.7	92.9	75.4
1932	80.1	89.4	67.2	76.5	70.3
1933	81.8	99.0	78.7	83.3	93.1

Sources: Banco Central de La Republica Argentina, *Cuentas Nacionales: Series Historicas*, vol. 3, (1976); R. Zerkowski and M. A. Veloso, "Seis Decadas de Economia Brasileira atraves do PIB," *Revista Brasileira de Economia*. 36, 3, (1982); United Nations, *Economic Survey of Latin America, 1949* (New York, United Nations 1951); CEPAL, *Series Historicas del Crescimiento* (Santiago, United Nations 1978); C. Bolona, "Estimaciones Preliminares del Producto Nacional," mimeo., Universidad del Pacifico. Statistics on population in the 1930s for Peru were not available. Its population growth rate is estimated as 1.8 percent in the 1940s and 3 percent in the 1970s. To obtain the numbers in column 5, we assumed that the Peruvian population growth was 1.8 percent in the 1930s.

The contraction of income provoked by the fall in exports was combined with capital flight and a reduction in the money supply. These effects were worsened by the fact that policymakers tried to maintain the gold standard and imposed strong contractionary measures on their countries in their initial reaction to the crisis. In Argentina and Chile, for instance, credit was restricted and interest rates increased. In Chile, the nominal exchange rate remained constant. In Argentina, real government spending started to increase only in 1935 when a program of massive road construction was implemented.

Peru suffered from common balance of payments troubles, but the effects were muted and short-lived, due to default on the foreign debt in 1932 (which doubled the import capacity overnight) and the fast recovery of export earnings. Half the coastal population in Peru earned their living from cotton and benefited from an international price support scheme initiated in the United States to protect U.S. farmers. The early revival of both cotton and petroleum exports was followed by a wave of renewed mining. Recovery in Peru thus was not linked to domestic fiscal and monetary policies. Instead, government spending declined more rapidly than export earnings during the early depression years. With the interruption of external borrowing, government expenditure fell by 50 percent between 1928 and 1931. It was cut by another 32 percent in 1932, while taxes were increased to finance aid for the unemployed. Public works programs began to expand only in 1936.

Brazil provides an interesting example of compensatory expenditures. The key to understanding the behavior of the Brazilian economy in the 1930s is the coffee support policy and, to a lesser extent, the promotion of cotton cultivation, which acted as Keynesian stimulants. By holding the income of the export sector at a high level, the government enabled the manufacturing sector to expand as the exchange rate was devalued.

As public protest against deflation mounted, most Latin American countries suspended normal servicing of the external debt and asked foreign creditors to reschedule payments. The exchange rate was devalued, and exchange controls isolated the domestic economy from external pressures. Domestic credit expansion took the form of increased loans by the central bank to the government, development institutions, agricultural and mortgage banks, and various producers' associations. Government spending also rose in response to natural disasters, civil disturbances, and border wars, such as the war between Peru and Colombia over Leticia and the second Chaco War between Bolivia and Paraguay in 1932, the political turmoil in Chile and Cuba during "socialist" governments over 1931–1933, the São Paulo rebellion of 1932, and a severe drought in northeastern Brazil.

Real devaluations made import substituting activities profitable by raising the local cost of imported goods. A real exchange rate is defined as the ratio of domestic prices to foreign prices, with both prices measured in the same currency. A real devaluation means that foreign prices in domestic currency increase relative to domestic prices.[5] In the mid-1930s, real exchange rates in some Latin American countries suffered a 70 percent depreciation relative to their levels in the 1920s. The Brazilian real exchange rate, for example, depreciated 43 percent between 1929 and 1931. At the same time, output per capita fell by 11 percent. This evidence supports the hypothesis that price elasticities are low in the short run (and thus devaluations are relatively ineffective in stimulating a fast recovery). Over time, however, real devaluations and expansionary fiscal policies took effect, and recovery began. Although devaluations

Chapter 3

THEORIES, IDEAS, AND OPINIONS

1 DIVERGENT OPINIONS

Economists can certainly agree on a broad outline of the problems facing Latin America: incomes are too low to guarantee adequate living standards, and they are not growing rapidly enough; income distribution is far from equal, and pockets of extreme poverty persist even in countries where average income is high compared with other developing regions; sporadic bouts of hyperinflation erode investors' confidence and arbitrarily redistribute income; balance of payments crises are persistent, and debt has sunk hopes for future growth. Defining these problems is easy; identifying acceptable solutions is not. Prescriptions for Latin American afflictions have generated heated debates among economists.

Many radical policy prescriptions find endorsement in Latin America, perhaps because the problems are so extreme and the need for solutions so urgent. Minor revisions of policy are unlikely to overcome malnutrition, hyperinflation, or fiscal insolvency. Debates about solutions to the region's problems spill over into the political arena; politicians mix economic theories in rhetoric meant to justify or oppose new policies. Latin America's experiments with radicalism have ranged from socialism to neoconservative liberalization.

At least two reasons account for the persistence of controversies about appropriate solutions to Latin America's problems. First, economic knowledge is imperfect. The data themselves are scarce and unreliable. Policies that seem to work in one context may fail in another; institutional differences do matter and can make it difficult to apply experiences from one place in another. For example, the effect of an exchange rate devaluation on export production depends on wage contracts, indexation rules, the strength of unions, access to credit from the local banking institutions, the capacity of shipping ports, and the extent of corruption among border police, to name just a few variables. Given the complexity of economic behavior, no economist can offer ready-made solutions to Latin America's problems with perfectly predictable results. Economists may agree in the abstract on which mistakes to avoid, but faced with a concrete situation, they may strongly disagree about the required reform. Economists agree that overvaluation should be avoided but disagree about whether the Mexican peso is overvalued today.

The second reason for debate over prescriptions for Latin America is that all programs have political ramifications. In promoting solutions to one problem—unsustainable external imbalances— economists implicitly support the impact of that policy in other areas, such as income distribution. One recommends devaluation to promote exports, while another opposes it on the grounds that food prices will rise and burden the poor. Different political priorities and uncertain consequences of policies generate fierce debates. In the example, neither economist knows with certainty by how much exports will grow or food prices will rise in response to a devaluation. The first economist may in fact be more oriented toward the immediate needs of the poor but estimates that a devaluation will strongly increase exports and only negligibly affect food prices.

Complex theoretical and empirical analyses try to resolve arguments, adding insight and new information. Bit by bit, these minor points form the basis of policy recommendations. If implemented, these policies can have an important impact on how people live. Because no economist is politically neutral, economic advice is inextricably linked with political perspectives.

2   WHY IS LATIN AMERICA UNDERDEVELOPED?

A Radical View

Dependencia as an explanation for underdevelopment emerged as a major school of thought in Latin America in the late 1950s. In conventional economic jargon, countries depend on trade and foreign technology; the world grows more interdependent because of increasing foreign investment. In such conventional views, there is nothing wrong with dependence. For the *dependencia* school, however, dependence describes characteristics causing underdevelopment. Its theorists introduced a dichotomy between core and periphery, or in more recent years, between North and South. Dependency is described as a situation in which the periphery can act only as a reflex of the expansion of the core economies.

Marxian dependency theory argues that capitalism places insuperable barriers before the working class. Without access to capital, workers cannot compete with the dominant firms. Elites are unlikely to act against their own self-interest to give the poor more power. Instead, the military serves to shore up the existing class structure. Union organizers are the first to feel the effects of repression. Nor will significant change come through international agencies, whose primary function is to sustain the dominance of the developed world. Only a very dramatic, revolutionary shift in the structure of political power will bring progress to the working class.

Dependency theory covers a wide range of interpretations and analyses. One of the earliest *dependencistas* was Paul Baran. He asserted that the economic development of the underdeveloped regions is inimical to interests in advanced capitalist countries. Thus, to avoid such development, advanced countries formed alliances with precapitalistic elites in the developing world to inhibit industrialization. The surplus produced in the underdeveloped countries is expropriated by foreign capital or squandered on imported luxury consumption by the elites. This process necessarily generates stagnation and demands a political solution. André Gunder Frank completed this analysis by arguing that the only political solution is a socialist revolution.

Fernando Henrique Cardoso and Enzo Faletto, before building up their own theory of dependency, claimed that the earlier school was mistaken in believing that capitalist development was not possible in the periphery. By 1967, when they wrote *Dependencia y Desarollo en America Latina*, industrialization was indeed a reality. Their interpretation shares with the previous school the view that the central dynamism of the Latin American economies lies outside their own countries, and thus their options are limited by the development of capitalism at the center. But they also emphasize the exploitative, unequal, and antagonistic patterns of social organization in Latin American countries.

An influential school of thought led by Raul Prebisch flourished in Santiago at the Economic Commission for Latin America (ECLA). Its starting point was the idea that the world is composed of two poles, the center and the periphery, and that the structure of production in each differs substantially. In the center, the structure of production is diversified; in the periphery, the structure is specialized in the sense that the export sector concentrates on a few primary products, with production confined to an enclave, having limited backward and forward linkage effects with the rest of the economy. The export sector, with relatively high productivity of labor, coexists with subsistence agriculture, with very low productivity.[1] Three tendencies mark the development of the periphery: unemployment of the labor force, external disequilibrium, and deterioration of the terms of trade. To escape these tendencies, the structure of production in the periphery has to be transformed. The essential element in this transformation was to be the ISI.

Dependencia theorists are harsh critics of foreign investment and MNCs. The international distribution of the gains from foreign investment has been at the center of a sharp debate throughout the postwar period. Neoclassical economists primarily see benefits in a policy of openness to capital flows. Foreign direct investment enhances the potential national income over time by increasing investment that cannot be financed with local savings, and it pumps up local production. Capital inflows add to the economy's productive capacity and thus potentially increase welfare. The literature on economic development in the neoclassical vein has emphasized that the gains from foreign investment go beyond this increase in productive capacity. Specifically, three additional positive effects are identified:

1. Foreign firms bring with them superior technology. Such direct investment comes with technical assistance and training possibilities.

2. Foreign direct investment increases competition in the host economy. In the presence of imperfect competition, goods are underproduced. The entry of a new firm reduces prices and leads to an increase in industrial output, with favorable welfare effects.

3. Foreign direct investment in a country's manufacturing export sector gives advantages in terms of foreign market access. These advantages stem from the foreign firms' experience in international markets or from their differential ability to gain market access abroad.

The market access argument is important in the context of trade restrictions in export markets. To the extent that foreign firms, by virtue of their residence, gain access where a developing country cannot, they become a vehicle for gains from trade. Of course, the question of the distribution of the rents arises.

A country may also obtain larger gains from trade if, rather than operating an export industry on its own, it draws on foreign firms for scale economy. This argument assumes that the country can, in fact, capture part of the rents stemming from the scale economy advantages enjoyed by the foreign firms.[2]

Starting with Singer (1950), discussion centered on the question of whether capital-importing developing countries actually benefited (or benefited relatively more than the capital exporters) from capital imports.[3] The basic thesis of this literature is that capital imports are invested in the traditional commodity export sector, with two consequences. First, the capacity expansion and productivity growth tend to be reflected in declining relative export prices. This terms of trade deterioration raises the possibility of net welfare losses. Second, unlike the manufacturing sector, primary commodity production offers little stimulation to the rest of the economy. Thus, foreign investment merely establishes an enclave rather than exerting a pervasive development effort.

The *dependencia* school shares this view and argues that the historical concentration of foreign investment in Latin America in the primary sector (extraction of minerals or production of agricultural exports) has benefited international capitalists far more than nationals. Moreover, foreign investment has failed to improve substantially the technological base of the economy because sophisticated capital and skilled technicians mainly come from abroad and limit spillover effects.

Dependency theory sees MNCs as unambiguously harmful, for a number of reasons:

• MNCs may lower domestic savings and investment by stifling competition, failing to reinvest much of their profits, and generating income for groups with a high propensity to import. By importing intermediates from overseas affiliates rather than buying them from indigenous firms, MNCs inhibit the expansion of local firms.

• In the long run, MNCs may cause foreign exchange shortages. The external accounts can deteriorate as a result of substantial importation of intermediates and capital goods. This problem is especially important when the MNC produces primarily for the domestic market. Repatriation of profits, interest, royalties, and management fees can add to this deterioration. The smaller are the original capital inflows, the larger is the local contribution of local bank credit, and the larger is the profit repatriation, the greater will be the negative impact on the external accounts.

• MNCs may contribute to the reduction of government revenues because of liberal tax concessions, investment allowances, disguised public subsidies, and tariff protection provided by the host government.

• MNCs may exacerbate income inequalities by promoting the interest of a small number of well-paid modern sector workers against the interest of nonskilled laborers by widening wage differentials. They can also divert resources away from needed food production and into the manufacture of sophisticated products catering to the demand of local elites. By establishing themselves in urban areas, they can exaggerate the existing inequality between rural and urban areas.

• MNCs may bring into the host country inappropriate products and stimulate inappropriate consumption patterns through advertising. They also use inappropriate technologies of production given the relative supply of factors of production. As a result, local resources tend to be allocated to socially undesirable projects.

• Intrafirm transactions may create opportunities for under- or overinvoicing of exports and imports in order to shift profits for tax purposes and to evade foreign trade taxes or exchange controls. It is especially difficult to fix an exact price for technology transfer if technology is transferred as one element of a package of resources provided by direct investment.

Dependency theory also argues that foreign investment has a profound impact on Latin America's social and political relations. Local managers of foreign firms create a bourgeois elite whose interests are tied to the success of the foreign firm. This class opposes unions, minimum wage legislation, and taxes on firms to finance social services. They also form the front line of resistance to expropriation. Their conservative voices are joined by those of the landed aristocracy who fear that any move to expropriate foreign assets might throw into question a broader range of property rights and trigger agrarian reform. Society becomes polarized. The working class and peasants confront a powerful local elite that depends on military repression to sustain the status quo.

Despite this long list of negatives, what may be bad a priori need not emerge in reality if the host government has the political commitment and instruments to avoid or mitigate such possibilities. Few countries are willing to allow MNCs unrestricted access to their territories today, and most recognize that direct investment might well be a valuable resource. Even the Sandinista regime made an effort to draw in foreign capital.

Mainstream Interpretations

The most common causes of underdevelopment cited by conventional economists are market size, slow capital accumulation, shortages of foreign exchange or skilled labor, and poor political organization. Few economists believe that there is a single barrier to growth. They explore the mechanisms through which these factors might affect output, but each weighs problems differently in assessing the impact of a policy on economic performance.

Although the various schools of thought on mainstream development theory appear in opposition to one another, it is absurd to align oneself with a single concept of development, however strong one's political allegiances. Economic ideas that survive the test of time contain a grain of truth even if not the single definitive answer to eliminating underdevelopment. Rather than perpetuate the misconception that economists themselves fall into easily identified intellectual camps, the goal of this section is to present an overview of ideas that compete (or should compete) within economists' minds.

The Big Push

Why are there so few shoe factories in Honduras? Because too few people can afford to buy shoes to justify investment in a factory. If an individual entrepreneur sets up a shoe factory, the employees will not spend enough on shoes to sustain the operation. Income in the rest of the country is too low to create enough demand to attract investment. If one could simultaneously establish several factories, producing a variety of goods, employment in them could raise consumer demand enough to maintain a healthy stream of profits, thereby inducing further investment and economic growth.

The view that demand in developing countries is too small to justify investment often assumes the existence of economies of scale in modern industries and oligopolistic market structures. Consequently, prices are sticky because firms avoid setting off price wars with one another. If demand slows, the price mechanism does not help to restimulate the economy. In a recession, such as the one caused by the recent debt crisis, a drop in demand will lead to a drop in output and employment.

The existence of economies of scale also supports the argument that small plants designed to meet local demand would be inefficient; demand must hit a minimum threshold before any investment is warranted. The implication is that governments should act to create demand. Increased government spending is justified on the grounds that it not only helps stimulate immediate economic growth but induces a long-run expansion of the economy by attracting more investment. This rapid expansion of demand is referred to as the big push.

Within this framework, supply-side shortages of capital were acknowledged as a constraint on growth early on. However, they were seen as a consequence of inadequate incomes and low savings, which in turn resulted from low incentives to invest in a demand-deficient environment. Government investment and higher incomes would not only invite more investment but would also increase savings, easing capital bottlenecks.

In Latin America, public enterprises dominate a wide range of economic activities, including banking, transport, and mining industries. Between 1985 and 1988, public investment accounted for more than half of total investment in Bolivia, for approximately half of total investment in Argentina, Chile, and Colombia, and for more than one-third of investment in Brazil, Uruguay, and Venezuela. In many countries, the explanation for the participation of government in production lies in the absence of a private sector capable of undertaking major projects.

Demand stimulation is controversial, but even critics of big government tend to agree that government spending in infrastructure and public goods is a good idea. Empirical evidence shows that there is an important complementarity between public and private investment. Government investment in fixed capital induces private investment because it increases productivity by providing infrastructure and services.

Complementarity between private and public investment does not rule out the possibility that an increase in total government spending (rather than just investment) could crowd out private investment. An increase in total spending not financed by an increase in taxes causes a deficit. A fiscal deficit financed by borrowing from the local credit market pushes up interest rates and reduces the availability of credit to the private sector.

If lack of faith in the fiscal soundness or political longevity of a regime makes it difficult to float government bonds, deficits are financed by printing money, which has a more immediate impact on the price level. Sustained excessive spending can easily set off high inflation. Even if many economists agree that temporary deficit spending is justified to stimulate the economy, they strongly disagree on whether inflation can be risked in trying to promote growth. And until recently in Latin America, they even debated whether deficits and inflation were connected. (Chapter 6 explores this issue by examining the debate between structuralists and monetarists.)

Foreign Aid

Foreign aid can serve as an alternative way to raise incomes and demand. The Alliance for Progress was the Kennedy administration's attempt to provide aid on a scale grand enough to enable Latin America to reach a self-reinforcing pattern of growth (box 3.1). Its failure to affect Latin American growth has been blamed on inadequate funding, the inability of Latin America to absorb aid rapidly, and a dampening of local entrepreneurial initiative in response to aid. Since then, smaller-scale aid programs have often been justified

Box 3.1
The Alliance for Progress

The Charter of Punta del Este, which formally inaugurated the Alliance for Progress, was signed on August 17, 1961. Until 1958, the United States consistently rejected proposals for an inter- American bank, stabilization schemes for export commodity prices, and Brazil's president Juscelino Kubitschek's Operation Pan America. The violently unfriendly reception to Vice-President Richard Nixon in Peru and Venezuela in 1956 and Fidel Castro's takeover in Cuba in January 1959 made the United States aware of economic stagnation, inflation, and distributional issues in Latin America. The Inter-American Development Bank was established in April 1959, and President Kennedy's proposal for an Alliance for Progress came six weeks after his inauguration.

on the basis of their power to stimulate markets and attract investment.[4] Table 3.1 shows the amount of aid received by Latin American countries in 1988.

As prospects for aid dimmed in the 1970s and Organization of Petroleum Exporting Countries (OPEC) dollars glutted credit markets, commercial loans became an important means of financing fiscal stimuli. Foreign credit enabled many Latin American regimes to stem the contractionary consequences of higher oil costs and financed remarkable booms in the oil exporting countries. Critics claim that the debt crisis itself is evidence of the failure of stimulative policies to solve Latin America's problems. While it is possible that capital flight, concentration of the borrowed funds in a few hands, and exchange rate overvaluation ruined the contribution of deficit spending to growth, the lesson from this experience is not new: demand stimulation may help growth in the short run but will not, in and of itself, overcome structural barriers to long-run growth.

Export Promotion

The World Bank supports export promotion as a market-oriented means of stimulating demand. If local demand is inadequate to justify construction of a shoe factory, why not try to sell shoes abroad? Not only could the export market justify investment in large plants with low average costs, benefiting domestic consumers,

Table 3.1
Concessional loans and grants from official sources to Latin American
countries, 1988

	Millions of dollars	Percentage of GNP
Argentina	152	0.2
Bolivia	392	9.1
Brazil	210	0.1
Chile	44	0.2
Colombia	61	0.2
Costa Rica	187	4.0
Dominican Republic	118	2.5
Ecuador	137	1.3
El Salvador	420	7.7
Guatemala	235	2.9
Haiti	147	5.9
Honduras	321	7.3
Mexico	173	0.1
Nicaragua	213	n.a.
Panama	22	n.a.
Paraguay	76	1.3
Peru	272	1.1
Uruguay	41	0.5
Venezuela	18	0.0

Note: Including multilateral agencies but excluding military aid.
Source: World Bank, *World Development Report* (Washington, D.C.: World Bank,
1990).

but it would provide jobs and income to stimulate domestic demand.
Furthermore, export earnings would finance imports of goods that
cannot be efficiently produced domestically.

Latin America has been very slow to adopt this strategy. Resistance lies in the difficulty of accepting its implied policy initiatives:

• Devalue to encourage exports.

• Cut real wages to compete in world markets.

• Reduce government spending to prevent inflationary erosion of
the exchange rate.

• Eliminate protection of domestic firms to force them to compete internationally.

Consumers of imported food and an upper class addicted to trips to Disneyworld object to the devaluation. Workers object to the cut in wages. Bureaucrats resist the paring down of government staff. And firms with market power based on protectionism fear the effects of competition.

Critics contend that the combination of lower real wages and fiscal contraction will induce a recession. Promoters of export-oriented growth acknowledge that the program may induce a short-run recession but argue that long-run growth rates will rise.

Opponents of export promotion also claim that export expansion is possible only after production for the domestic market is well established, as the history of automobile production in Japan and Korea demonstrates. They argue that firms first need experience in their domestic market, preferably with protection, to develop the sophistication to enter world markets.

Protectionism in the developed countries is also said to make it difficult for Latin American countries to expand through export promotion.

Whatever their merits, demand-driven-growth arguments remain important in the policymaking arena. They underlie explanations used to oppose austerity in debt-ridden countries. By dampening domestic demand, austerity reduces incentives to invest and slows the growth in capacity needed to make debt repayment possible.[5]

What is missing in the demand-driven-growth approach is a realistic sense of resource availability. It has produced substantial budget deficits that created financial instability throughout Latin America.

Savings and Foreign Exchange

An approach to development more prevalent among economists than policymakers emphasizes that growth cannot take place without an increase in the resources for production. In the absence of technical progress, output growth is limited by the rate of capital formation (which depends on the savings rate) and the rate of labor force growth. In labor-abundant developing countries, this model implies, capital shortages constrain growth. So dominant is this theory of growth that the terms *developed* and *less developed countries* became synonymous with the distinction between capital-rich and capital-poor countries.

If the savings rate is too low, output is being used to satisfy current consumption rather than to expand the economy's capital stock and its capacity for future production. Far from stimulating consumption through deficit spending, governments should be encouraging higher savings rates, taxing to finance public investment in infrastructure, and promoting stronger banking institutions to offer credit to entrepreneurs.

The long-run-growth rate of a savings-constrained economy can also be increased through foreign aid or commercial borrowing. Within this framework, there is a strong argument for funneling aid and loans directly into investment rather than consumption (unless one views food subsidies for the poor as investment in the development of a healthy, more productive work force). The apparent failure of borrowed funds to contribute to growth is usually pinned on its misuse for current consumption.

The two-gap model adds a foreign exchange constraint to the savings constraint. The key assumption associated with a foreign exchange constraint is that less developed economies cannot produce all types of goods necessary for production. Sewing machines, lathes, backhoes, and computers may need to be imported. This analysis assumes limited substitution between factors of production: without foreign exchange to buy sewing machines, the country cannot expand its output of shoes. Although shoes can be sewn by hand and ditches dug with shovels, those who emphasize the importance of foreign exchange shortages assume that substitution is difficult. Use of manual labor dramatically slows the production process, and in some cases, workers lack the accuracy and technical capacities of machines. In addition, essential raw materials, such as petroleum, may be in short supply in the developing country.

A binding foreign exchange constraint implies that the economy has the savings rate to support investment but that domestic output is not easily exchanged for essential imported factors of production. Reasons for poor export performance range from domestic problems like inadequate development of ports, weak marketing skills, and overvalued exchange rates to foreign monopolistic control of markets and protectionism abroad.

Belief in the dominance of a foreign exchange constraint can generate divergent policy prescriptions. Liberals have argued that aid and loans from abroad can provide foreign exchange to support growth. If foreign credit is used to increase the less developed countries' (LDC) capital stock, gains in output generated through foreign credit can provide a basis for repayment of borrowed credit.

The more market-oriented view has been that growth depends on increased competitiveness abroad. Thus, promotion of greater export orientation through devaluations, reduced export taxes, and wage cuts can provide the foreign exchange needed to import goods that cannot be made at home.

A somewhat different twist on the same line of analysis is that growth depends on an opening of markets in the developed world. Demands for reduced protectionism or, better, preferential access to protected markets (where high prices prevail) would stimulate LDC growth. Calls for "trade not aid" or "trade, and aid" from Third World leaders have persuaded wealthier countries to implement some special quotas for developing countries.

An alternative proposition that follows from the foreign exchange constraint analysis is that developing countries should try to overcome the causes of their dependence on foreign exchange. Arguments for protectionism in the early postwar period were consistent with the notion that foreign exchange constrains growth. Supporters of import substitution programs argued that developing countries must acquire the capacity to produce more sophisticated goods to escape dependence on foreign markets. Governments should encourage domestic production of basic goods like steel and cement and, lacking private interest in these sectors, establish state-run enterprises to get basic industries off the ground. In order to accumulate the technology to produce more sophisticated goods, they should also encourage assembly of cars, trucks, and electrical appliances through protectionist tariffs and quotas. Until the late 1960s, import substitution strategies dominated Latin American economic plans.

Although enthusiasm for import substitution as an overall strategy for growth has faded, protectionism persists throughout Latin America and is often justified on the ground that it reduces dependency on export earnings. Critics of import substitution invoke the principle of comparative advantage: a policy of self-sufficient growth underperforms export-oriented strategies because of differences in factor endowments underlying international productivity differences. (We explore a host of issues associated with import substitution in the 1950s and 1960s in chapter 4.)

Human Capital

Human capital shortages are often seen as a critical barrier to growth. The basic argument is that more physical capital or foreign exchange may not improve growth rates if the country lacks enough skilled workers to put these resources to work. The policy prescription is obvious: governments should direct more attention to education. The most common criticism of increases in educational spending is that programs are often misdirected, training superfluous lawyers, accountants, and social scientists instead of mechanics, engineers, and medical technicians.

A broader version of the skill constraint argument is that the poor cannot work productively if they are hungry most of the time, and poor children cannot develop their full mental abilities if they are malnourished. Not only should education be publicly financed, but programs should be put in place to subsidize basic goods consumed by the poor.[6] Given the extensiveness of poverty throughout Latin America, any serious effort to overcome this barrier to growth would involve substantial public spending and income redistribution. Critics claim that although such programs may be desirable on humanitarian grounds, malnutrition is not the main cause of slow growth but a consequence of it.

Laissez-Faire

A different perspective on development comes from economists with faith in the market. Conservatives stress that growth has mainly been hampered not by lack of resources but by massive government interference with market mechanisms. Governments try to satisfy politically powerful unions with minimum wage legislation and thereby raise costs above internationally competitive levels. To assuage business, they offer protection from foreign firms but in doing so cut off incentives to produce cheaply and efficiently. Inefficiency is also evident in government-owned factories, which lack managerial initiative. Overvalued exchange rates prevent the development of a strong export sector and contribute to balance of payments crises. They also combine with protectionist quotas to generate a morass of bureaucratic delays that stymie business. Deficit financing of excessive government interference in the economy has fueled inflation and discouraged investment. Even foreign aid comes under fire: food aid depresses local food prices and hurts domestic production, while foreign credit dampens domestic incentives to save.

The remedy for this malaise is a general dismantling of government programs and intervention—what has come to be known as economic liberalization and deregulation. The primary policy targets are privatization of government enterprises, repeal of minimum wage laws, elimination of tariffs and quotas, reduced spending on social welfare programs, and incentives for investment in the form of lower taxes and stronger protection of private property.

Critics of this school argue that the history of Latin America provides ample evidence that economic development cannot occur without government help. Even if one believes that private investment is the engine of growth, at the very least governments should provide goods with positive externalities to firms: roads, ports, police, elementary education. More broadly viewed, social welfare programs and minimum wage legislation provide political stability that is essential to attract investment. Because the short-run distributional consequences of the laissez-faire agenda tend to favor the rich, critics claim that liberalization is merely a ploy for promoting the interests of the wealthy rather than a strategy for overall economic growth.[7]

3 PRESCRIPTIONS

By their nature, theories of development imply policy prescriptions. We would be fools not to use the knowledge we accumulate, but resolving differences among theories is difficult. They are not easily testable; rarely is one strategy fully implemented, and even then evaluation of its results is debatable.

To pretend that policies are aimed at the general good but often fail to deliver on their promises is ingenuous. Policy prescriptions have different effects on various social groups. Employed workers who benefit from minimum wage legislation and social service programs are obviously unlikely to support laissez-faire theories of development, and few farm owners cheer the prospects of agrarian reform. Income distribution and the history of grabbing power through force in Latin America belie any notion that policymakers intend to act in the interest of the majority. In the end, policies reflect economic logic that is or is not sound, a constantly changing global context, and the political allegiances of those who institute the policy.

Economic theories about Latin America's development tend to fall into two broad categories: interventionist and laissez-faire.[8] In principle, most theories can serve the interests of poor Latin Americans. In practice, each has shown its vulnerability to abuse.

Interventionist models tend to emphasize the need for government involvement to overcome barriers to growth. Governments should act to create jobs, support minimum wages, and sustain demand. Austerity is somewhat self-defeating since recessions reduce investment and stunt growth. A second justification for an active government lies in the argument that resource bottlenecks constrain Latin American growth. Historically, shortages of skills and technology were the basis for investing heavily in joint ventures with foreign firms to produce vehicles, appliances, and pharmaceuticals. With the help of borrowed funds, growth was to overcome these barriers and ultimately generate enough foreign exchange and savings to service the debt. Today intervention is seen as essential to mitigate the effect of the debt crisis on poor Latin Americans and to provide a stimulus for new growth.

Active government intervention has been associated with heavy deficit spending, much of it financed by printing money. The result is hyperinflation. Capital borrowed in the 1970s did not yield the anticipated effect on output; having seen little gain in their income, Latin Americans now face higher bills. What went wrong? Public expenditures were too wasteful and concentrated too heavily on consumption, including subsidies of basic goods, instead of on investment. Laissez-faire agendas for growth argue that government interference with natural market mechanisms has hampered Latin American development.

A relatively new body of literature argues that a shift toward laissez-faire would actually favor the poor. Elimination of the repressive regulations that favor elite industrialists would free small business to grow rapidly. Potential growth is in the eye of the beholder; where de Soto sees a budding entrepreneur holding out roses on the street corner, others see a kid who could use an education, some free health care and a chance to feel that life is not simply a scramble for survival.[9] In fact, the peasant who has no land and cannot feed her children is interested not in theories to explain her condition but in programs that will solve her problems. Less is gained in debating ideology than in finding policies that work.

FURTHER READING

Palma, G. "Dependency and Development: A Critical Overview." In D. Seers, ed., *Dependency Theory: A Critical Reassessment*. London: Frances Pinter Publishers, 1981.

Lall, S. "Is Dependency a Useful Concept in Understanding Development?" *World Development* 3, no.11 (1975): 799–810.

Wiarda, H. "Misreading Latin America Again." *Foreign Policy* 65, no. 1 (1987): 135–153.

Chapter 4

FROM IMPORT SUBSTITUTION TO TRADE LIBERALIZATION

Protection used to be the rule in Latin America. Today radical change is underway as economies open to trade and investment. In 1990, under pressure from the United States, Brazil relented and allowed Microsoft to sell its MS-DOS 3.2 in a market that was once reserved solely for domestic firms. Mexico revised its requirement that cars have 60 percent of their value domestically produced. Struggling to overcome a reputation for bureaucratic red tape, Argentina courts foreign investment in assembly industries.

This chapter discusses exchange rates and commercial policies in Latin America. After reviewing basic concepts, we examine the pros and cons of import substitution industrialization. We also discuss the consequences of ISI, failed and successful attempts at trade liberalization, and the recent trend toward free trade agreements.

For fifty years, Latin America pursued an inward-looking strategy, supported by the United Nations's ECLA under Raul Prebisch's leadership. Exchange and trade restrictions—such as multiple exchange rates, protective tariffs, import licenses, quotas, and export taxes—served to limit trade flows and to reserve local markets for domestic producers. The goal was to provide a training ground for industry, which might eventually compete internationally. Hard experience proved that development policies that pay little attention to trade imbalances are unsustainable. Distortions in the relationship between international and domestic prices led to a host of inefficient firms that served domestic consumers poorly and drained foreign reserves. Yet the protectionist policies associated with ISI played an important role in stimulating economic development in Latin America. Certainly viable alternatives to the ISI strategies of the 1940s and 1950s were not present. Moreover, Latin America enjoyed high growth rates prior to the 1970s.

As Latin American countries continued to rely heavily on tariff and nontariff trade barriers well beyond the early stages of industrialization, local industry failed to become competitive in the world market. The implications were twofold: Latin Americans paid high prices for domestically produced goods of poor quality and lacked foreign exchange to pay for essential imports. The region's imports and exports of goods in the 1950s and 1960s grew well below the world average (tables A.1 and A.2 in appendix A). Forced to confront chronic external imbalances, by 1990 most Latin leaders talked loudly of introducing trade reforms in their countries.

1 EXTERNAL POLICIES

Openness Measures

A country's propensity to trade depends on its size. Small countries, in general, produce fewer goods and thus rely on exports to pay for essential imports. Bigger countries tend to be more self-sufficient. Worldwide, the countries with the lowest ratio of trade to GDP have more than 100 million people (figure 4.1). In Latin America, the two largest countries, Brazil and Mexico, are also the least open to trade. The smallest countries, such as Honduras and Costa Rica, are the most open (table 4.1).[1]

The propensity to trade also depends on a country's exchange rate policy, its import restrictions, and the incentives to export. Although it is changing, Brazil is still a highly protected economy. Size and protection make Brazil's ratio of imports and exports to GDP one of the lowest in the world.

Nominal and Real Exchange Rates

The analysis of trade issues, such as the performance of the export sector and import growth, requires measures of international competitiveness. But competitiveness is hard to pin down because quality and technological sophistication are as important as price. Real exchange rates are an important, if only partial, determinant of competitiveness and behave quite differently from nominal ex-

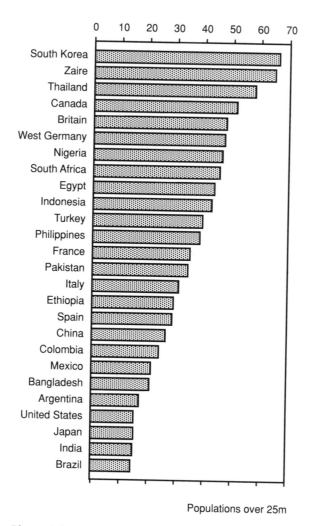

Populations over 25m

Figure 4.1
Exports plus imports as a percentage of GDP, selected countries, 1988.
Source: World Bank, *World Tables*, Washington, D.C.: World Bank, 1990.

Table 4.1
Ratio of trade to GDP (combined value of exports and imports of goods
and services as a percentage of GDP), Latin American countries,
1970–1980

	1970	1980
Highly open		
Venezuela	45	108
Honduras	59	96
Costa Rica	63	90
Relatively open		
Chile	39	80
Ecuador	33	78
El Salvador	42	74
Nicaragua	52	74
Bolivia	43	72
Dominican Republic	43	60
Uruguay	27	59
Moderately open		
Haiti	27	54
Argentina	21	51
Colombia	34	47
Guatemala	29	47
Peru	30	46
Paraguay	25	46
Mexico	20	44
Less open		
Brazil	16	30

Note: These ratios include imports and exports of services. They are not comparable
to ratios that include only imports and exports of goods.
Source: Inter-American Development Bank, *Economic and Social Progress in Latin
America: The External Sector* (Washington, D.C.: IDB, 1982).

change rates. A commonly used definition of the real exchange rate
is the nominal rate deflated by the ratio between domestic prices and
foreign prices. If country A's currency is the peso, then its real
exchange rate in dollar/peso terms is:

$$\text{Real exchange rate} = \frac{\text{Prices of country A in pesos}}{\text{Foreign prices in dollars}} \times (\text{Dollar/peso exchange rate}).$$

By this measure, an increase in the real exchange rate denotes a real
appreciation. Real appreciation of the local currency implies that
one dollar buys fewer hours of labor in an assembly plant or in the
fields. The result is that coffee, blue jeans, and soybeans cost more
to produce and the country loses price competitiveness in international markets. Conversely, a reduction in the real exchange rate
denotes a real depreciation and an increase in competitiveness.[2] In
figures 4.2 to 4.5, an increase in the real exchange rate denotes a
strengthening of local currencies relative to the dollar and, thus, a
weakening in competitiveness.[3]

Nominal devaluations seek to generate a real devaluation and
thus increase competitiveness and improve the external position of
the country. If inflation proceeds more rapidly than nominal devaluations, the local currency will continue to appreciate in real terms.
In early 1988, Nicaragua devalued the cordoba by 3,000 percent, but
with inflation running at over 10,000 percent, the currency continued to appreciate in real terms. In order for the nominal devaluation
to achieve a real depreciation, policies that accompany the devaluation must not accelerate inflation.

In the 1950s, fixed exchange rates and domestic inflation created
overvaluation of real exchange rates throughout Latin America. The
adoption of a crawling peg in the 1960s in Colombia, Chile, and
Brazil offered an escape from the problem of overvaluation, but even
they faced renewed overvaluation as policymakers sought to avoid
a free-fall of the currency.

Figures 4.2 to 4.5 show the real exchange rates of Argentina,
Brazil, Chile, and Mexico between 1970 and 1989. The instability
of the Argentine economy is illustrated by the extreme oscillations
of its real exchange rate. Its extraordinary swings reflect economic
policy mistakes as well as external shocks. The outstanding episode

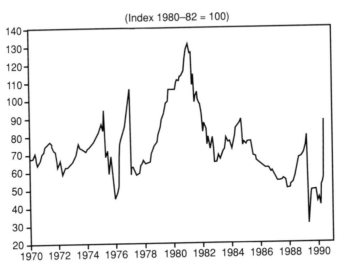

Figure 4.2
Index of the real exchange rate, Argentina, 1970–1990.
Source: Morgan Guaranty Trust Company, *World Financial Markets*, various issues. Note: Morgan Guaranty defines the effective real exchange rate as domestic prices/foreign prices, as we do in the text. A movement upward indicates a real appreciation.

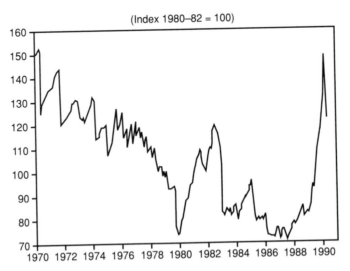

Figure 4.3
Index of the real exchange rate, Brazil, 1970–1990.
Source: Morgan Guaranty Trust Company, *World Financial Markets*, various issues.

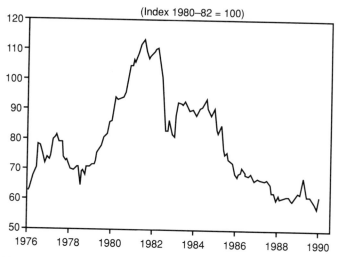

Figure 4.4
Index of the real exchange rate, Chile, 1970–1990.
Source: Morgan Guaranty Trust Company, *World Financial Markets*, various issues.

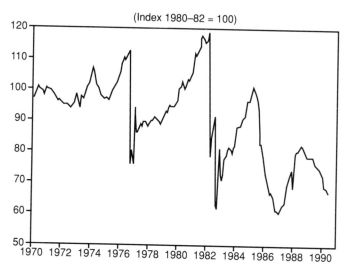

Figure 4.5
Index of the real exchange rate, Mexico, 1970–1990.
Source: Morgan Guaranty Trust Company, *World Financial Markets*, various issues.

is the neoconservative regimes' appreciation of 1979–1981, which was followed by the collapse of the peso.[4]

Overvaluation can be sustained in the medium run only if policymakers introduce import controls, as in the 1950s and 1960s, or if they can borrow abroad, as in the 1970s. In recent years, a few Latin American countries have been able to avoid depreciation in the short run by sticking to an external debt moratorium. Ultimately the trade imbalances associated with overvaluation tend to create black markets for foreign exchange. In cases of extreme hyperinflation, even governments find it difficult to transact business at absurd exchange rates.

Why have Latin American policymakers allowed overvaluation to persist? During the heyday of ISI, overvaluation served as a subsidy on essential imported inputs for industry. Import licenses were used to clear foreign exchange markets. In the 1970s, Southern Cone countries adopted fixed exchange rates in an effort to stem inflation by imposing discipline on price setters, who would have to compete with cheaper imports. They also hoped that fixed rates would provide a benchmark to which inflationary expectations could converge. (We discuss these fantastic overvaluation episodes of the late 1970s in chapter 7.)

Politically, devaluation can bring about massive protests. A devaluation increases the cost of all imported goods, including food and gasoline. The export sector (and producers of goods that compete with imports) get a boost, but this does not readily translate into higher wages in a labor-surplus economy. Industries that rely on imported inputs see their costs rise and lay off workers. As import-dependent industry gained power under ISI, the opposition to devaluation became formidable.

Mexican Exchange Rates

The behavior of Mexican exchange rates is fascinating. From the mid-1920s to the early 1930s, the exchange rate was fixed in terms of gold, but silver coins were the main medium of exchange and fluctuated with regard to gold. In practice, this system acted as a flexible exchange rate. Between 1925 and 1934, the nominal exchange rate changed every year. It was then fixed for seven years. Starting in 1950, with one interruption in 1954, Mexico had a fixed nominal rate for twenty-five years. In the twenty years between 1955 and 1975, the real exchange rate appreciated slowly but continuously in response to modest inflation.

By 1975 overvaluation of the Mexican peso had become a serious issue. Inflation increased because of government spending and, later, a rise in oil prices. As a result of overvaluation, the current account deteriorated, and the external debt increased.[5] From 1974 to 1976, the public external debt doubled from $11 billion to $21 billion. Part of the increase in external debt financed capital flight. Finally, unable to sustain the currency against capital flight, President Luis Echeverria devalued the exchange rate to the dollar for the first time in twenty-three years, from 12.5 to 19 pesos in 1976.

By the early 1980s, overvaluation and capital flight were once again major problems (figure 4.5). Increased openness of the Mexican economy, resulting from oil exports and a growing external debt, made the economy especially vulnerable to external shocks. The first came with the rise in world interest rates, which dramatically increased the cost of servicing the debt. The second was the fall of oil prices in 1981. Instead of adjusting macroeconomic policy to these shocks by reducing spending and realigning the exchange rate, the government opted to borrow more. Access to foreign capital was plentiful, but few believed these policies were sustainable. Capital flight increased once again. The external public debt jumped to $52 billion.

By early 1982, the exchange rate could no longer be maintained. The central bank pulled out of the foreign exchange market, causing an immediate devaluation of 70 percent. In August, faced with the erosion of the country's foreign reserves, the government adopted a dual exchange rate system in an attempt to avoid the inflationary pressures of massive devaluation. It also nationalized banks and established exchange controls for the first time since a failed attempt to impose exchange controls in 1930. A black market developed. Thereafter the peso continued drifting downward, first in the black market and then in the official market, until its value stabilized with the new administration of President Miguel de la Madrid and an austerity program guided by the International Monetary Fund (IMF).

Use of a dual exchange rate regime instead of a fixed rate is usually based on the notion that it will allow a country to protect the commercial rate and domestic prices from fluctuations caused by speculation against the domestic currency. Early analytical work conveyed the impression that a dual exchange regime could isolate the production side of the economy from disturbances in the capital market. Experience has since shown that separating the two markets is difficult. Interest rates and relative prices serve as important channels between the two markets. In equilibrium, the two rates have to depreciate at the same pace. The merits of dual exchange rates thus depend on whether they help adjustment to crises in the short run by averting bankruptcies and by isolating the budget deficit from rapid deterioration.

In the Mexican case, the first effect seemed present: private businesses had access to the controlled exchange rate to service their external debts. The question of its impact on the budget is unclear. The government gained mainly because essential imports were bought at the controlled rate, and thus it may have avoided subsidies to imported foodstuffs, whose prices would have skyrocketed otherwise. On the other hand, the government had to buy exchange in the free market to service its own debt. To know whether the dual rate system actually favored the budget, one would have to calculate the government balance for goods and services transacted under each category and estimate the alternative single exchange rate.

If there is a lesson to be learned from the Mexican experience, it is that imbalances that are left to accumulate for too long are extremely painful to correct. Oil discoveries in the late 1970s permitted policymakers to postpone correction of overvaluation, price distortions, and misallocation of resources. Adjustments to the adverse shocks of the early 1980s were extremely costly. Real wages in the 1980s fell by approximately 50 percent, and signs of recovery were only starting to be seen in 1989.

Commercial Policies

Latin American countries have historically maintained highly protective trade regimes. Protection was introduced as a major instrument of industrialization and took the form of tariffs, total prohibition of certain goods, quotas, and discretionary licensing of imports. Table 4.2 shows the ratio of import duties to total tax revenues and the ratio of import duties to total imports. This gives only a partial picture of how much protection is in place because it measures tariff

Table 4.2
Import duties, Latin American countries, averages for 1978–1984
(percentage)

	Import duties/ total tax revenue	Import duties/ total imports
Argentina	8.2	16.3
Brazil	3.0	6.8
Colombia	14.9	11.4
Costa Rica	9.8	4.9
Mexico	5.5	9.4
Nicaragua	15.9	9.3
Venezuela	7.9	9.2

Source: Margaret Kelly et al., *Issues and Developments in International Trade Policy*
IMF Occasional Paper no. 63 (Washington, D.C.: International Monetary Fund, 1986).

Table 4.3
Nominal and actual tariff rates, Brazil, 1982 (weighted averages,
percentage)

	Nominal	Actual
Total imports, except fuels and wheat	47.5	13.7
Total imports	22.4	5.9

Source: Heloisa Correia e Aloisio de Araujo, *Politica Brasileira de Importacoes: Uma Descricao* (Rio: INPES/IPEA, 1984).

revenues on only goods that were imported. Goods subject to very high tariffs never get imported, and other goods are simply not allowed in.

In many Latin American countries, nontariff barriers are more important than tariff barriers. We illustrate with the case of Brazil. Table 4.3 shows the legal and implemented average tariff rates. The former are considerable, averaging 47 percent, excluding the non-dutiable fuel and wheat imports. But actual tariff rates, measured by the ratio of duties to total imports, are only 6 percent. The explanation is straightforward: if imports are permitted at all, they are almost always exempt from tariffs or receive large rate reductions. Import licenses rather than tariffs serve to exclude goods. There is a large degree of administrative discretion in the allocation of licenses; a foreign car will enter freely for use in one firm, while another firm's petition to admit the same type of car is denied. The arbitrary nature of this discretion increases inefficiency.[6]

2   IMPORT SUBSTITUTION INDUSTRIALIZATION

From the 1930s to the early 1960s, a growth strategy known as import substitution industrialization (ISI) dominated economic planning in Latin America. Although the region has long since undergone a reversal of the ideology associated with ISI, the economic structure in place today contains vestiges of this attempt to achieve industrial self-sufficiency. Factories constructed under ISI continue to operate today, and policies from this era remained intact well into the 1980s despite disillusionment with them. As antecedents to current economic problems in the region, ISI policies have had a profound effect.

The Great Depression backed many Latin American countries into an ISI strategy by default. The drop in international commodity prices left Latin Americans with little foreign exchange to spend on imports, forcing them to produce substitutes for imported essentials. This is not to imply that the crash stimulated growth in the region; real incomes plummeted with lower export earnings. However, political agitation in urban areas prompted governments to finance new industrial projects to create employment. Protectionist barriers were also erected to cope with balance of payments problems and protect local jobs.

World War II accelerated industrialization. Capacity shortages existed throughout the industrialized countries. Latin Americans enjoyed a recovery in the demand for their raw materials and were even able to compete in some markets for manufactured goods. At the same time, they were unable to import goods with their new export earnings. Unsatiated domestic demand stimulated expansion in the region's industrial capacity.

These secular influences on policy were complemented by the support of intellectuals who viewed ISI as a means of escaping dependence on unstable world markets. Although ISI was well underway as a strategy of development by then, R. Prebisch's work in 1949 for ECLA, arguing for changes in the structure of production in the periphery, became the classic doctrine of this growth model.

Arguments in Favor of ISI

Economists joined politicians in their support for ISI, calling attention to the lack of foreign exchange as an important constraint on growth. In a world where the terms of trade moved against traditional primary export products, domestic production would have to substitute for nonessential imports, freeing foreign exchange for needed inputs. Moreover, while technical progress in agriculture would leave labor unemployed, industry could absorb the growing population with increasing productivity and incomes. In the microeconomic sphere, markets in developing countries were thought to operate imperfectly, failing to make full use of an economy's resources. Expansion of domestic production required protection against imports and active government support in reducing barriers to industrial growth. The most common rationales in favor of ISI follow.

Volatility of Primary Commodities Prices

Primary commodity markets are unstable, and the concentration of exports in primary goods is risky. Good harvests worldwide can lead to a collapse of agricultural prices, especially in markets for tropical commodities, which do not benefit from price stabilization programs.

Mineral prices are also unstable; demand is highly sensitive to recessions in industrialized markets because metals like copper are heavily used in construction and new equipment. This instability is exacerbated by speculative stockpiling.

Latin American countries have seen their markets in guano, cochineal, cotton, rubber, hemp, tin, and copper erode as a result of innovation. Technological change also destroys markets for manufactured goods, but critics of primary export dependence argued that retooling factories for new products is generally easier than shifting the use of natural resources.

Declining Terms of Trade

The Prebisch-Singer hypothesis argued that there is a structural tendency for the terms of trade of developing countries to deteriorate because of the concentration of their exports in primary commodities. The terms of trade of Latin America are defined as:

$$\frac{\text{Latin American}}{\text{Terms of Trade}} = \frac{\text{Dollar Price of Latin America's Exports}}{\text{Dollar Price of Latin America's Imports}}$$

Figure 4.6 shows Latin America's terms of trade between 1930 and 1985, figure 4.7 shows the price of nonfuel primary commodities relative to industrialized goods, and figure 4.8 shows the price of metals relative to industrialized goods. This data tend to support the Prebisch-Singer hypothesis, but studies using different end points often reject it.

Underlying the deteriorating terms of trade observed by Singer and Prebisch are several factors:

• Demand for primary goods expands less rapidly than demand for industrial goods due to a lower income elasticity (Engel's Law). A 10 percent increase in world income does not raise demand for coffee by 10 percent. In the long term, there is a shift in consumption to goods that involve more skill and less raw material.

• The technological superiority of the industrial countries means that their exports embody a more sophisticated technology and their prices embody profits from innovation, including the development of synthetic substitutes for primary commodities.

• The structure of labor markets is different in industrial and developing countries. In industrial countries, technical progress leads to higher factor incomes rather than lower prices of exports. In developing countries, productivity gains are not translated into higher wages because of widespread unemployment; instead, prices decline. An increase in productivity thus benefits overseas consumers rather than developing country producers.

Dynamic Nature of Resource Endowments

The theory of comparative advantage, which underlies arguments for free trade, implies that countries gain by exporting goods that intensively use their relatively abundant factors. In Latin America, these are natural resources and labor. The theory fails to take into account, however, the dynamic nature of resource endowments. Developing countries are capital poor, but capital is not a natural endowment; it is accumulated in response to market conditions. Supporters of protectionism argued that concentration in labor-intensive exports would simply trap workers in low wage industries.

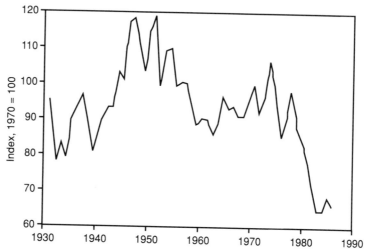

Figure 4.6
Latin America's terms of trade, nonoil exporting countries, 1930–1985.
Source: Economic Commission for Latin America and the Caribbean,
*Preliminary Overview of the Economy of Latin America and the Caribbean,
1985* (Santiago: United Nations, 1985, 155)

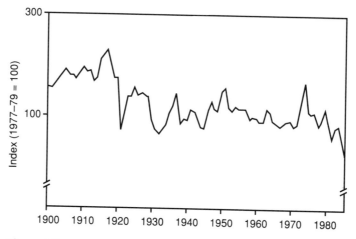

Figure 4.7
Price of nonfuel commodities/price of industrialized goods, 1900–1986.
Source: E. Grilli and M. C. Yang, "Primary Commodity Prices, Manufactured
Goods and the Terms of Trade," *World Bank Review* 1 (January 1988) 14.

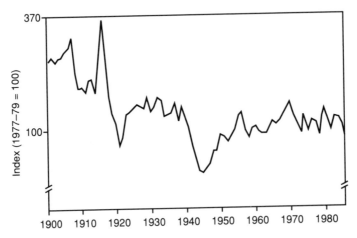

Figure 4.8
Price of metals/price of industrialized goods, 1900–1986.
Source: E. Grilli and M. C. Yang, "Primary Commodity Prices, Manufactured Goods and the Terms of Trade," *World Bank Review* 1 (January 1988) 16.

Governments must provide incentives—protection and financing—to attract investment in factories and equipment, shifting the resource balance from capital poor to capital rich.

Infant Industry

A related argument is that efficiency improves with experience. Whereas developed countries have moved well along the learning curve, Latin American industrialists are just starting out. The point of protection is to enable the firm to acquire the experience necessary to be competitive and perhaps eventually to export its product.

Caveats against infant industry protection were no different in Latin America than elsewhere: how can governments identify potentially competitive firms that merit protection? How long should consumers pay triple the international price of a washing machine for the sake of establishing a washing machine industry in Colombia? And if this industry is so promising, why won't private investors absorb the initial costs needed to establish the firm? For the most part, Latin American policies of protection have done little to ensure long-run competitiveness. This stands in contrast to Asian NICs, which made success in export markets a condition for continued government support. An exception is Brazil, which set an eight-year limit on protection given to its computer industry.

Linkages

Promoters of ISI argued that key industries have positive spillover effects. An automobile assembly plant generates demand for parts and steel, stimulating domestic production. As more supplier industries grow, bottlenecks that stymie other industries are eased. But the private sector may not be in the position to set this kind of growth in motion. Without a supply of steel, potential owners of a tool factory do not enter business, yet entrepreneurs considering construction of a steel plant reject the idea for lack of apparent demand. Government intervention is necessary to break this knot of inaction.

Elasticity Pessimism

ISI offered a solution to balance of payments deficits, at least in the short run. The assumption is that it is easier to cut imports by blocking their entry than it is to entice producers to increase exports. Policymakers who believe a real devaluation will have little positive impact on the trade balance are called elasticity pessimists. They are bound to be right in the very short run. A real devaluation takes time to work because resources must be transferred from nontraded goods to traded goods. But it is now widely believed that a real devaluation helps the external account in the medium run.

Export promotion might also face restrictions abroad. In 1982, for instance, almost half of Brazilian exports to the European Community and to the United States were affected by trade restrictions in these regions (table 4.4).

3 IMPLEMENTATION OF ISI

In practice, ISI differed from protectionism in industrialized countries. Whereas protectionism in developed countries has typically been aimed at helping specific industries, ISI was adopted as an economy-wide strategy. Moreover, the goal of ISI was to establish new industries, not simply to protect existing firms. Governments were expected to play an active role in the economy, with benefits

Table 4.4
Manufactured exports affected by trade restrictions abroad as a percentage of exports by destination, Brazil, 1982

Australia	4.7
Canada	22.0
Chile	1.5
European Community	44.7
United States	43.6

Source: S. Anjaria, et al., *Trade Policy Issues and Developments*, IMF Occasional Paper, no. 38 (Washington, D.C.: International Monetary Fund, 1985).

extending beyond the small number of workers already employed in industry.

The main tools used to implement an ISI strategy were import licensing, tariffs, overvalued exchange rates, and direct government investment in key industries. Import licensing enabled the government to control the composition of imports in order to promote specific activities. Essential goods—mainly food, capital goods, and intermediate inputs—were given preference, while imports of final consumer goods were discouraged with administrative red tape. Essential goods entered under lower tariffs and at preferential exchange rates. Multiple exchange rate systems served as an important mechanism for subsidizing favored goods.

Governments themselves constructed plants in heavy industries—steel, cement, utilities, and airplanes—where the amount of start-up capital involved was thought to discourage private investment. New plants in automobiles, pharmaceuticals, and grain processing were set up as joint ventures with foreign firms. Foreign firms provided access to technology, while government ownership limited the repatriation of profits abroad.

Latin American governments also stimulated industry through low interest rates and easy access to credit under soft monetary regimes. Publicly owned enterprises subsidized intermediate goods like electricity and steel by running in the red. Price ceilings on wage goods, especially food, helped to keep down labor costs for urban employers.

4   CONSEQUENCES OF ISI

The ISI model made sense, but it downplayed market forces and confronted three major limitations:

1. Protection led to overvalued exchange rates and hence to slow export growth.

2. In sectoral terms, import substitution policies exaggerated industrial growth at the expense of agriculture. Relatively capital-intensive manufactures absorbed only a fraction of the labor force, which grew with urban migration, placing pressure on government to serve as an employer of last resort.

3. As revenues from primary export taxes failed to increase, subsidies to industrial investment and growing government responsibilities put pressure on the budget. Monetization of the deficit led to persistent inflation.

ISI policies also had positive effects. They did indeed stimulate industrialization in Latin America. Table 4.5 shows the declining share of the labor force employed in agriculture. The counterpart of this phenomenon was the increasing relative importance of manufacturing. Some industrialization would have occurred anyway, but the marked shift of resources into industry contrasts sharply with

Table 4.5
Share of the labor force employed in the agricultural sector, Argentina, Brazil, Chile, and Mexico, 1930–1980 (percentage)

	Argentina	Brazil	Chile	Mexico
1930			43	65
1940		70	41	63
1950	26[a]	61		
1960	20	52	31	55
1965	18	48	27	50
1980	13	31	16	37

a. 1947.
Sources: Mitchell, B. R., *International Historical Statistics* (Detroit: Gale, 1983) and James Wilkie, ed., *Statistical Abstract of Latin America*, vol. 27 (Los Angeles: UCLA Latin American Center Publications, 1989).

the slow development of manufacturing before World War I. At the height of ISI's influence in the mid-1950s, industrial growth rates were high not only relative to agriculture but to industrial performance in developed countries as well. Furthermore, to the extent that reduction of dependence on world markets was a goal of ISI, import coefficients in the region did drop (table 4.6), although this change was misleading because the region remained dependent on inputs of essential goods.

Although difficult to measure, the ISI phase probably had a positive effect on the development of attitudes of social responsibility toward the poor. (Chapter 8 on populism returns to this issue.) The idea that an increased supply of skilled labor was necessary for industrialization justified more spending on education. The stronger voices of union activists helped to establish at least some minimal social security programs. And greater expectations were placed on governments to provide infrastructure to support industrialization.

One can ask whether these gains would have occurred anyway, given the prosperous world economic climate of the late 1940s and 1950s, but at least the ideology associated with ISI ran in their favor. Critics of ISI argue that the poor lost out on growth that would have occurred had Latin American countries followed a policy of laissez-faire. It is hard to conjecture about growth under this hypothetical alternative, but even had overall growth rates been higher, one wonders how output would have been distributed, given the history of Latin American class relations prior to the ISI period.

A close look at the industrialization process shows a checkered pattern of success and failure, sometimes even within the same sectors. The Brazilians and Mexicans managed to establish successful automobile industries, but the Chileans and Peruvians wound up with a host of inefficient assembly operations. Efficient steel production was established in Argentina and Brazil, but attempts failed elsewhere. As a generalization, assembly of consumer durables went well, while few countries succeeded in getting capital goods and intermediate input industries off the ground. Perhaps because of their larger domestic markets, Brazil and Mexico managed better than other countries in the region (table 4.7).

Table 4.6
Value of imports of goods and services as a percentage of GDP, Latin
American countries, 1928–1988

	1928	1938	1948	1958	1970	1978	1988
Argentina	18	12	11	6	10	14	17
Brazil	11	6	7	6	7	8	12
Chile	31	15	12	10	17	29	46
Colombia	18	11	11	8	19	18	22
Mexico	14	7	9	8	10	13	24

Sources: Joseph Grunwald and Philip Musgrove, *Natural Resources in Latin America
Development* (Baltimore: Johns Hopkins University Press, 1970) and World Bank,
World Tables (Washington, D.C.: World Bank, 1989).

Table 4.7
Imports as a percentage of total supplies by categories, Brazil and Mexico,
1949–1960

	Consumer goods	Intermediate goods	Capital goods
Brazil			
1949	9.0	25.9	63.7
1959	1.9	11.7	32.9
Mexico			
1950	2.4	13.2	66.5
1960	1.3	10.4	54.9

Source: Werner Baer, "Import Substitution and Industrialization in Latin America:
Experiences and Interpretations," *Latin America Research Review* 7 (1972): 95–122.

5   CRITICISMS OF ISI

Problems with import substitution strategies became increasingly
apparent by the late 1950s. Criticisms came from both the left and
the right. Leftists argued that ISI increased Latin America's dependency on imports, put power in the hands of industrialists and
MNCs, and perpetuated the exploitation of peasants. Conservatives
argued that the strategy misallocated resources; instead of enjoying
rapid growth rates through export promotion, Latin American gov-

ernments were creating hopelessly inefficient industries that depended on huge bureaucracies, which in themselves were a drain on the economy. Díaz-Alejandro's evaluation of the Argentine situation at the end of 1955 summarizes the most important criticisms:

> The corporate-state mentality of the Perón regime had resulted in an economy with a low capacity to transform, where producers, workers and consumers expected the government to shield them from undesirable trends arising from the market. The price mechanism became a tool to redistribute income rather than to allocate resources. The structure of production showed some glaring imbalances after years of neglecting marginal adjustments. Severe bottlenecks had been allowed to develop in transportation, electricity, the supply of machinery and equipment, oil and rural goods; in most cases, the government had neither allowed the price mechanism to reflect these imbalances in a steady fashion nor taken effective measures to remedy them by public investment. The system of protection not only created quasi-monopolistic positions but also hampered new exports of manufactures. Efficient activities that had export potential were often forced to buy costly inputs from inefficient domestic sources. . . . Detailed government controls over the allocation and terms of credit, plus inflation, gave rise to a distribution of loanable funds that bore few links to either the entrepreneurial capabilities of borrowers or the social profitability of projects.[7]

Uneven Protection

The overall level of protection is measured by the effective rate of protection (ERP). ERPs measure the degree of protection accorded to value-added in domestic industries, taking into account the level of protection afforded to both inputs and output. Value-added is the value of a firm's sales minus the cost of materials it buys to produce its goods:

$$\text{ERP of industry } i = \frac{\text{(Value-added in domestic prices)}}{\text{(Value-added in international prices)}} - 1.$$

For a given level of nominal protection, the lower the protection of inputs is to an industry, the higher is the degree of effective rate of protection. Conversely, if the inputs to an industry are heavily protected, the effective rate of protection of the industry could be low although the nominal protection may be high. Brazilian agriculture in the 1970s, for example, suffered from tariff protection given to fertilizer and farm machinery. The more heavily an industry uses untaxed imported inputs and enjoys protection on its final output, the greater the protection is likely to be. Under ISI, effective rates of protection tended to favor investment in assembly industries rather than in basic goods. Parts for refrigerators and cars entered with low duties, while high tariffs kept out imported final goods. Thus, it is not surprising that the backward linkages that planners had hoped for failed to materialize. In some periods, the presence of multiple exchange rates compounded the distortions due to uneven effective protection.

Estimates of effective rates of protection in different industrial sectors around 1970 in Argentina, Brazil, and Chile are reported in table 4.8. Table 4.9 shows average ERPs for the manufacturing sector in twelve Latin American countries. The tables should be interpreted with care because of the lack continuity in data and the differences in methodology. With these caveats in mind, observe that before 1975, Chile had not only large effective rates of protection but also a huge dispersion of ERPs across industrial sectors. Generally a larger dispersion of ERPs will lead to greater distortion across sectors.

High levels of effective protection and overvalued exchange rates contributed to a situation in which domestically produced goods were often priced well above world prices. In 1969, the Chilean domestic price of electric sewing machines, bicycles, home refrigerators, and air conditioners was, respectively, three, five, six, and

Table 4.8
Effective rates of protection by industrial sector around 1970, Argentina, Brazil, Mexico, and Chile (percentage)

	Argentina, 1969	Brazil, 1967	Mexico, 1970	Chile, 1967
Food products	-15	40	32	365
Textiles	143	162	45	492
Footwear	121	60	40	34
Wood products	178	25	12	-4
Industrial chemicals	82	42	62	64
Electrical machinery	165	97	88	740

Source: Anjaria et al., *Trade Policy Issues and Developments*; World Bank, *Chile: An Economy in Transition* (Washington, D.C.: World Bank, 1979).

Table 4.9
Average effective rates of protection in the manufacturing sector, Latin
American countries, around 1970 (percentage)

Argentina	27
Brazil	66
Chile	217
Colombia	29
Costa Rica	22
Dominican Republic	124
El Salvador	44
Guatemala	31
Honduras	59
Mexico	49
Nicaragua	53
Uruguay	384

Source: Anjaria et al., *Trade Policy Issues and Developments.*

seven times higher than international prices.[8] At these relative
prices, any consumer with access to foreign exchange and import
licenses would buy foreign goods. At the same time, producers
enjoyed profitable domestic markets but did not stand a chance of
exporting.

Overcapacity

ISI was also marked by overcapacity in many industries.[9] The typical
plant size exceeded domestic demand and operated at high average
cost. This was especially evident in the automobile industry. In the
late 1960s, Latin America had ninety firms producing 600,000 cars,
or an average annual output of just 6,700 cars.[10]

Agriculture

Agriculture was seriously hurt by ISI. Credit was diverted to industry, making it difficult for farmers to finance seasonal costs or
investment in irrigation and equipment. Public expenditures on
roads, water, and electricity services were biased toward urban areas.
Little effort was made to integrate the peasantry into the modern

sector through technical assistance and land reform. Overvalued exchange rates reduced the profitability of agricultural exports and at the same time made it difficult to compete with cheap imports of food. Price controls were used to keep wages down for urban employers, at the expense of farmers. Not only did Latin America become increasingly dependent on imported food, but its traditional source of foreign exchange, the agricultural sector, could not keep up with the need for foreign exchange.

Budget Deficits

The heavy involvement of governments in setting up new industries and providing credit to private firms contributed to public deficits. Subsidies and bureaucratic growth added to expenditures, while the failure to promote export growth cut into revenues from a sector that traditionally has paid a large percentage of taxes. In the absence of easy borrowing from abroad, monetary expansion financed deficits and spurred inflation.

Interest Rates

The use of low interest rates to encourage investment had two negative side effects: industry was excessively capital-intensive and savings rates were low. Large savers with connections abroad shifted their wealth to foreign banks. Allocation of scarce credit at negative real interest rates became subject to arbitrary bureaucratic decisions that often reflected inefficient, even corrupt, choices.

Labor

Progressive governments of the period supported labor through minimum wage legislation, but promotion of capital-intensive industries resulted in a two-tiered labor structure: those who had jobs enjoyed relatively good pay, but many workers were either unemployed or forced into the traditional sectors neglected by governmental emphasis on modernization. Labor is a relatively abundant factor in Latin America, but ISI programs failed to take advantage of this resource. At the same time, very high population growth rates contributed to underemployment. Industrial employment could not keep up with the growth in the labor force.

Foreign Direct Investment

Joint ventures with foreign firms brought in the same technology used in industrialized countries. Capital-intensive plants employed few unskilled workers. Expatriates filled highly skilled jobs, causing disappointment in the progress at which local workers gained technologically advanced skills. These joint ventures often involved a ban on exports; foreign firms had no interest in trying to coordinate international marketing decisions with Latin American governments. Yet despite these criticisms of foreign involvement, foreign firms provided capital necessary to finance some major investments. The ISI experience perpetuated a love-hate relationship between Latin Americans and multinational firms. On the one hand, Latin Americans objected to the extraction of profits and the enclave nature of foreign operations, but on the other, they saw MNCs as sources of technology and capital vital to the realization of economic independence.

6   THE END OF THE GOLDEN YEARS

Ironically, these complaints about import substitution emerged in the 1960s, a period of relatively strong growth in Latin America. The average real rate of growth in the region exceeded 4.5 percent between 1940 and 1968. By comparison to the 1.2 percent rate of the 1980s, the ISI years seem golden. Average inflation rates were also relatively low; whereas 100 percent inflation was shocking in the 1950s, triple-digit inflation was common in the region during the 1980s. The ISI era was also marked by important improvements in literacy rates, mortality rates, and access to electricity and water. Yet disappointment was understandable, particularly by the early 1960s; on a per capita basis, Latin American income rose only 2.1 percent per year between 1960 and 1967, significantly less than the 3.7 percent growth of per capita income in developed countries and the 6.4 percent growth rate characteristic of Asian developing countries. Inflation rates were high relative to the rest of the world. Perhaps most indicting was the fact that the Southern Cone countries, which had applied ISI most thoroughly, had postwar growth rates below the regional average.

As theorists argued the demerits of ISI, some practical factors intervened to draw this phase of Latin American economic planning to a close. On a political level, labor unions had gained enormous strength under ISI. Demands for higher wages and improved benefits threatened the share of income going to the upper tiers of the class structure. Government efforts to placate worker demands through fiscal expansion fueled inflation, further eroding the support of the wealthy. Growing balance of payments problems made it impossible to squeeze more real output from the economy to keep everyone happy. Class tension was erupting into full-fledged political crises.

The first failed attempts at reversing ISI policies occurred in the late 1950s as conservative regimes briefly took control in Chile (1956–1958) and Argentina (1959–1962). In the 1960s, other countries, notably Brazil and Colombia, recognized the limits of ISI and introduced modifications to commercial policy. Crawling-peg exchange rate systems accommodated high domestic rates of inflation and averted the overvaluation earlier so predominant. Explicit concern for inducing nontraditional exports produced special export-subsidy programs in many countries after 1965. In the context of a more buoyant international market, such reinforcements produced positive results, and export growth and diversification in the region increased (see appendix A).

At the same time, borrowing became an option for several countries. From the end of the 1960s but notably after 1973, governments could finance both more imports and larger public sector deficits. The commitment to industrialization remained, and that meant an intrusive role for the public sector even under the "orthodox" policies pursued by military governments. In Brazil's "miracle" between 1968 and 1974, the large domestic market still dominated production decisions.

This period of adaptation and relatively successful adjustment of the earlier model came to an end with the international disequilibrium brought by the oil price rise in 1973. Mounting indebtedness and deterioration of domestic policy in a more difficult external environment marked the postoil shock.

7 TRADE REFORM

Changes in the international economic environment in the 1970s led to important splits in the region's economic history. While we can generalize about import substitution throughout the region in the mid-twentieth century and comment on the uniformly dismal experience of the debt crisis in the 1980s (admitting a few exceptions among the smaller countries), the experiences of Latin American countries in the 1970s are less consistent. Although import substitution was deemed inefficient, the policies that were adopted in the wake of its demise depended to a large extent on how successful a country was in its export markets.

The oil-importing countries did not fare well. Military regimes in Chile (1973), Argentina (1976), and Uruguay (1974) ushered in the end of inward-looking ISI strategies. Austerity measures took hold. Although the military regimes favored the elite, the tension that preceded the coups gave these regimes support that reached into the very classes bound to bear the brunt of stabilization programs. Unemployment, price hikes, and political repression were silently accepted by many as a bitter but potentially viable alternative to failed populist agendas.

Stabilization called for lower real wages, cuts in government spending, incentives for private investment, devaluation, and reduced protectionism. The market liberalization programs in Argentina and Chile in the 1970s were intended to improve industrial efficiency and hasten the transition from ISI to industrial exporting. Trade was opened up: in Chile, tariffs were reduced from an average rate of 94 percent in 1973 to an average rate of 33 percent in 1976. By mid-1979, all tariff rates had been reduced to 10 percent. However, the exchange rate was allowed to appreciate in real terms in both countries. The outcomes were surging consumer imports (table 4.10), partial deindustrialization, and financial bubbles that collapsed with disastrous consequences.

Mexico represents a more recent example of trade reform. After 1985, Mexico not only joined the General Agreement on Tariffs and Trade (GATT) but also engaged in a substantial trade liberalization. Trade reform complemented privatization and deregulation as measures to increase domestic competitiveness. Table 4.11 shows the progress of trade liberalization.

In the 1950s, development economists overemphasized the need for state intervention to promote investment and growth. In the 1980s, the fashion turned 180 degrees to favor nonintervention, privatization, and liberalization. It is now widely recognized that in small countries, import substitution policies (based on quantitative

Table 4.10
Share of consumer goods in total imports, Argentina and Chile,
1970–1985

	1970	1975	1980	1985
Argentina	4.7	3.0	13.4	4.5
Chile	5.8	3.7	15.6[a]	7.5

a. 1981.
Source: Wilkie, *Statistical Abstract of Latin America.*

Table 4.11
Mexican trade restrictions, 1985–1989 (percentage)

	1985	1989
Import license coverage	92.2	22.3
Maximum tariff	100.0	20.0
Average tariff	23.5	12.5

Source: R. Dornbusch, "U.S.-Mexico Trade Relations," *Challenge* 33 (December 1990): 52–55.

restrictions, differentiated tariffs, and a lack of commitment to competitive exchange rates) lead to disaster. Even large countries must avoid extended overvaluation.

The question remains of how fast trade liberalization should proceed. An argument can be made in favor of a rapid transition, as Carlos Salinas has attempted in Mexico. First, fast-moving reform avoids a drawn-out process that allows opponents time to organize and lobby for reversal as transitional setbacks emerge. Second, the sooner the benefits of reform begin, the better are the prospects for sustainability. And third, clear and decisive steps strengthen credibility.

Not everyone would argue in favor of a rapid transition. There are steps that can be taken immediately without costs, especially the replacement of quantitative restrictions by tariffs. Such a move is not adverse to stabilization because it is revenue enhancing. But once protection has shifted to tariffs, slow reduction of tariffs helps to ease adjustment in the industrial sector. Chile's rapid trade liberalization caused widespread bankruptcies, and the government refused to take responsibility for the ensuing social costs. Tariff reduction works better in times of booms and in times of trade surpluses. In Chile and Mexico, trade liberalization brought a rapid increase in imports and a much slower export expansion, creating trade deficits and the belief that the exchange rate might be out of line. Such evidence reinforces the argument for gradual reduction of tariffs.

The speed of liberalization also depends on how fast the real exchange rate can be devalued. Keep in mind the late-1970s experiments in the Southern Cone. Massive capital inflows lead to real appreciation; the exchange rate is not out of equilibrium, but trade imbalances persist as capital inflows finance imports. The experiments in Argentina, Chile, and Uruguay demonstrate that liberalization is ineffective if large capital inflows move the exchange rate in the wrong direction.

Latin America is not frozen under protectionism (table 4.12). Neoliberal doctrines are reviving in the region, spreading the belief that import substitution was pushed too far and that countries will benefit in the long run by opening up their economies.

Can exchange rates and trade policies guarantee growth? Development involves sustained capital accumulation, a diffusion of new technologies, sound infrastructure, incentives and financing for education and skill development, and enough momentum in the domestic economy to escape the pitfalls of dependence on a few exports (to say nothing of political freedom and equity). Trade and macroeconomic policies are important, but prodevelopment policies play an essential role in growth.

Common Markets?

Latin America's major trade partner is the United States, but intraregional trade is increasingly important (tables 4.13 and 4.14).

In the 1950s Costa Rica, El Salvador, Guatemala, Honduras and Nicaragua took steps toward economic integration. In 1960, the Central American Common Market (CACM) provided for free trade within the region (except for a list of exempt items, mainly agricultural) and the harmonization of tariffs rates to a common external tariff schedule. After several years, it also provided for harmonized tax policies, but the market's chief goal was to free intraregional trade to stimulate production of goods formerly purchased from outside, especially industrial goods.

Table 4.12
Protection and trade liberalization in the 1980s, Latin American
countries

Bolivia	Replacement of complex, highly protective system by single uniform tariff of 20 percent in 1985; subsequently reduced gradually to 10 percent
Chile	Trade liberalization in 1970s; tariffs increased to 35 percent in response to 1982 crisis but subsequently reduced in stages to 15 percent
Peru	Multiple exchange rate system used to provide high level of protection; widespread import licensing
Argentina	Liberalization between 1976 and 1981, followed by new protection; intent to liberalize since 1987; tariffs reduced to maximum 40 percent in 1989
Brazil	Rationalization of tariff structure and reduction of tariff rates in 1988; import licensing almost universal by 1989; quantitative restriction removed in 1990; intent to reduce all tariffs to 10 percent by 1994
Mexico	Import licensing almost universal in 1982 and still covered 92 percent of production by 1985 but abolished by 1989; phased but rapid reduction of tariffs as well
Colombia	Gradual and reluctant import liberalization, reversing increase in protection over 1980–1984; proposal to reduce licensing under discussion
Venezuela	Radical import liberalization initiated in 1989; most important prohibitions abolished and tariffs reduced to maximum of 80 percent
Costa Rica	In 1986 Central American Common Market countries rationalized their common trade regime by converting specific to ad valorem tariffs and reduced mean external tariff from 53 percent to 26 percent; in 1987, Costa Rica (alone) reduced average external tariff to 16 percent

Source: John Williamson, *The Progress of Policy Reform in Latin America* (Washington, D.C.: Institute for International Economics, 1990).

Table 4.13
Destination of Latin American exports, 1961–1979
(percentage of total exports)

Countries and regions buying Latin American goods and services	1961–1963 average	1977–1979 average
United States	37.2	35.0
European Community	29.4	21.4
Japan	3.3	4.1
Canada	3.2	3.0
Middle East	0.2	1.4
Regional countries	8.4	15.9
Others	18.3	19.2

Note: Includes Caribbean countries.
Source: Inter-American Development Bank, *Economic and Social Progress in Latin America: The External Sector* (Washington, D.C.: IDB, 1982).

Table 4.14
Origin of Latin American imports, 1961–1979
(percentage of total imports)

Countries and regions selling goods to Latin America	1961–1963 average	1977–1979 average
United States	41.8	32.9
European Community	28.1	19.4
Japan	3.7	7.9
Canada	3.0	2.5
Middle East	1.8	9.8
Regional countries	10.7	16.9
Others	10.9	10.6

Note: Includes Caribbean countries.
Source: Ibid.

After a phase of euphoria, difficulties developed in the late 1960s. Especially Honduras, but also Costa Rica and Nicaragua, felt that free trade favored Guatemala and El Salvador, with their larger industrial bases. Acrimony between Honduras and El Salvador, growing out of migration from the latter to the former, exploded into a brief war between the two countries. Honduras withdrew from the CACM. Despite this blow, Central American integration remained substantial until regional violence erupted in the late 1970s. The elimination of tariffs on most products represented in itself a remarkable achievement, in addition to the rapid expansion of intraregional trade.

By contrast, trade liberalization under the Latin American Free Trade Association (LAFTA), established in 1960, proved to be extremely limited. The wider range of size and development of the eleven countries in LAFTA posed greater problems for unbalanced gains from free trade.[11]

Impatience with the slow pace of integration within LAFTA led Bolivia, Colombia, Chile, Ecuador, and Peru to establish the Andean Pact in 1969. Venezuela joined in 1973, and Chile withdrew in 1976. The Andean Group initially saw a surge in intra-Andean trade, but by late 1975, there were serious disagreements within the Group over the set of common external tariffs to be adopted and sectoral development plans.

Argentina and Brazil now hope they can avoid the clashes that led to failure in past attempts at Latin American integration. At talks in Buenos Aires in July 1990 President Fernando Collor de Mello and President Carlos Menem promised to create a genuine Brazil-Argentine common market by the beginning of 1994, and they hope Chile, Uruguay, and Paraguay will join them. They are building on the experience of other attempts at integration in Latin America.

The United States has also shown an interest in establishing a free trade zone covering the entire Western Hemisphere. In 1990, progress in the direction of a Mexico-U.S.-Canada free trade agreement was moving much more quickly than anyone could have imagined. Success will depend on whether U.S. workers see their jobs threatened by the movement of factories south; some argue that firms are already fleeing to Asia and that there is more chance of holding on to some jobs if production remains in the hemisphere. The prongs of the proposal require the countries of the region to open their economies to free trade and foreign investment. Tighter environmental regulation may also turn out to be a key requirement (box 4.1).

At its worst, integration may set up the same trade barriers that caused problems in the past, within somewhat extended borders. At best, it can give the region bargaining power that it lacks without unity. Latin leaders seem to believe that if they integrate their economies with the rest of the world—their own hemisphere in particular—they have a better chance of improving their countries' welfare.

Box 4.1
Pollution, Policy, and the Free Trade Pact

The founders of Latin America's major cities had a proclivity for basins that trap air pollution. Today a downtown block of Santiago has the worst air quality in the world, children in Mexico City tell stories of dead birds falling from smoggy skies, and even tiny Tegulcigalpa suffers from inversions that trap pollution among the mountains that surround it. The recent trend toward less powerful central governments will not overcome the tendency of business to compound existing agglomeration by locating close to large markets.

In 1989, Mexico City instituted its "One Day without a Car" program; license plate colors designate one weekday during which the corresponding car cannot circulate. Smog abated, and people suddenly found it possible to cross town in less than an hour. The success of the program reflects both Mexicans' willingness to sacrifice in the face of a common crisis and the effectiveness of extremely stiff fines. In 1991, the government took the costly step of shutting down a Pemex refinery identified as the worst industrial polluter in the Valley of Mexico. The cost of constructing an alternative plant elsewhere was estimated at $500 million.

U.S. farmers and industrialists have argued that weaker environmental regulation in Mexico would give that country an important cost advantage under a U.S.-Mexico free trade pact. The elimination of tariffs—about 10 percent on tomatoes and 35 percent on melons—would reduce barriers that enable U.S. farmers to compete with Mexico's lower wages and weak laws regarding pesticides. Unions have been quick to jump on the environmental bandwagon. Mexicans know only too well that their environmental laws lag those in the United States but argue that growth anticipated under the free trade pact is essential to finance environmental protection.

FURTHER READING

Baer, W. "Import Substitution Industrialization in Latin America." *Latin American Research Review* 7, no. 1 (1972): 95–121.

Corbo, V., and J. de Melo. "Lessons from the Southern Cone Policy Reforms." *Research Observer* 2 (no. 2) (July 1987).

Economic Development and Cultural Change (April 1986). Special Issue: "Growth, Reform and Adjustment: Latin America's Trade and Macroeconomic Policies in the 1970s and 1980s."

Williamson, J. *The Progress of Policy Reform in Latin America.* Washington, D.C.: Institute for International Economics, 1990.

Chapter 5

DEBT

The debt crisis is pervasive. The man on the street is out of a job because it caused a recession. Children cannot read because it forced a cut in education budgets. Trees are felled because it increased the need to grow export crops. Not a problem in Latin America is discussed without reference to the debt crisis. Latin America (including the Caribbean) owes $430 billion, or $1,000 per person. Per capita GDP is $2,000 per year. Can Latin America pay?

A debt crisis arises when countries fail to meet their interest payments. External interest payments can be financed by three alternative sources:

$$\text{Interest payments} = \text{Noninterest current account} + \text{Net increase in debt} + \text{Other net capital inflows.}$$

1. The noninterest current account surplus is the difference between exports and imports, adjusted for repatriation of profit, transportation and insurance services, money sent home by migrant workers, and other factors. Ideally interest payments are possible because productive investment of debt has generated growth and current account surpluses. In Latin America, neither emerged from the 1970s loans. The current account surpluses that eventually developed in the 1980s were the result of import contraction rather than new growth.

2. New debt issues can be used to pay interest and amortization on existing debt. Borrowing to finance interest payments is considered a bad practice, but banks willingly let Latin American countries further indebt themselves in this way in the 1970s.[1] New lending to cover old debts abruptly stopped in the early 1980s.

3. Other capital inflows, specifically direct foreign investment, can provide the foreign exchange needed for interest payments. Unfortunately, as bankers lost faith in Latin American solvency, so did investors.

A debt crisis can arise for different reasons. First, domestic fiscal and political disorder translates into deficits in the noninterest current account balance. Second, world economic shocks to a country's terms of trade hurt export earnings or increase import costs. Third, nondebt capital inflows that financed interest payments and trade deficits suddenly dry up. And fourth, rolling over of debt (principal and interest) is disrupted by a loss of confidence on the part of the world capital market.

These disturbances tend to come together. When a country's terms of trade deteriorate, investment opportunities are much less attractive, and hence investment capital from abroad dries up. Knowledge of a nation's financial problem makes competitive bondholders leery about buying new debt issued to tide that country over the difficulty. The inevitable outcome, as Latin America's financial history amply demonstrates, is an interruption of debt service.[2]

Table 5.1 shows the debt held by major Latin American countries at the end of 1989. Four-fifths of the debt is held by six countries: Brazil, Mexico, Argentina, Venezuela, Peru, and Chile. These are the players the banks watch. Although other countries owe less money, their debt is high relative to GDP. Bolivia's debt/GDP ratio is the highest in the region. (Appendix B contains a comparison of Latin America with other regions.)

Who can pay? When the debt crisis began, creditors kept a close eye on a number of debt indicators: the ratio of debt to income, the ratio of interest payments to export earnings, and the ratio of debt service (interest plus principal payments) to export earnings, on the grounds that exports reflected dollars available for repayment. It has since become clear that payment and creditworthiness bear little relationship to these ratios. The willingness of an individual bank to roll over loans to a country depends on other banks' doing the same. During 1989, net commercial lending to Latin America was negative because repayments exceeded disbursements. And all Latin American countries except Chile and Colombia were in arrears.

Since the debt crisis erupted in 1982, per capita GDP has fallen nearly 1 percent per year. Average GDP per capita at the end of 1989

Table 5.1
Debt and debt service, Latin America and selected countries, 1989

Country	Debt outstanding, 1989 ($ billions)	Debt ratios, 1988 (percentage)	
		Debt/GNP	Interest/exports
Argentina	61.9	60.5	27.5
Bolivia	5.8	135.5	17.2
Brazil	112.7	30.7	36.1
Chile	18.5	96.6	15.1
Costa Rica	4.6	100.0	13.4
Ecuador	11.5	113.3	12.7
Honduras	3.4	81.9	15.6
Mexico	102.6	58.0	27.3
Peru	19.9	47.3	5.6
Uruguay	4.5	50.1	18.3
Venezuela	34.1	57.7	24.1
Latin America[a]	434.1	53.6	22.3

a. Includes the Caribbean.
Source: World Bank, *World Debt Tables, 1989-90* (Washington, D.C.: World Bank, 1990).

was more than 8 percent below its level in 1980, earning for the 1980s the reference as the lost decade (table 5.2). Excluding debt-for-equity swaps, foreign investment in Latin America declined 43 percent in the seven years to 1989, compared to the preceding seven years. Investment in physical capital declined as people became pessimistic about Latin American solvency, leaving the region with an even less competitive capital base than it held at the end of the import substitution industrialization era. Even if the debt crisis is resolved now, its implications will go well beyond the 1980s.

1 LESSONS FROM HISTORY

Latin American countries emerged from colonialism not with silver spoons in their mouths but with debt on their hands. Wars of independence were costly and brought about the first instances of default in the 1820s. By 1828, all Latin American countries except Brazil had defaulted. They received no new loans during the next

Table 5.2
Income, investment, and consumption per capita, Latin American
countries, 1981–1989

	Average annual growth rates (percentage)		
Country	Income per capita, 1981–1989	Consumption per capita, 1981–1989	Investment per capita, 1981–1989
Argentina	-2.9	-3.0	-12.9
Bolivia	-3.4	-3.0	-8.2
Brazil	0.0	0.0	-3.5
Chile	1.0	0.2	0.2
Colombia	1.7	1.1	-0.9
Costa Rica	-0.7	-0.9	-2.6
Ecuador	-0.1	-0.4	-7.2
Honduras	-1.4	-1.1	-6.7
Mexico	-1.1	-0.9	-5.9
Peru	-3.1	-2.6	-7.6
Uruguay	-0.8	-0.3	-8.8
Venezuela	-3.1	-3.0	-9.8
Latin America[a]	-1.0	-1.1	-5.4

a. Includes the Caribbean.
Sources: ECLAC, *Preliminary Overview of the Economy of Latin America and the Caribbean, 1989* (New York: ECLAC, 1989); Inter-American Development Bank, *Economic and Social Progress in Latin America, 1990 Report* (Washington, D.C.: IDB, 1990).

three decades while creditors tried to resolve the debts of independence, with the help of European military pressure. Indeed, Mexico's
invasion by France, Britain, and Spain in 1862 and its subsequent
rule by Emperor Maximilian were the result of Mexico's default on
foreign debts. Commodity booms after mid-century led to the
revival of lending. Wars and railroad construction burned up this
new money rapidly; when the international crash of the 1870s
arrived, only the wealthiest Latin American countries avoided
another default.[3] The 1890s brought a major collapse in Argentina
and Brazil.

The 1890s Crisis

In the 1880s, money markets in London, Paris, Brussels, and Berlin were competing with one another for the privilege of taking up ventures and floating loans in Argentina as new technologies made possible more extensive trade in grains and meat. At any other time, such loans would have been regarded as of doubtful security, considering both the financial and political instability of Argentina.

When debt service difficulties developed in 1890–1891, Argentina's debt was more than three times its GDP. Its failure to service the debt brought down Baring Brothers, the English banking house. Rapid intervention by the Bank of England prevented a major collapse. A settlement named the Arreglo Romero was reached in 1893, granting Argentina a decade-long moratorium on principal payments and substantially reduced interest payments. For their part, European bankers took advantage of the collapse of Argentine-owned enterprises to increase their role in key industries. A surge of new foreign investment spurred rapid recovery.

Even as the crisis developed in Argentina, bankers readily lent to Brazil. The boom in Brazil led to a proliferation of new enterprises in early 1890s and excessive money creation on the part of the government. Economic and political instability in Brazil were, in fact, on the rise as early as 1891. As the price of coffee plummeted, the day of reckoning arrived for many bubble companies. Shares that once sold at a high premium now could not find buyers even at less than half the paid-up capital.

The crisis in Brazil did not actually lead to default; however, the milreis underwent rapid devaluation, adding heavily to the cost of servicing the foreign debt. The hope that financial affairs in Brazil would improve with the coming to power of the new president, Dr. Campos Salles, soon gave way to the question of whether national bankruptcy could be avoided. As it became evident that the financial position of the Brazilian government was desperate, restructuring of the debt was organized under conditions that required tight monetary policy. Despite its domestic unpopularity and resulting rebellion against it, the finance minister, Joaquim Murtinho, imposed a contractionary policy similar to today's IMF austerity plans. Combined with improvements in external conditions, the program stabilized the exchange rate after 1903. The cost, however, was severe recession.

Rising coffee prices and a favorable balance of payments attracted a new surge of foreign investment and renewed loans. The doubling of coffee prices between 1906 and 1912 and the rubber boom provided the impetus for rapid recovery.

The Crisis of the 1930s

The stock market crash of 1929 was anticipated in Latin America by a decline in commodity prices two years earlier. With the crash, Latin American countries found it impossible to market goods in Europe and the United States. Between 1930 and 1932, a wildfire of coups and revolution swept through nearly every country in the region. Defaults began in 1931 but not before Latin America had exported roughly $1 billion in capital.

Among the large countries, only Argentina managed to maintain full payment of its debt. Bolivia, Chile, Peru, and Brazil suspended payments in 1931; Costa Rica, Panama, the Dominican Republic, Uruguay, and Colombia either defaulted or partially suspended payments the following year. Mexico had already been in default since 1914. For most countries, default was an inevitable result of lower export earnings as developed markets collapsed.[4]

World War II gave large Latin American countries the bargaining power to resolve this debt crisis. Britain depended heavily on Argentine meat for its military. The United States was concerned about potential alliances with the Axis powers because large communities of German immigrants resided in Argentina, Brazil, and Chile. Mexico's leverage derived from its potential assistance in the war; a quarter of a million Mexicans served in the U.S. Army and many more crossed the border to ease the wartime labor shortage. Mexico and Brazil were especially successful in negotiating financial concessions in the 1940s. Mexico reduced its debt by 90 percent, and Brazil cut its obligations by 63 percent.

Is History Repeating Itself?

A complete comparison of today's debt crisis with that of the depression is beyond the scope of this survey, but some points are worth highlighting:

• The 1930s, just like the 1980s, presented a situation of simultaneous, widespread debt service difficulties. The roots of the crises lie not only in debtors' policies but also in global economic conditions.

• By comparison with the 1930s, the decline in world trade and prices in the 1980s was very small.[5] Trade remained relatively open in the 1980s. By comparison, in the 1930s worldwide trade restriction was the rule. Instead, the very sharp increase in interest rates at the start of the 1980s contributed a disturbance not characteristic of the debt crisis of the 1930s.

• Debt problems of the 1980s were primarily concentrated in Latin America and the Philippines. By contrast, in the 1930s many European countries, including Germany, went into default. Creditor countries themselves in the 1930s experienced widespread domestic defaults of their municipal debts. Bank closings, foreclosures, and mass unemployment were the rule worldwide.

• Most debt before the depression took the form of bonds. In the 1980s, commercial bank loans and official credits constituted most of the debt. The earlier bondholders were primarily represented by protective councils, which negotiated on behalf of the bondholders and recommended settlements after lengthy periods of suspension of debt service. Their resources and clout were limited. In the 1980s, governments and international institutions were at the center of the rescheduling process from the very beginning. The existence of standby credits and the framework of IMF programs facilitated rescheduling, compared to 1930s-style suspension of debt service. Debt problems of the developing countries were seen as a threat to the banking system and to the stability of international finance. The highest levels of government have thus been involved in negotiations.

• Investment income accounted for a much more significant share of total investment income payments in the interwar crisis than in the 1980s. For example, in 1935, direct investment amounted to 70 percent, 35 percent, 53 percent, and 50 percent of the total foreign obligations of Argentina, Brazil, Chile, and Mexico, respectively. By comparison, in 1983 these shares were 12 percent, 22 percent, 18 percent, and 13 percent, respectively. Foreign direct investment does not create fixed obligations in foreign exchange. Unlike commercial lenders, direct investors bear the risk of losses if a project fails.

• Five years after the earlier debt difficulties emerged, Latin America looked better than it does today. Through 1990, recession was the rule all over Latin America, with a clear recovery only in Chile. By contrast, after 1933, growth had increased per capita income in many countries. The world economic environment at the time was surely not more favorable, although default was easier. Were policies better?

2   THE 1980s DEBT CRISIS

The oil shock of 1974 enabled the Latin American countries to depend more heavily on credit. Oil exporters deposited their earnings in the commercial banks of developed countries, but higher oil prices caused a recession in OECD countries and reduced demand for credit. Left with excessive liquidity, bankers eagerly lent to the Third World.

Oil-importing Latin American countries gambled that higher import bills would be short-lived, and therefore they borrowed to avoid adjustment. They also counted on unusually high commodity prices to continue. Coffee prices tripled between 1975 and 1977. Cotton, sugar, tin, and beef also experienced brief price spikes in the 1970s. A spate of new commodity cartels formed with the goal of duplicating OPEC's success.

Oil exporters justified borrowing on the grounds that wealthy future generations could well afford debts incurred to alleviate current poverty. Even relatively cautious economists advised Venezuela and Mexico to borrow against their oil assets for investment in industry and education.

On the domestic front, budget deficits increased vastly, exchange rates were overvalued, and capital flight and excessive consumer imports were the rule. Low real international interest rates made the spending spree all the more attractive. Moreover, lenders paid little attention to creditworthiness and made excess accumulation of debt possible.

The essential ingredients in the outbreak of the debt crisis came together between 1979 and 1981. The United States and other OECD countries shifted to tight money and dramatically raised interest rates (table 5.3). This directly increased Latin American debt, much

Table 5.3
International interest rates, 1974–1984

Year	U.S. prime rate, real terms	London interbank offer rate, real terms
1974	-2.2	-1.9
1975	-2.9	-3.1
1976	-1.3	-2.0
1977	-1.4	-1.8
1978	1.7	1.1
1979	3.2	2.6
1980	3.0	2.0
1981	8.1	6.0
1982	6.8	5.3
1983	5.5	4.6
1984	6.9	6.1

Note: The financial terms of lending are higher than reported in this table because they include a spread. In 1975 and 1976, all publicized variable-rate Eurocurrency loans to Latin American countries paid a spread higher than 1 percent.
Source: Robert Devlin, *Debt and Crisis in Latin America, The Supply Side of the Story* (Princeton: Princeton University Press, 1989).

of which carried floating interest rates. Whether pulled by higher interest rates or pushed by gnawing concern about local stability, Latin Americans shifted their money abroad; new lending made its way back to Miami. Capital flight started well before the crisis actually erupted.

High interest rates also induced another recession in OECD countries, depressing the export earnings of debtors. In 1981–1982 the group of countries that subsequently rescheduled their debts experienced an 8.5 percent decline in export volume and a 7.6 percent fall in export prices.

Other factors contributed to the crisis. The second oil shock in 1979 caused trouble for importers, especially Brazil. The Southern Cone countries' experiments with preannounced exchange rates led to overvaluation and balance of payments problems. Argentina's military expenditures, first to prepare for war with Chile and then to fight the Malvinas war with England in 1982, created major fiscal deficits. Throughout the region, the delicate transition from military to civilian rule made austerity measures politically impractical.

In contrast to the 1970s, automatic financing of deficits was no longer easily available. Debtors could not pay, and creditors would not lend, the 1982 debt crisis was ready. In August 1982, Mexico was unable to meet scheduled payments and declared a moratorium. In short order, many other countries followed. Causes of the crisis were both external and internal. Table 5.4 shows the sources and magnitudes of external shocks for seven Latin American countries.

There were actually three different situations among Latin American debtors (table 5.5). The first group, which includes Brazil and Mexico, borrowed in the 1970s largely to finance an excess of imports over exports and to pay interest. To its credit, Brazil also invested heavily in new capital formation. Before 1982–83 interest payments were automatically financed by new lending, as were negative net exports of goods and services. Once commercial lenders rationed credit, however, this was no longer possible. Now debtors had to run noninterest surpluses to finance at least part of the interest payments. Table 5.5 shows the dramatic turnaround of net exports of goods and services from large deficits to large surpluses in Brazil and Mexico. Governments used both devaluations and restrictive fiscal and monetary policies to reduce demand for tradables and to produce the external surpluses. The result was a deep recession.

Table 5.4
Sources and magnitudes of shocks for seven Latin American debtors, 1979–1982 (U.S. $ billions except where indicated)

| Country | Impact of changes in terms of trade | | Impact of high real interest rates | Impact of low export demand | Total Impact | |
	All trade	Oil trade			billions of U.S. dollars	As percentage of GDP
Colombia	-4.3	-0.9	-0.9	-1.6	-6.8	-4.9
Brazil	-31.7	-17.9	-8.9	-7.9	-48.5	-4.6
Chile	-1.9	-1.4	-1.5	-1.5	-4.8	-4.6
Argentina	-6.2	-0.6	-3.7	-3.6	-13.4	-3.0
Peru	2.3	1.2	-0.8	-1.1	0.4	0.5
Mexico	22.5	21.0	-8.4	-2.4	11.7	1.6
Venezuela	24.0	29.4	-4.6	-0.3	19.1	7.8

Source: Thomas Enders and Richard Mattione, *Latin America, The Crisis of Debt and Growth* (Washington, D.C.: Brookings Institution, 1984).

Table 5.5
Net exports of goods and nonfactor services, selected countries, 1970–1988
(annual average, U.S. $ billions)

	1970–74	1975–79	1980–81	1982–83	1984–85	1986–87	1988
Brazil	-1.9	-3.6	-3.8	0.6	11.1	7.5	18.1
Mexico	-0.7	-1.2	-5.2	10.1	11.4	8.0	4.1
Argentina	0.4	1.0	-2.0	3.1	4.2	1.1	3.5
Venezuela	2.0	-1.0	4.3	2.3	6.3	0.2	-3.0
Peru	-0.1	-0.2	-0.1	-0.4	0.9	-0.7	-0.5

Source: World Bank, *World Tables, 1989–90* (Washington, D.C.: World Bank, 1990).

A second group of countries, which includes Argentina and Venezuela, borrowed to finance capital flight; they did not run large trade deficits in the 1970s. (Table 5.7 shows an estimate of assets their residents hold abroad.)

Finally, there are countries, such as Peru, that have been unable to sustain positive net exports in the 1980s and are running large arrears.

Two phenomena leading to the crisis warrant discussion: overvaluation and capital flight.

Overvaluation

Overvaluation is a good example of how external economic conditions and internal policymaking interacted in contributing to the debt crisis.

At different times during the period 1978 to 1982, a number of countries in Latin America experienced strong real appreciation of their currency, followed by balance of payments crises and real depreciation. Figure 5.1 presents the real exchange rates of Argentina and Chile as extreme examples of this process.

The explanation of this experience begins with the recognition that the monetary authorities in these countries followed a conscious policy of avoiding exchange depreciation or, as in the case of Chile, a policy of outright fixing of the exchange rate, as a means of stopping inflation. The real appreciation, in turn, led to a current account deterioration. At least in the initial phase, these deficits

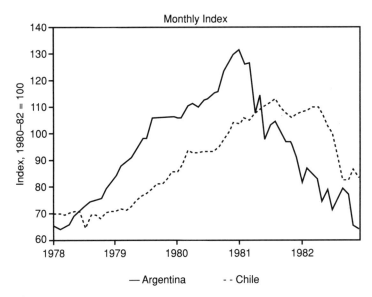

Figure 5.1
Real exchange rate indexes, Argentina and Chile, 1978–1982.
Source: Morgan Guaranty Trust Company, *World Financial Markets*, various
issues.

could be financed by private capital inflows and subsequently by
official borrowing abroad. The availability of foreign borrowing thus
supported overvaluation in the 1970s. Did mismanagement cause
the debt overhang? To some extent, the availability of credit made
policy errors possible.

Table 5.6 shows the current account effects of the overvaluation.
Of course, the current account also reflects other variables, specifically world interest rates and commodity prices; nonetheless,
overvaluation was accompanied by significant increases in current
account deficits. The case of Chile reflects, in the most striking way,
how overvaluation and access to financing, combined with trade
liberalization, can induce a capital import spree. Overvaluation,
combined with elimination of tariffs and quotas, led to a massive
increase in import spending, especially in the area of durables. The
sharply increased purchases of durables reflected not only an adjustment to the price reduction brought about by appreciation and
liberalization but also an expectation that the low price was unlikely
to persist. Although lenders eagerly supported these policies, the

Table 5.6
Current account and real appreciation, Argentina and Chile, 1976–1981 (percentage)

	Argentina		Chile	
	Ratio of the current account to exports[a]	Real appreciation rate[b]	Ratio of the current account to exports[a]	Real appreciation rate[b]
1976	14	34	5	13
1977	17	-29	-22	3
1978	25	10	-38	-16
1979	-6	25	-26	11
1980	-48	10	-34	14
1981	-43	-25	-88	10

a. A minus sign indicates a deficit.
b. A minus sign indicates a depreciation of the real effective exchange rate.
Source: Joseph Ramos, *Neoconservative Economics in the Southern Cone of Latin America* (Baltimore: Johns Hopkins University Press, 1986).

borrowing binge was thoroughly counterproductive; the large deficits did not reflect high rates of investment.

The point of the discussion is that access to the world capital market can be a source of important and costly policy errors. Whether these errors are initiated primarily by spontaneous lending disturbances or by the ability of governments to finance extravagant exchange rate experiments remains an open question. The fact that the experiences were exceptionally costly is beyond doubt.

Capital Flight

Argentines, Mexicans, and Venezuelans hold dollar deposits and other assets abroad worth nearly as much as their countries' debt. Capital flight is arguably an important cause of the debt crisis, and its reversal is its most promising solution. The foreign assets held by Latin Americans range from cash (actual dollar bills) to deposits in Miami, Zurich, and Panama, real estate in California, and shares of Fuji stock held with a Cayman Island depositary.

Investors face three broad concerns in choosing their assets: inflation/exchange rate risk, which leads investors to shift from domestic currency to foreign currency assets; political risk, which leads investors to shift assets out of the country to a safe haven; and tax reasons, which involve taking assets underground or to foreign tax shelters. These concerns tend to overlap, with different considerations being paramount at any given time. The basic portfolio problem, stated in terms of a choice between domestic and foreign (by denomination and possibly location), involves the comparison of rates of net return. Foreign assets are more attractive than home assets if the expected return from tax evasion and expected depreciation exceeds the home rate of after-tax return. If investors are risk averse, then diversification considerations also influence portfolio choices.

Expected depreciation is important in the context of periods of overvaluation. When it is widely perceived that an extreme devaluation lies ahead, capital flight becomes massive. This is the case especially when capital movements can take place at the official exchange rate. This was, in fact, the case in Argentina and in Mexico during several overvaluation episodes. Postponing a devaluation then implies large reserve losses.

Taxation is also an issue. Nonresident assets in the United States and elsewhere are untaxed. When political instability threatens assets in developing countries, it is doubly worthwhile to send capital abroad.

The broadest measures of capital flight encompass all additions to external assets, except official reserves, as well as errors and omissions recorded in the balance of payments. This presumes that any private investment abroad is disadvantageous to the domestic economy. Another approach is to measure foreign assets that yield no recorded repatriation of income. In this case, retention of income abroad is considered indicative of flight concerns. The "hot money" measure adds net short-term capital outflows of the nonbank private sector to recorded errors and omissions to measure funds that respond quickly to changes in expected returns or risk.

The difficulty of defining capital flight is exacerbated by problems in the actual data, which reflect underinvoicing of trade, undisclosed military imports, and the lack of detailed statistics on foreign asset holdings by residents of a debtor country. Table 5.7 shows one recent estimate for capital flight from Latin America.

There are principally two channels through which Latin Americans have acquired external assets. The more obvious way applies

Table 5.7
Capital flight, Latin American countries, 1973–1987

	Capital flight 1973–1987	Stock of foreign assets, 1987	Foreign assets as a percentage of external debt, 1987
	(millions of U.S. dollars)		
Argentina	29,469	43,674	76.9
Brazil	15,566	20,634	18.3
Colombia	1,913	2,994	19.5
Mexico	60,970	79,102	73.3
Peru	2,599	4,148	23.0
Uruguay	83	902	21.3
Venezuela	38,815	48,027	131.5

Source: M. Pastor, "Capital Flight from Latin America," *World Development* 18 (January 1990): 1–18.

where the central bank allows transfers abroad at the official exchange rate. Because capital controls are cumbersome, and in some countries very ineffective, some governments (Argentina and Mexico) in fact authorize transfers at the official exchange rate.[6] In these instances, massive capital flight can occur in response to a ripe overvaluation.

The second channel takes the form of misinvoicing trade transactions. Overinvoicing of imports and underinvoicing of exports are the means by which foreign assets can be accumulated and then sold in the black market. Evidence from Latin America supports the view that misinvoicing peaks during periods preceding major alignments in exchange rates. Because capital flight and duty evasion work in the same direction, export underinvoicing tends to be rampant. Estimates of underinvoicing are available from a comparison of import values of trade partners with the export value of a particular exporting country. Using these trade data, Cuddington reports that in the period 1977–1983 the percentage of underinvoicing of exports averaged the following: Argentina, 19.6 percent; Brazil, 12.7 percent; Chile, 12.8 percent; Mexico, 33.6 percent; and Uruguay, 27.8 percent.[7]

Capital flight imposes four costs. First, it destabilizes macroeconomic management.[8] To stem capital flight, real exchange rates must be on the defensive side, and interest rates need to be sufficiently high to reward asset holders for the "risk" of holding domestic assets. Taxes on capital are also suppressed. Thus, the middle and upper classes get their assets protected at the expense of wage earners.

Second, capital flight means that residents use less domestic currency and more foreign currency. To the extent that seigniorage (money creation) is used to finance budget deficits, reduced demand for domestic currency implies increased inflation.

Third, capital flight undermines tax morality. Underinvoicing of exports is invariably reflected in reduced tax payments. Once assets are abroad, it would be quite exceptional if taxes were paid on the earnings. Moreover, external assets become convenient vehicles for the payment of fraud and bribes.

Finally, when a certain percentage of gross national product (GNP) is transferred abroad year after year, fewer resources are available for domestic investment. Rather than financing imports of capital goods, export earnings finance the building up of external asset positions. The reduced capital formation implies slower growth, with negative consequences for labor.

There are few effective policy options that stop capital flight and are politically acceptable. An obvious step is to raise interest rates and undervalue the exchange rate. But high real interest rates deter investment, and devaluations cause inflation and a lower standard of living for workers. Policymakers must therefore devise more narrowly targeted controls on capital flight.

Until recently, capital controls have been relatively effective in Brazil and Korea, but they are considered almost entirely ineffective in Argentina and Mexico. Part of the difficulty lies in porous geographic borders. Networks to avoid controls also become increasingly sophisticated as the public adjusts to instability.

An alternative to capital controls is a dual exchange rate: setting one rate for approved commercial transactions and a separate one for capital account transactions. Mexico's experience has shown that a dual rate buffers transitory shocks, but significant differences between the two rates cannot be sustained in the long run.

Industrialized countries could also help reduce capital flight from developing countries by collecting taxes on expatriate asset holdings. For the time being, developed countries have actually gone in the opposite direction by eliminating taxes on nonresident assets, thus providing outright incentives for capital flight.

3 SOLUTIONS TO THE DEBT CRISIS

In 1982, the world economy was in dismal shape: economic activity was more depressed than at any other time since the Great Depression, interest rates stood at their highest levels in decades, the real price of commodities was sharply depressed, and the dollar was too strong. These conditions were not expected to persist. Recovery of the world economy would bring rising demand for exports, higher commodity prices, declining real interest rates, and a weaker dollar. This favorable global outlook suggested that the burdens of debt service would almost surely vanish. A muddling-through strategy, initiated by the U.S. Federal Reserve, the U.S. Treasury, and the IMF, operated on the assumption that debtors would regain their creditworthiness with a combination of internal adjustment and more favorable world conditions. A return to voluntary lending could be envisaged only if debtors cooperated with the system, servicing debts to the fullest extent possible. It seemed to be in the interest of debtor countries to do their best to promote a return to voluntary lending.

The debt situation has evolved in a very different direction from these expectations. Voluntary lending has not reappeared, and the chances that it will soon are remote. The muddling-through strategy, even with the enhancements of the Baker and Brady plans, in which banks accepted modest reductions in debt, has failed.

What went wrong with muddling through? First, real interest rates did not decline as much as expected.[9] Given the sensitivity of debt to interest rates, high interest rates represent a major barrier in resolving the crisis.

Second, real commodity prices were expected to recover from what was thought to be a cyclical low; in fact, however, they kept falling. The real price of nonoil commodities was still 30 percent below its 1980 level in 1988. It became increasingly clear that much of the decline in real commodity prices was not cyclical but was rather an irreversible decline due to overcapacity on the supply side and commodity-saving innovation and substitution on the demand side. In the case of agricultural goods, immense productivity growth and increasing self-sufficiency of traditional importers, as well as price support policies in industrial countries, led to worldwide oversupply.

Third, there was the transfer problem, that is, problems that result from the attempt to transfer resources representing a significant share of GDP from debtors to creditors. Five aspects of the transfer problem deserve emphasis:

1. As debtors increase their exports to service their debt, they depress their own terms of trade.

2. The effort to service public debts rather than to roll them over strains budgetary resources and leads to inflationary money creation. If domestic debt is issued to acquire resources for external debt service, deficit problems are merely postponed.

3. The effort to transfer resources abroad requires an improvement in competitiveness, which is itself inflationary. Rather than falling absolutely, wages decline in real terms as prices rise. The better organized labor is, the harder it is to avoid indexing wages and the more inflationary are devaluations aimed at improving competitiveness.

4. These aspects of the transfer problem interact: the devaluation needed to generate a trade surplus raises the cost of debt service in terms of domestic currency. Relative to the domestic tax base, the higher cost of debt service creates an even worse public finance problem. External debt service is then financed either by inflationary money creation or by increases in domestic public debt. The real value of the domestic public debt is much higher today than in 1981. Thus, a domestic public debt problem arises as a by-product of efforts to contain external indebtedness (table 5.8)

5. The trade surplus required to finance debt service can come out of reduced consumption (public or private) or reduced investment. When investment declines, as has been the case in Latin America, there is concern about sustaining growth. Since 1982, Latin America has been transferring resources abroad at an average rate of more than 4 percent of GDP. Although per capita consumption has declined, most of the transfer is occurring at the expense of domestic investment. As table 5.2 shows, investment in the region plummeted with the debt crisis, dimming the prospects for ending insolvency through growth.

Table 5.8
Consolidated debt of the public sector, Brazil and Mexico, 1981–1989
(percentage of GDP)

Year	Brazil			Mexico		
	External	Domestic	Total	External	Domestic	Total
1981	19	15	34	27	13	40
1982	25	20	45	61	24	85
1983	51	29	80	57	20	77
1984	51	34	85	46	19	65
1985	51	36	87	56	20	76
1986	32	23	55	92	27	1.19
1987	55	37	92	90	26	1.16
1988	70	57	1.27	47	22	69
1989[a]	73	83	1.56	38	25	63

Note: Consolidated debt outstanding at the end of the year divided by GDP.
a. Preliminary.
Source: Banco de Mexico and Banco Central de Brasil.

In short, the cost of servicing the debt has led to depressed living standards, hyperinflation, sharply reduced investment, and the prospect of reduced long-term growth. The inability of governments to sustain payment is reflected in the deep discount for Latin American debt in the secondary market (table 5.9). The ratios of debt to exports and debt to GDP of problem debtors have risen since 1982, and creditworthiness has deteriorated. Eight years of adjustment have made debtor countries look worse rather than better. There is no indication of a return to voluntary lending and even countries with no rescheduling problems (e.g., Colombia) experience difficulties borrowing in the world market.

Beyond Muddling Through

The basic problem to solve is how to reverse the outflow of real resources from debtor countries. New transfers of capital are needed to finance growth. Yet as long as existing debts are judged to be bad, commercial banks will be reluctant to put up new money to finance even the interest bill. Moreover, existing debt stands in the way of raising capital from investors who so far have not been involved, such as insurance companies, because existing debt has a prior claim on debtor resources. Direct investment is also stunted by existing debt, because these depressed economies yield low profit on new investment.[10] Finally, if the debt collection process provokes a political backlash in the debtor nations, there is no assurance that a fine distinction will be drawn between uncooperative banks holding on to long-dead debts and new investors. In short, until the problem of old debt is resolved, fresh capital resources will be very limited.

Among the many schemes to solve the debt problem, we highlight a few: debt swaps, buybacks, a financing facility, and interest capitalization or recycling. Three of these schemes center around the fact that prices of developing-country debt show large discounts in the secondary market (table 5.9). These schemes attempt to pass on to debtor countries some of the reduction in loan value implicit in these discounts.

Debt Swaps

In 1988, PSV Eindhoven, the European soccer champions, used a debt swap to pay the fee of a Brazilian center-forward, Romario Farias. PSV is owned by Philips, a Dutch company. Philips bought Brazilian bank debt with a face value of $5 million for $4 million in cash in the secondary market. Philips sold the loans to the Brazilian Central Bank, received $4.7 million cruzados, and paid Vasco da Gama, Farias's Brazilian club. Philips saved $1 million, the bank that sold its loan at a discount got rid of an unwanted piece of its portfolio, and both Farias and his club are happy with the deal. But after taking off a slice of its foreign debt at a discount price, Brazil has even more inflation, and investment is unchanged. Were it not for this deal, Philips would have paid Farias's fee in dollars badly needed to liberalize imports or to invest in capital goods.

How do swaps work? In a debt-equity swap, a firm buys a claim from a bank in the secondary market. The claim is then presented to the debtor country's central bank for payment in local currency, at a discount. The proceeds are used for investment in the debtor country. When the transaction is complete, a bank has sold off (at a discount) a claim for dollar cash, a foreign firm has acquired a real

Table 5.9
Secondary market prices for debt of major Latin American debtors, 1986–1990
(percentage of face value)

	Argentina	Brazil	Chile	Colombia	Mexico	Peru	Venezuela
1986							
April	65.8	77.0	67.5	83.0	58.0	22.0	77.5
August	66.0	75.0	68.5	83.0	58.0	22.0	75.0
December	64.0	74.0	68.5	84.0	56.0	21.0	73.5
1987							
April	59.0	63.0	69.0	84.0	58.0	15.0	73.5
August	42.0	43.0	59.0	80.0	48.0	8.0	59.0
December	36.0	46.0	53.0	63.0	50.0	8.0	58.0
1988							
April	29.0	50.0	59.0	65.0	51.0	8.0	55.0
August	22.5	46.5	60.0	66.5	46.5	6.0	50.0
December	21.5	39.5	59.0	57.0	41.5	5.0	38.0
1989							
April	17.3	37.8	59.5	54.0	42.8	4.0	39.0
August	15.0	31.5	64.5	62.5	43.3	4.5	39.4
December	12.3	23.5	60.5	65.0	36.0	6.3	35.5
1990							
April	13.3	28.0	64.3	64.0	41.2	5.3	44.5
August	14.3	18.0	70.0	63.0	43.8	4.8	46.0

Source: *Latin Finance*, no. 23 (December 1990).

asset in the debtor country, and the central bank has reduced its dollar liabilities but suffers an increase in domestic monetary liabilities or in domestic debt.

Debt-equity swaps have been used to finance purchases of existing firms, to induce investment in new operations, and to unload burdensome state corporations. For example, in 1990, Argentina reached an agreement to sell its state-owned telephone company to two groups led by the Bell Atlantic Corporation and Telefonica de España. Argentina was to receive $214 million in cash and $5 billion in debt paper. It would draw down its external debt and eliminate a source of $50 million in red ink from its monthly budget.

Chile, with a debt of approximately $20 billion, swapped $6 billion between 1985 and 1988. Both Mexico and Brazil swapped large amounts in the late 1980s. Brazil then shifted to policies that discourage swaps (table 5.10).

Why Do Governments Resist Swaps?

Hard-pressed to meet interest due on its debt, a country might be tempted to cut its interest bill by carving down the stock of outstanding debt and repaying it at a discount. Such deals look good for everybody: creditor banks get more than the secondary-market valuation of their Latin American loan exposure, debtors pay less than they would through official channels, brokers make nice commissions, and investors get their equity cheap. But debtor governments have good reasons to resist these swaps because of their impact on inflation, the budget, and capital flight.

Whether debt-equity swaps are beneficial for the debtor country depends on two considerations. First, it is important to determine whether the investment that takes place is an extra investment or one that would have taken place anyway. In the latter case, the debt-equity swap is costly because the central bank does not receive dollars that could have been used for import liberalization or other uses. Moreover, concessions made to attract additional investment affect investment that would occur in the absence of swap subsidies. Mexican finance minister Pedro Aspe spoke out forcefully against

Table 5.10
Debt conversions, Argentina, Brazil, Chile, and Mexico, 1985–1989 (millions of U. S. dollars)

	Argentina	Brazil	Chile	Mexico
1985	469	537	313	769
1986		176	987	1,023
1987	35	1,800	1,983	3,804
1988	1,330	9,175	2,905	6,670
1989[a]	500	4,000	2,000	6,000

Note: Debt-equity and debt-debt swaps (transactions that convert debt claims on the debtor country to another form) and debt repurchases.
a. Preliminary.
Source: World Bank, *World Debt Tables*.

swaps on the grounds that they stop investment; in the Mexican resort of Cancun, hotels stand half finished as investors wait for the subsidies they expect from a renewed debt-equity program.

The second consideration is whether the discount at which the central bank redeems its external debt is large enough to offset the extra interest cost incurred on domestic debt issued as a counterpart. By assumption the debtor is illiquid. The interest cost on new debt will typically exceed the interest on old debt, and hence refinancing raises interest costs unless the discount on conversion is sufficiently large. When new money is generated for the conversion, inflation rises. The Brazilian central bank monetized more than $1.8 billion worth of swaps in 1988, the equivalent of one-third of its monetary base.

After initial optimism, the impression is now widespread that relatively little additional investment has taken place, and invariably the cost of refinancing has raised interest burdens. As a result, debt-equity swaps are losing momentum. Whatever the merits of swaps, and there may well be some in the form of creating a favorable investment atmosphere, these schemes cannot play a major role in resolving the debt problem.

The Green Solution: Debt-for-Nature Swaps

Debt-for-nature swaps both reduce the debt and save the environment. International environmental groups buy discounted debt on the financial markets and turn this over to debtor governments, which then commit local currency to create a national park. The conservation group does not own the park; the government does. There is no loss of sovereignty over national resources, the government pays domestic currency to protect domestic property, and the earth is a bit greener.

Debt-for-nature swaps have been set up in Bolivia, Costa Rica, and Ecuador. In Costa Rica, nearly $70 million in debt was converted for conservation purposes. Parks throughout the country—including Braulio Carrillo, Guanacaste, La Amistad, Corcovado, and Barra Honda—receive funds through swaps. The program also funds a major reforestation program and environmental research.

Costa Rica cut its first deal in August 1987. At the time, its debt traded for 35 cents on the dollar in secondary markets. Under the debt-for-nature swap, the government accepted $5.4 million in debt at 75 percent of face value and converted it into bonds paying a fixed interest rate of 25 percent. In other words, for each $35 it spent, the World Wildlife Fund (WWF) bought $100 of Costa Rican debt, for which the government was willing to commit $75 in local currency conservation bonds. WWF thus more than doubled the value of the money it offered by engaging in a debt swap.

Why do debtor countries insist on discounting the face value of bonds in debt-for-nature swaps? Costa Rica, for example, recognized only 30 percent of the face value of debt when the secondary debt price fell to 16 cents on the dollar. The reason is that governments would gain nothing from the deal if they did not discount. Like debt-equity swaps, nature swaps impose a fiscal burden on debtors that typically carries inflationary consequences.

Suppose WWF comes to the government with a $1 million bond. The floating exchange rate is 80 colones per dollar. If Costa Rica were to give WWF 80 million colones, the cost to the government would be no different than if it had bought $1 million on the local exchange market to repay Citibank.

If the government had intended neither to repay the $1 million principal nor to buy a park for 80 million colones, this deals represents a net increase in fiscal expenditures of 80 million colones. In return it reduces its debt and gets a new park, neither of which were necessarily top priorities; it also gets a fiscal deficit that generates inflation. The 80 million colones will have to come out of the budget somewhere—by cutting spending on health programs, for example.

If the government had intended to repay the debt (in contrast to secondary market expectations), the deal does not change Costa Rica's fiscal picture, although the country gets a new park. A net saving in fiscal costs occurs only if the government were planning to buy the park and repay the debt.

Several limitations of debt-for-nature swaps have already emerged. Success depends on park management expertise and a genuine commitment on the part of the government to support protection of conservation land. Legislative delays and the power of local timber companies seriously compromised the value of Bolivian agreements. Elsewhere, critics charge that swaps simply lead to "paper parks." Debt-for-nature swaps give conservation groups very little power to enforce agreements with debtor countries. One would expect them to look for governments that are relatively stable and accommodating, but these countries may offer the least discounting of debt on the secondary market. Some trade-off between cost and risk has to be made.

So far, debt-for-nature swaps amount to a very small amount of money relative to total debt. Costa Rica's program, the largest to date, has amounted to less than 5 percent of its external debt. Multilateral organizations like the World Bank cannot directly engage in swaps that compromise the face value of debt, so funding depends on relatively small nonprofit organizations.

In theory, these swaps could serve as a model for debt-for-health, debt-for-education, and debt-for-land-reform programs. The main constraints are the capacity of the nonprofit community to finance these deals and the ability of the debtor to absorb more debt without inflationary consequences. Given the fiscal consequences of swaps, debtor countries have to consider which deals to favor. Should they agree to convert debt for a park or debt for a new Ralph Lauren jeans factory? The latter generates foreign exchange; saving trees does not.

Buybacks

An alternative form in which the secondary market has emerged as a solution is for debtor countries to offer their creditors buybacks of the debt. This can occur directly in the secondary market, the case of Bolivia being an example. With the help of friendly governments, Bolivia has bought back its external debt at a small fraction of the face value. For major debtors, by contrast, debt conversion would take the form of a new bond offer that involves conversion of existing debt, at a discount, into new bonds. If successful, such a conversion would reduce the face value of debt outstanding and hence interest payments. This is what happened during the 1940s in many debt adjustment plans. One issue in these conversion offers is how to make the new bonds attractive. The new bonds would obviously be attractive if they had seniority; however, existing creditors have no incentive to part with the seniority of their own claims.

A Debt Facility

A third possibility involves a facility organized by creditor governments. The facility would take over from banks LDC debts at a discount in exchange for debt guaranteed by creditor governments. The claims thus acquired would be renegotiated with the debtor countries, passing on the discount and restructuring the debt in terms of maturity and grace period as well as contingency payments. The only risk is inability or unwillingness of debtors to meet their now-reduced and tailored debts.

This proposal for a facility encounters three difficulties. The first is the reluctance of taxpayers in developed countries to assume the guarantee. The second is how to force banks to relinquish their claim rather than hold out from the debt reduction process in order to exercise their full claim. The third involves moral hazard and fairness. Specifically, countries without debt problems would see an incentive to behave poorly to get the benefits of debt reduction. There is also the question of whether resources of developed countries (including the World Bank) should be used to solve problems of middle-income countries and banks rather than those of exceptionally poor countries. This issue arises because poor countries have only debts to governments and would not benefit from this mechanism.

All of the schemes that involve discounting of debt are limited by the fact that banks have so far discounted only a small fraction of their Latin American debt. Until 1986, they avoided discounting because regulatory rules would require them to write down all similar debt to its market value. This barrier has been lifted, but the banks remain unwilling to compromise their negotiating power on the debt they continue to hold. Consortium agreements also constrain individual banks from breaking ranks to dump their debt on secondary markets.

Interest Relief

An alternative route is to seek relief on interest payments rather than principal. Here two possibilities have been suggested. One is to capitalize interest payments automatically. In such a situation, payments beyond a certain interest rate, say 5 percent, would be added to the principal of the loan. Such capitalization might also be geared to export or import prices of key commodities, such as oil in the case of Brazil or Mexico. Another version of interest relief would provide for payment of interest in local currency, available for the creditors to invest in the debtor country's economy. This scheme avoids the problem of generating trade surpluses (at the expense of investment) and the associated crowding out of investment and inflationary problems. Creditors would use the interest payments to buy assets or lend, thus allowing investment and growth to resume. The scheme has as its rationale the idea that some countries, specifically Brazil, would be in a position to service their debts in a few years (by trade surplus or new capital inflows) if they could enjoy a period of reconstruction.

Interest capitalization or recycling of interest is attractive when problems of debt service are temporary. They are not of much help, however, when there is a problem of insolvency. In that case, adding to the burden of debt does not improve creditworthiness. Unfortunately, there is no objective criterion for solvency or ability to pay. In virtually all cases, sufficiently drastic adjustment would generate the surpluses required to service debts. The difficulty is the social and political cost.

The Brady Plan

In 1985, U.S. treasury secretary James A. Baker proposed that fifteen developing countries be supported with $29 billion in new loans from the World Bank and private banks if these countries introduced free market policies. Neither side cooperated sufficiently, and the Baker Plan fizzled.

U.S. treasury secretary Nicholas Brady then offered a plan in 1989 that asked banks to forgive part of their loans to debtor countries in exchange for limited guarantees of repayment, financed by the World Bank and the IMF. The plan also called for banks to make new loans to help fund growth. For their part, debtors would be required to undertake polices favoring private investment. Calculations suggest that with the $30 billion to $35 billion available, total relief would amount to $6 billion annually, or 15 percent of the debt service owed by the nineteen largest debtors among all developing countries. This amount represented 1 percent of their GNP and was considered too small.

Banks were hardly eager to participate. None was convinced the economies would recover enough to warrant throwing good money after bad. Nor were they eager to lose bargaining power with debtors that could repay. Venezuela was cited as a potential beneficiary of the Brady plan when violence erupted in response to austerity measures, yet it held enough reserves of gold, foreign currency, and oil to service its debt. Large banks complained that they were being forced to grant debt relief that would subsidize smaller banks that did not participate in the plan. Despite their resistance, banks were enticed into coming up with a deal for Mexico when the government threatened to force them to write down loans to market value.

The Brady Plan gave Mexico some relief. In exchange for guaranteed interest payments, banks chose between swapping old loans for new thirty-year bonds with a 35 percent discount on face value but a variable interest rate, swapping loans at par for bonds at a fixed 6 1/4 percent interest rate, or lending new money. The IMF, the World Bank, Japan, and Mexico came up with $10 billion in guarantee funding. In the end, Mexico shaved an estimated $1.5 billion from its interest bill. The agreement also had favorable effects on domestic investors, and domestic peso interest rates dropped in the weeks following the announcement. However, the agreement did not fulfill the expectations of relief that could be obtained.

Under the Brady Plan, Costa Rica also managed to conclude agreements, although they were less dramatic. Costa Rica's debt strategy is a three-act story with a happy ending. After following a path similar to other Latin American countries and experiencing the costs of a recession resulting from a traditional renegotiation of its debt (1983–1985), Costa Rica moved to its own strategy in 1986. The country realized—and succeeded in convincing the international financial community—that it would not be able to grow if it had to continue servicing its debt according to the contractual terms. It unilaterally decided to service short-term debts and debts to the IMF and the World Bank, while imposing a nonconfrontational moratorium of payments on medium and long-run commercial bank debt. Finally, in 1990, Costa Rica obtained substantial debt reduction.

Because of its democratic traditions and its relatively favorable social indicators in regard to Latin American countries with higher incomes per capita, Costa Rica has been showcased as an example for other nations in the region. It now stands as an example for its prudent adjustment and determination in obtaining relief without giving in to creditors' pressure.

Can other countries follow Costa Rica's example and obtain relief through the Brady Plan? The banks are far from eager to participate, and the U.S. government has increasingly less leverage over them as they write down Latin American debt voluntarily. Moreover, the deal puts pressure on debtors to accept debt-equity swaps and offer investment incentives. Unenthusiastically received and underfunded, the plan holds limited promise.

FURTHER READING

Devlin, R. *Debt and Crisis in Latin America: The Supply Side of the Story.* Princeton: Princeton University Press, 1989.

Dornbusch, R. *The Road to Economic Recovery.* New York: Twentieth Century, 1989.

Marichal, Carlos. *A Century of Debt Crises in Latin America: From Independence to the Great Depression.* Princeton: Princeton University Press, 1989.

Sachs, J., ed. *Developing Country Debt and Economic Performance.* Vol. 2. Chicago: Chicago University Press, 1990.

Chapter 6

INFLATION

Latin America has a longstanding reputation for its battles with runaway inflation. The most notorious example is Bolivia's recent hyperinflation. Between May and August 1985, Bolivian inflation reached an annualized rate of 60,000 percent, the seventh worst case of hyperinflation in world history. Shopkeepers found themselves rushing into the street to exchange pesos for dollars as soon as they made a sale; to wait even an hour could mean a noticeable loss. Although none of Bolivia's neighbors has managed to match this experience, three-digit inflation rates are a recurrent problem in the region.

The cost of very high inflation in terms of economic growth is substantial. Uncertainty about prices brings about short horizons for production decisions and concentration of assets in inflation hedging. The economic structure that results emphasizes finance at the expense of production. Hoarding and speculation displace real production. As one Nicaraguan described the response to the 30,000 percent inflation rate in his country in 1988; "It's a hussle economy. Everyone is out to beat the market and no one is producing anything."

Capital flight also rises with inflation. The World Bank estimates that capital flight from Argentina between 1974 and 1982 amounted to 72 percent of the country's external debt, implying that if the Argentine government were able to restore confidence in the local currency, most of its foreign exchange crisis would be resolved.

Although the extreme cases of inflation in Latin America have caught world attention, inflation rates in Latin America have differed widely over time and among countries. On the whole, inflation rates have increased markedly during the 1980s. Table 6.1 divides the Latin American countries (except Cuba and Nicaragua) into three groups. During the twenty-five years between 1960 and 1985, the high inflation countries experienced average inflation rates of more than 30 percent per year. All the countries in this group are found below the equator. The low inflation countries had average inflation rates below 10 percent during the 1960–1985 period. Almost all countries in this group are situated in Central America.

After 1985, Bolivia and Chile (which used to be among the most inflationary economies in Latin America) brought inflation under control, in contrast with most other countries in the region, where inflation increased further. Figure 6.1 shows the decline of inflation in Chile, and figure 6.2 shows how Mexican inflation rates, which historically were very low, increased in the 1980s. Table 6.2 shows the annual inflation rates in countries subject to acute inflation acceleration after 1985.

One single model could hardly explain the behavior of inflation in all these countries. This chapter looks at different theories and describes various experiences with inflation in Latin America. The first section reviews the longstanding debate between monetarists and structuralists about the causes of inflation. Over time both schools have evolved but neither has yet to offer a complete diagnosis of inflation. Consequently, prescriptions for reducing inflation invariably fail at the combined task of achieving price stability and growth.

Further progress in explaining inflation depends on integrating the insights offered by conflicting points of view. In the second section of this chapter, we address five concepts central to understanding inflation: seigniorage models, foreign exchange crises, dollarization, capacity constraints, and indexation.

1 MONETARISM VERSUS STRUCTURALISM

In the 1950s and 1960s, two schools of thought, monetarism and structuralism, dominated the analysis of Latin American inflation. Monetarists argued that the main cause of inflation was deficit spending financed by money creation. Structuralists argued that inflation had its roots in real shortages of key goods in the economy and struggles between different groups in society to increase their

Table 6.1
Inflation rates, Latin American countries, 1960–1989
(percentage per year)

	1960–1969	1970–1979	1980–1985	1986–1989
High inflation countries				
Argentina	22.9	132.8	335.5	1,392.1
Bolivia	6.3	15.9	2,251.5	28.7
Brazil	45.8	30.5	142.0	795.6
Chile	25.1	174.0	23.8	18.3
Peru	9.8	26.5	97.3	1,169.2
Uruguay	50.1	59.3	48.9	73.0
Weighted average[a]	36.6	53.7	224.0	844.8
Middle inflation countries				
Colombia	11.2	19.3	23.1	24.8
Costa Rica	2.0	10.4	34.2	16.8
Ecuador	4.2	11.9	25.6	49.9
Mexico	2.7	14.7	56.4	84.1
Paraguay	4.3	11.1	17.0	25.4
Weighted average[a]	4.7	15.3	45.1	63.5
Low inflation countries				
Dominican Republic	1.3	9.2	16.9	32.6
El Salvador	0.4	9.4	15.2	22.9
Guatemala	0.5	8.9	8.2	16.7
Haiti	2.2	9.2	10.6	0.9
Honduras	1.9	6.6	8.8	6.0
Panama	1.0	6.0	5.0	0.4
Venezuela	1.1	6.6	12.9	42.3
Weighted average[a]	1.1	7.9	11.9	24.0

a. Weights equal the share of each country's population in its group.
Source: International Monetary Fund, *International Financial Statistics* (Washington, D. C.: IMF, various issues).

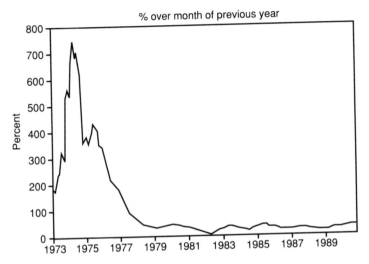

Figure 6.1
Inflation rate, Chile, 1973–1990.
Source: IMF, *International Financial Statistics* (Washington, D. C.:
International Monetary Fund, various issues).

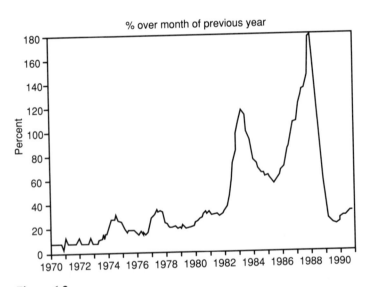

Figure 6.2
Inflation rate, Mexico, 1970–1990.
Source: IMF *International Financial Statistics* (Washington, D. C.:
International Monetary Fund, various issues).

Table 6.2
Inflation rates, selected countries, 1985–1990
(percentage per year, December–December)

	1985	1986	1987	1988	1989	1990[a]
Argentina	385	82	175	388	4,924	1,833
Brazil	228	58	366	993	1,765	2,360
Ecuador	24	27	33	86	54	48
Mexico	64	106	159	52	20	30
Nicaragua	334	747	1,347	33,603	1,690	8,500
Peru	158	63	115	1,723	2,777	8,292
Uruguay	83	76	57	69	89	130
Venezuela	6	12	40	36	81	32

a. Preliminary.
Source: ECLAC, *Preliminary Overview of the Economy of Latin America and the Caribbean* (New York: ECLAC, 1991).

shares of national income. The debate focused not only on the theoretical causes of inflation but its appropriate solutions, which invariably involve political consequences. According to the monetarist view, to stop inflation, deficits must be cut and free enterprise encouraged. In general, structuralists are more inclined toward government intervention in the economy to overcome supply constraints. In recent years, structuralism has also put more emphasis on the inertial forces that sustain inflation.

Monetarism

Monetarism explains inflation as the result of too much money chasing too few goods. The most common explanation for sustained money growth is the financing of budget deficits by money creation. Inflation is a monetary phenomenon in the sense that it could not persist without sustained money growth. Table 6.3 and figures 6.3 and 6.4 illustrate this by showing a striking positive correlation between inflation and money growth in Latin America.[1] The observation that sustained inflation is always accompanied by monetary expansion is the basis for the hypothesis that monetary expansion causes inflation. This leaves open the question of what determines money growth (discussed later in this chapter). Monetarists see

Table 6.3
Average inflation and money growth, Latin American countries, 1965–1985 (percentage per year)

	Inflation rate	Money growth rate
Bolivia	528.1	360.2
Argentina	137.3	120.9
Chile	82.1	97.7
Brazil	62.1	63.8
Uruguay	53.4	51.5
Peru	36.4	38.5
Mexico	19.7	22.6
Colombia	17.1	20.8
Costa Rica	12.4	18.6
Ecuador	12.1	19.0
Paraguay	9.8	15.4
Dominican Republic	7.9	10.3
El Salvador	7.3	9.2
Haiti	6.8	11.3
Venezuela	5.9	13.2
Guatemala	5.5	9.5
Honduras	5.3	10.3
Panama	3.9	9.1

Source: IMF, *International Financial Statistics.*

government deficits as the cause of the problem; structuralists see deficit spending and money creation as a necessary response to inflation caused by bottlenecks in the economy.

If government expenditures exceed tax collections, the government must finance its deficit by borrowing or by printing money. The financing of the government budget deficit can be written as:

Budget deficit = sales of bonds + external borrowing
                    + increase in money base.

There are two possible links between the budget deficit and money growth. First, the government may directly finance the deficit by increasing the money stock, as often occurs when the central bank is not independent. Second, an increase in the budget

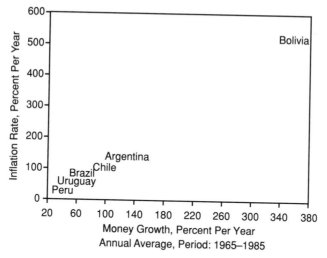

Figure 6.3
Inflation and money growth in high-inflation countries, 1965–1985.
Source: IMF, *International Financial Statistics* (Washington, D. C.:
International Monetary Fund, various issues).

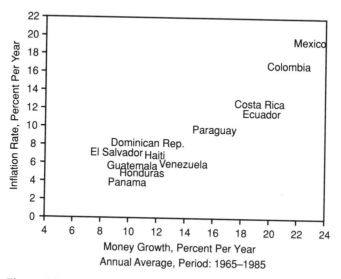

Figure 6.4
Inflation and money growth in low-inflation countries, 1965–1985.
Source: IMF, *International Financial Statistics* (Washington, D. C.:
International Monetary Fund, various issues).

deficit financed by the sale of domestic bonds will increase interest rates. If the central bank wants to keep interest rates low in order to encourage investment, it will increase money growth, indirectly financing the deficit through the printing press.[2]

In the view of monetarists, deficit spending not only causes inflation, but it makes very little contribution to real growth in the economy. A central assumption in the monetarist model is that economies naturally move toward an equilibrium with all markets clearing and full employment of resources. Any increase in aggregate demand that the government creates by raising spending (and the stock of money) will manifest itself in the long run in higher prices, not higher output. Because resources tend to be fully employed, deficit spending can only raise prices in the long run. Short-run increases in output may occur but only so long as people fail to anticipate price increases. Once inflation is built into the public's expectations, an increase in the money supply merely increases the level of prices. This reaction can be extremely fast if people anticipate the consequences of money growth or have learned from past experience with inflation. Thus, for example, the rapid takeoff of inflation in Argentina after the Austral Plan failed to stabilize the economy without austerity in 1986 is partly the result of Argentines' past experience with hyperinflation.

Because monetarists generally assume that private individuals allocate resources more efficiently than government, deficit spending hurts the economy not only by forcing people to adjust to rapidly changing prices but also by substituting public consumption for private consumption and investment. The traditional monetarist solution to inflation is to limit money creation to the economy's real rate of growth. To the extent that shortages of goods are also a factor causing inflation, monetarists argue that liberalization, or a freeing of markets from government intervention, will increase output.

Structuralism

The structuralist interpretation of inflation was developed in the 1950s and 1960s at ECLA. It claimed that different sectors of the economy develop at different speeds, giving rise to bottlenecks. Shortages in sectors that fail to grow as rapidly as the rest of the economy generate price increases that may be transmitted throughout the economy.

An important bottleneck to which structuralists often point is low productivity growth in the agricultural sector. During the process of industrialization, there is a shift of workers from agriculture to industry. The failure to address the need for credit, technical assistance, and land reform, as well as the export bias of large producers, leads to stagnant food production. As the industrial sector grows, the demand for food increases faster than its supply. Basic food prices increase, and urban workers insist on higher nominal wages. Industry tries to recover the cost of higher wages by raising prices, and economy-wide inflation is set in motion.

Similarly, inflation results when basic supplier industries (steel, cement, petroleum refining) fail to grow as rapidly as industry as a whole. Shortages of key inputs raise production costs and are passed on in the form of higher prices of final goods, which, in turn, generate worker demands for increased wages.

Three factors make this situation possible. First, the inadequate purchasing power of exports prevents the economy from importing sufficient food to keep urban food prices down. Structuralist explanations for slow growth in the export sector are linked to the Prebisch hypothesis and arguments for import substitution industrialization (described in chapter 4).[3]

Second, labor markets are neither homogeneous nor competitive. Despite widespread underemployment of unskilled workers, the skilled workers that industry needs are well enough organized to demand wage increases when rising prices threaten their standard of living.

Third, industry is able to pass on price increases because most markets are oligopolistic. The small size of the local market relative to efficient minimum scale prevents competitive pressure in most industries. Instead, price is often a markup over cost. Any increase in the wage bill is passed along in the form of higher prices.

In short, neither workers nor industrialists accept a decline in real income when shortages occur. Behind inflation lies the struggle of different groups in society trying to maintain, or even increase, their share of the pie.

In the structuralist view, inflation is ratified by monetary policy, which accommodates these forces in order to maintain employment. Accommodation refers to expansion of the money supply in response to inflation. If prices rise because of underlying structural forces, more cash is needed to cover nominally larger transactions. Were the monetary authorities to refuse to accommodate this demand by restraining credit, slower growth would follow. Yet industrial growth was seen as essential to achieve the skills and economies of scale necessary for Latin America to become internationally competitive.[4]

Structuralists have been inclined to accept inflationary pressure as a necessary consequence of growth. Some dampening of inflation has been sought in wage and price controls, which effectively serve as a truce in the struggle for changes in the share of income going to labor and capital. The social pact concluded in Mexico in 1988 was an attempt to establish this truce with the cooperation of workers and industrialists rather than to impose controls by government fiat.

In the past, structuralists have also lobbied for investment in areas where bottlenecks occur, particularly in supplier industries with high capital costs, where the private sector might shy away from risk. Deficit spending aimed at relieving bottlenecks in the economy could contribute to long-run growth, even if it were financed by money creation and higher inflation rates.

Discussing definitions and labels is always arbitrary and risky. Nonetheless, box 6.1 lists some beliefs and characteristics commonly attributed to monetarists and structuralists. Even economists who once held up the banner of monetarism or structuralism will not agree with all of their listed attributes and will agree with one or two propositions listed under the opposing column.

By now, most economists agree that inflation can be induced by both demand and supply shocks, that sustained inflation requires sustained money growth, and that the workings of inflation depend on the institutional and structural characteristics of each economy. Recent models of inflation have become more sophisticated, incorporating into their framework a better understanding of the importance of seigniorage, exchange rates, foreign debt, and indexation schemes. While models of inflation increasingly overlap in their methodology, they diverge quite a bit on the weight assigned to various factors and the expected speed of adjustment. Since empirical tests so far have not been strong enough to reject different hypotheses, economists continue to develop their analyses and policy recommendations partly based on subjective judgment and political priorities.

Box 6.1
The Monetarist/Structuralist Debate

Monetarists	Structuralists
1. Inflation is bad.	1. Inflation is not as bad as the slow growth that accompanies tight monetary policy.
2. The main source of inflation is excess demand due to budget deficits financed by money creation.	2. The main sources of inflation are structural imbalances and rigidities accommodated by passive money.
3. To reduce inflation, one must cut domestic credit creation.	3. Costs of reducing inflation are large. Use of incomes policy and price freezes are recommended.
4. Monetarists prefer to work with full employment models.	4. Structuralists emphasize unemployment.
5. Monetarists are usually identified with conservative groups in society.	5. Structuralists are thought to be progressive reformers.

Because inflation is increasingly viewed as a phenomenon linked to balance of payments problems, the proposed solutions for inflation have become closely intertwined with stabilization programs. Throughout the 1970s and 1980s, monetarists were associated with either IMF stabilization programs (often tagged as orthodox) or global monetarism. The main difference between the two is a matter of exchange rate policy. Orthodoxy recommends devaluation along with budget cuts on the theory that inflation leads to overvaluation of the exchange rate, further aggravating balance of payments problems. Global monetarism calls for guaranteeing a fixed exchange rate to reduce inflationary expectations while sharply cutting government deficits to avoid overvaluation through inflation.

By contrast, while structuralists have increasingly acknowledged the need for fiscal discipline, they have also put more emphasis on the role of inertial inflation caused by conflict over income shares. The changes in this school of thought have been substantial enough that few economists now identify themselves as structuralists, preferring instead the term *interventionist* or *inertialist*. Their view is that tight monetary policy and fiscal contraction can force the economy into a sharp recession with high unemployment yet still fail to correct inflation caused by the indexation process. The measures proposed by this new poststructuralist school have been baptized as heterodox and are discussed in chapter 7. In brief, heterodoxy calls for a combination of fiscal consolidation, monetization to avoid rising interest rates, and an incomes policy to reduce conflict over the share of income accruing to labor and capital.

Dudley Seers observed in 1970 that the controversy between monetarists and structuralists "is not just a technical issue in economic theory. At the heart of the controversy are two different ways of looking at economic development, in fact two completely different sets of value judgments about the purposes of economic activity and the ends of economic policy, and two incompatible views on what is politically possible."[5] Today the gap between orthodoxy or global monetarism and heterodoxy is every bit as wide.

2   FIVE FACTORS IN THE INFLATION PROCESS

Five concepts are essential to the analysis of inflation: seigniorage, balance of payments crises, dollarization, capacity constraints, and indexation.

Seigniorage

The government's ability to buy goods and services by printing money is called seigniorage. As the sole supplier of cash, the government is able to obtain goods and services in exchange for the money that it prints. Since no government uses a pure gold standard, an increase in the supply of cash is nearly costless to the government. The public accepts this money created by the government because they need it for transactions; other media of exchange (gold, cows) are usually too costly, too risky, or too inconvenient to use. Even if there is no inflation, a government enjoys some seigniorage as the economy grows and the need for cash increases.

When the government finances a deficit by creating money, it makes a claim on real output without reducing (by direct taxation) claims on output made by the private sector. If prices rise, either because the economy is already at full employment or because sector-specific shortages prevent an expansion of output, the purchasing power of the outstanding stock of money falls. The cash that people hold (their nominal balances) drops in value. To maintain the real value of their cash holdings, the public has to add to their nominal balances. Inflation acts like a tax: people are forced to spend less, while the government is able to buy real goods and services with the money it prints.[6]

Deficit finance inevitably leads to two types of vicious circles. First, if taxes are collected with a lag, inflation itself increases the budget deficit, inducing even larger increases in money.[7] Second, a sustained increase in money growth and inflation ultimately leads to a reduction in the real money stock. The reason is that a higher inflation rate raises the cost of holding cash. People are likely to shift some of their wealth into real goods (houses, consumer durables), a response that only increases inflationary pressures. In addition, they send their wealth abroad, reducing the amount of foreign exchange available in the economy and raising the cost of imported goods.

The amount of revenue the government can generate by printing money is shown in figure 6.5. When the economy is growing, the government can obtain limited revenue from seigniorage without causing inflation. Because the demand for money rises as real income grows, the government can print some money without raising prices. But as money growth rises above the real growth of income, inflation rises. Seigniorage increases but at a decreasing rate. This happens because people reduce their real holdings of the money base as it becomes more and more costly to hold. Thus, seigniorage increases less than proportionately with the increase in money growth and inflation. Eventually inflation will become so high that no increase in money growth can produce an increase in real seigniorage.

How much revenue do governments in Latin America obtain from the printing of money? Can we explain inflation in Latin America by making use of the model just described?

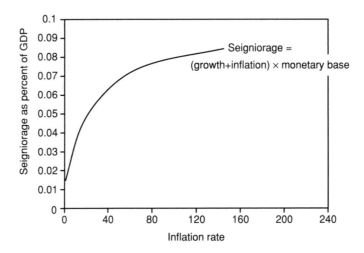

Figure 6.5
Seigniorage.
Source: IMF *International Financial Statistics* (Washington, D. C.: International Monetary Fund, various issues).

The classic illustration of seigniorage is a war economy where a government is unable to boost taxes and must finance its defense expenditures by printing money, as Nicaragua did between 1986 and 1990. Although news from Nicaragua during that period was dominated by political events, the important issue for Nicaraguans was the dramatic deterioration in their living standards. The proliferation of conflicting data makes an evaluation of the Nicaraguan economy difficult, but there is wide agreement that the economic nightmare stemmed in good measure from the contra insurgency. The toll was heavy in both lives and resources. Between 1988 and 1990, more than half of the national budget was devoted to defense. Much of the budget was financed by printing money, resulting in an acceleration of inflation.

At the beginning of the Sandinistas' rule in 1979, the exchange rate was 10 cordobas to the U.S. dollar. By February 1987, when the government exchanged the old bills for new ones at a rate of 1 to 1,000, the black market rate was 40,000 cordobas to the dollar. It was hoped that this monetary reform would stop inflation, which had reached 7,000 percent per year. With no substantial relief in the country's military and economic situation in sight, the government continued to run deficits, and inflation persisted. In 1988, the annual inflation rate in Managua reached 30,000 percent. Deficits were financed on the backs of workers as real wages fell by 75 percent.[8]

The Sandinistas lost the presidential election in 1990. Despite expectations of a turnaround after the inauguration of President Violeta Chamorro in April 1990, the economy continued to deteriorate amid large deficits and high military spending. Output shrank by 5 percent in 1990 (even more than during the last year of the Sandinista rule), while inflation continued. In January 1991, the cordoba (reissued by the Sandinista government at an exchange rate of ten to the dollar in 1988) traded at roughly 3.2 million cordobas to the dollar.

Table 6.4 shows the data for inflation and seigniorage elsewhere in the region. Seigniorage generally rises with inflation in Argentina, Mexico, and Chile. We cannot reject the hypothesis that governments in these countries use their ability to print money as a means of raising real revenue and in doing so accelerate inflation. In no case, however, does seigniorage seem to explain inflation fully, and in the case of Brazil, there is no apparent relationship between the two

Table 6.4
Seigniorage and inflation, Argentina, Brazil, Chile, and Mexico, 1978–1986 (percentage)

Year	Argentina ΔH/GDP	Inflation	Brazil ΔH/GDP	Inflation	Chile ΔH/GDP	Inflation	Mexico ΔH/GDP	Inflation
1978	4.2	175.5	2.0	38.7	3.4	40.1	3.6	17.5
1979	3.2	159.5	3.3	52.7	2.5	33.4	4.3	18.2
1980	3.0	100.8	2.0	82.8	2.4	35.1	4.9	26.4
1981	2.5	104.5	2.0	105.6	-0.7	19.7	5.5	27.9
1982	3.9	164.8	2.1	97.8	-1.7	9.9	10.9	58.9
1983	5.5	343.8	2.0	142.1	0.7	27.3	6.7	101.8
1984	5.1	626.7	2.7	197.0	0.8	19.9	5.8	65.5
1985	4.3	672.1	2.7	226.9	1.0	30.7	1.8	57.7
1986	2.6	90.1	3.6	145.2	n.a	19.5	1.8	86.2

Note: Seigniorage, ΔH, is the increase in the money base, H, defined as line 14 in *International Financial Statistics*, except for Argentina, where it is line 14a. Inflation is the annual change in consumer prices, line 64.
Source: Ibid.

variables. Nor does the existence of a relationship between the two variables explain why governments would turn to this source of revenue despite its destabilizing consequences. Clearly the inflation story is more complicated. Latin American experiences with inflation must be interpreted in the light of local financial markets, mechanisms for adjustment to inflation, and growing external debt.

Balance of Payments Crises

Inflation in Latin America since 1950 has been linked to the external balance. Easily financed current account deficits make for low inflation. A balance of payments crisis, originating in either a sudden fall in the terms of trade or a halt of capital inflows, generates an immediate jump in the inflation rate. This contrasts sharply with the conventional view of inflation linked simply to money growth and budget deficit finance.

The sharp jump in inflation rates throughout Latin America during the 1980s was linked to the debt crisis. In the preceding decade, governments were able to finance deficit spending by borrowing abroad. Interest rates on foreign loans were low, and obtaining credit was easy. Few governments felt an urgent need to resort to the printing press as a means of raising revenue in the mid-1970s.

With the rise in international interest rates and the sudden withdrawal of foreign lending in the early 1980s, Latin American governments were deprived of foreign capital to finance interest payments and noninterest deficits. The governments' answer to forced debt service has been increased taxes and reduced expenditures, but it has also been to incur higher budget deficits and to finance these by issuing domestically denominated debt or by printing money. It is no accident that Argentina, Brazil, and Bolivia experienced extraordinary inflation in the aftermath of the debt shock in 1982.

A terms of trade shock can also generate inflationary pressure. If the international prices of major export commodities drop—or if the price of an important import like oil rises—shortages of foreign exchange develop. Imported intermediate and final goods become scarce. The price of any good with imported components rises. Particularly where basic wage goods like food are imported, higher prices lead to demands for higher wages and ultimately generate inflationary pressure throughout the economy.

Another way in which a terms of trade shock can cause inflation is through the government budget. Many countries depend heavily on export taxes as a source of revenue. Mexico, Venezuela, Ecuador, and Bolivia, for example, earn much of their revenue from oil and mineral exports. Argentina taxes some of its agricultural exports. A decline in the world price of exports reduces tax revenues. If government expenditures are not reduced as tax collections fall, the primary budget deficit increases. Unless borrowing is possible, it is tempting to finance this increase in the deficit by printing more money.

A widely recommended response to a sudden loss of capital inflows or to a terms of trade shock is to devalue. By raising the price of traded goods in terms of the local currency, export production is encouraged and import demand is dampened. An improvement in the trade balance helps to generate the foreign exchange needed to service an external debt or to relieve shortages of imported goods. But devaluations also carry their own inflationary consequences. First, an increase in the price of imports raises the cost of any good involving imported inputs and directly increases the price of imported final goods; in response, well-organized workers insist on higher nominal wages.

Second, frequent devaluation may lead to the perception that further devaluations are likely. In this case, people shift their wealth into dollars, anticipating profits from reconversion after later devaluations.[9] Dollarization contributes to inflation.

Third, devaluations have an important impact on the domestic cost of servicing the external debt. Foreign debt service measured in domestic currency increases. For example, if the currency is devalued from 200 pesos per dollar to 230 pesos per dollar, the government must now offer more pesos to people who hold dollars in order to raise a dollar to pay foreign creditors. As a result, the budget deficit measured in local currency also increases. If the government prints more money to cover the higher cost of obtaining dollars, it stimulates inflation further.

Finally, devaluations can cut real growth in the short run by lowering the real wage rate and reducing domestic aggregate demand. The drop in real growth reduces the amount of noninflationary seigniorage that the government can collect. Moreover, the political consequences of recession are unpalatable.

Dollarization

As inflation rises and confidence in domestic money declines, people tend to substitute away from domestic money in favor of foreign money. The use of U.S. dollars by Latin Americans in place of domestic currency is referred to as the dollarization of Latin America.

There are several reasons for dollarization. In terms of transactions, it becomes difficult to keep measuring prices on a current basis when they change rapidly. Setting prices in terms of U.S. dollars becomes less costly than constantly changing price tags. Furthermore, any negotiation that involves a time lag is difficult to carry out unless discussions take place in terms of a more stable currency. If local interest rates do not keep up with inflation, there is also an incentive to store one's wealth in a foreign currency that will not lose its value so rapidly. Moreover, as inflation proceeds, devaluation or depreciation of the local currency is inevitable; without it, imported goods become increasingly cheap relative to domestic goods, and balance of payments problems develop. In anticipation of a devaluation, people will convert their money to dollars in order to be able to exchange them for more pesos after the devaluation.

To measure dollarization, we need to know to what extent U.S. dollars are used for transactions and speculation. There are no data on U.S. currency circulating in the region; however, we can use data for dollar-denominated bank deposits in Mexico and Bolivia to illustrate this phenomenon.

Figure 6.6 shows the ratio of dollar- to peso-denominated deposits in Mexico. This ratio rose from 5 percent in 1975 to 25 percent by the first quarter of 1977. With higher inflation, the ratio rose dramatically to 58 percent in 1982. Years of marked increases in the dollarization ratio have also been the final years of an administration. Both expectations of a devaluation and perceptions of possible changes in the economic regime play an important role in explaining the Mexican dollarization. At the end of 1982, when the government froze dollar-denominated deposits and introduced radical financial reforms, the ratio suddenly dropped. Dollarization no doubt continued, but by threatening to expropriate dollar deposits in Mexican banks, the government sent the phenomenon underground.

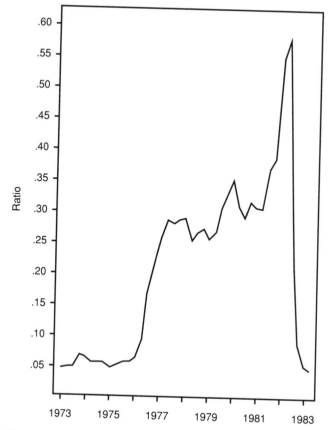

Figure 6.6
Dollar/peso deposit ratio in the Mexican banking system, 1973–1983.
Source: M. Melvin, "The Dollarization of Latin America as a Market Forced
Monetary Reform," *Economic Development and Cultural Change* 36 (April
1988), 549.

Figure 6.7 shows the ratio between dollar-denominated and Bolivian peso–denominated time deposits in Bolivian commercial
banks. The ratio increased from 10 percent in 1973 to more than 150
percent in 1982, a period during which inflation had risen from one
to three digits. In November 1982, domestic contracts denominated
in foreign currency were forbidden, and the ratio plummeted, eliminating the record of dollarization.

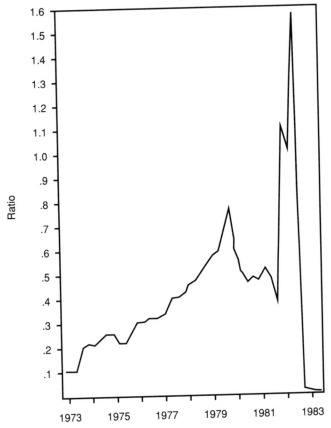

Figure 6.7
Dollar/peso deposit ratio in the Bolivian banking system, 1973–1983.
Source: M. Melvin, "The Dollarization of Latin America as a Market Forced
Monetary Reform," *Economic Development and Cultural Change* 36 (April
1988), 550.

As long as dollarization occurs, recorded or unrecorded, its cost
to the local economy is substantial. Dollars that could be used to
import real goods are instead used as a medium of exchange. Just as
gold is considered too valuable to serve as a medium of exchange in
industrialized countries, the use of scarce dollars in Latin America
is an inefficient use of resources. In addition, if local residents shift
their wealth out of the country, credit available to local investors
falls, and real growth suffers. Finally, the government's ability to

collect seigniorage from domestic money creation falls with dollarization because it no longer acts as the primary source of money in the economy. Indeed, by one estimate, the Argentine government supplied less than half the value of currency in the local economy in 1988 because Argentines used dollars so widely. The government's response to this loss of seigniorage is typically not a decrease in money creation but a frantic attempt to keep up real government spending by printing even more money.

The extent of dollarization depends on its context. The impacts of the terms of trade shock that reduced export tax revenues in the early 1980s in Mexico and Bolivia were quantitatively different. It is also true that the effects of dollarization are different depending on whether the inflation rate has previously been high or low. In countries with low inflation rates like Mexico, the share of the money base in output is large relative to other countries long used to inflation. In traditionally high inflation countries that have already been partially demonetized, the base on which the government can collect seigniorage is small. In those countries, a terms of trade shock that reduces tax revenues, combined with a flight from domestic currency, can easily lead to a hyperinflation, as it did in Bolivia.

What set off the stampede to dollars in Bolivia? The case of Bolivia shows how closely linked monetary policy and external imbalances can be in causing inflation. Between 1971 and 1978, Bolivia experienced relative stability under the regime of General Hugo Banzer. Some economic prosperity was achieved as a result of favorable terms of trade and heavy borrowing from international banks. At the end of this period, however, high international interest rates, falling commodity prices, and tight credit put an end to easy economic growth. By late 1980, access to international capital markets had dried up, and both the World Bank and the IMF had stopped lending. Shortly thereafter, the price of tin plummeted.

By 1982, inflation was running at almost 300 percent per year. Hernan Siles-Suazo took power that year as head of a leftist coalition. The government wanted to satisfy social demands and also had to meet larger debt service because of the increase in international interest rates in the early 1980s. However, it lacked the base to raise tax revenues, and international lending had dried up. Moreover, revenues from export taxes dwindled with the falling price of tin.

Thus, the deficit was met through an increase in money creation. While the country should have been adjusting to lower standards of living as borrowing became impossible and export earnings fell, strikes and lockouts put pressure on the government to make promises it could not keep. Hyperinflation followed.

Prices rose by a factor of fourteen in 1984 and kept soaring throughout 1985. Distortions in the economy became manifold. Tin miners smuggled ore out of the country to exchange it for dollars in Peru. Workers left their jobs early—if they came in at all—to join in the speculative hoarding of dollars and basic goods. Companies shifted their attention from production to financial scams. One firm borrowed dollars from the government with the stated intent of importing tractors, arranged to have empty crates shipped through customs, and sold the dollars on the black market. A mine owner who had subsidized heavy losses in mining with lucrative financial deals said, "Bolivians are learning that only a chump tries to make a profit producing something."[10] The exception was cocaine: more Bolivians turned to drug production to earn dollars.

The Bolivian hyperinflation hit the country during a period of intense political instability. The large deficits, which could not be financed by borrowing abroad after 1980, caused the government to print money and led to increasing inflation. Inflation itself increased the deficit because real tax revenues fell due to lags in tax collection. Total central government revenues fell from around 9 percent of GNP in 1981 to about 1.3 percent of GNP in the first half of 1985. Cuts in spending were made in public investment and then in international debt servicing. They came too late. At the peak of hyperinflation, the external debt was no longer being honored, but by then the tax system had collapsed. Revenues fell from 10 percent of GDP in 1978 to 2 percent in 1984.

The inflation stopped abruptly in October 1985 when President Victor Paz Estenssoro, who had just been elected, announced a stabilization program. The program reduced the fiscal deficit through a sharp increase in public sector prices, a reduction in subsidies to the mining industry, a public sector wage freeze, and a moratorium on debt service. Expenditures fell below taxes, and the exchange rate policy played an important role in the stabilization. By stabilizing the exchange rate, inflation could be made to revert to the US inflation rate. Nonetheless, GDP growth was negative in 1985 and

1986, as it had been since 1982, and economic recovery in the late 1980s was much slower than expected. The stabilization process was not without costs, an issue discussed in the following chapter.

Capacity Constraints and Supply Shocks

Inflationary pressure is not solely the result of money creation and crises in the external sector. Heavy fiscal spending can force an economy to its limits. Thus, wars have inflationary consequences not only because governments often finance them by printing money but also because they put a strain on the real capacity of the economy. In most Latin American countries, an expansion of demand is likely to wind up increasing the demand for imported goods. As a result, inflation will frequently be linked to balance of payments problems, even if an external shock is not a major root of the problem.

Government policy can also influence aggregate demand and prices through its role in determining wages. Populist regimes in Argentina, Peru, and Chile have often been blamed for inflation because they have given workers greater bargaining power by refusing to crush strikes. The real increase in wages raises consumption and often raises output too. But firms can pass on the higher wage costs because protectionism does not force them to remain internationally competitive, and inflation rises. The problem becomes more acute when populist regimes fail to recognize the capacity of the economy to respond to increasing demand. Continued increases in real wages, combined with expanded social programs, create a struggle over loaves of bread that refuse to multiply despite the proclamations of a charismatic leader. The inflation that occurred under President Salvador Allende is a good example of a crisis that developed as a result of several factors, including rapid stimulation of demand beyond the capacity constraint. (We discuss this problem in detail in chapter 8.)

If inflation is defined as too much money chasing too few goods, any shock that increases aggregate demand above full employment output, or decreases supply, contributes to inflationary pressure. Bad harvests, earthquakes, shifts in the political power of workers, and devaluations can fuel inflation. In Mexico and Brazil in the early 1980s, prices took off faster than the money supply, lending some credence to the argument that it is not the money supply per se that causes inflation but real shocks that drive up prices.

Indexation and Adjustment Intervals

Throughout Latin America but especially in the high inflation countries of the Southern Cone, contracts are written to include an adjustment for inflation. Minimum wage legislation assures workers that their wages will be periodically increased by the rate of inflation. This indexation is generally backward looking; that is, wages or contracts are adjusted for past inflation. Figure 6.8 illustrates an indexation system like the one that existed in Brazil between 1968 and 1986. In this case, legislation corrected wages for past inflation; the exchange rate was readjusted in short intervals by minidevaluations; interest rates, bonds, and rents were corrected for price increases through a system of indexation called monetary correction.

This indexation process makes inflation a self-perpetuating phenomenon. Current supply shocks are automatically transmitted to future periods. An oil price increase, a real depreciation, increases in indirect taxes, elimination of public sector subsidies, or increases

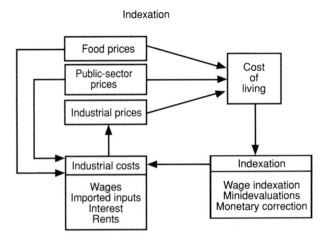

Figure 6.8
Indexation

in the real price of agricultural goods raise the current rate of inflation and are transmitted by indexation into increased inflation in subsequent periods.

Figure 6.8 shows how current inflation depends on past inflation through indexation of wages, the exchange rate, and public sector prices. Overspending or underspending (the level of aggregate demand in the economy) and supply shocks can set the inflationary process in motion. Indexation will keep it going. We can describe the inflation process as

Inflation today = Inflation yesterday + effects of the level of demand
+ effects of supply shocks.

In the vicious circle created by indexation, inflationary shocks, such as a devaluation or an increase in the public sector prices, are perpetuated. Inflation today repeats inflation yesterday. Adverse shocks push up prices today, and tomorrow prices will increase again simply because they are higher today. Indexation protects the real economy from the effects of inflation caused by rapid expansion of the money supply, but it makes adjustment to real shocks, such as an increase in the price of imported oil, more difficult. A devaluation aimed at raising the relative price of imported oil is quickly eroded in real terms under indexation.

In fact, to raise real prices or cut real wages in the presence of full indexation, the frequency of adjustment of prices and exchange rates has to be higher than the frequency of wage adjustments. Only then is it possible to beat the indexation, cutting the average real wage during the adjustment period by stepping up the rate of inflation. Indexation of the financial system, the tax structure, and the public debt implies that changes in the inflation rate are automatically and fully accommodated.

A slowdown in the growth rate of nominal spending cannot eliminate inflation from one day to the next. The lagged effects of past inflation will continue to raise prices. Even if an indexation system is not in place, high current rates of inflation create expectations of inflation for the future. The concept of inertial inflation refers to the difficulty of stopping inflation once it is in motion.

The most striking examples of inflation inertia are found in countries with formal indexation mechanisms—for instance, Brazil.

Figure 6.9 shows the history of the Brazilian inflation. In the five years between 1959 and 1964, increasingly populist administrations carried inflation from 10 to 100 percent. Sharp wage repression after the military coup brought inflation down to 20 percent by 1968, where it stayed until the first oil shock, when inflation jumped to 40 percent. There it remained until 1979. In the five years between 1980 and 1985, the government's failure to absorb the debt and oil shocks in a noninflationary manner pushed inflation from 50 to 220 percent.

Brazilian money growth lagged inflation from 1980 to the end of 1984. Inflation seemed to enjoy a life of its own. A committed monetarist might argue that inflation accelerated due to the expectation of faster money growth in the future, although current money growth was slow relative to the inflation rate. These expectations might have been fueled by the rapid accumulation of the debt and the prospect of increasing interest payments, but the facts seem more consistent with the view that inflation carries some inertia. Furthermore, a whole host of other factors contributed to the acceleration of inflation, including two large devaluations in 1979

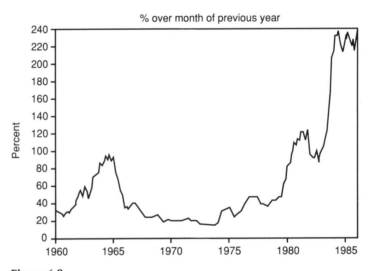

Figure 6.9
Inflation rate, Brazil, 1960–1985.
Source: Fundação Getúlio Vargas, *Conjunctura Economica*, various issues.
Rio de Janeiro: Fundação Getúlio Vargas.

and 1983, increases in the prices and interest rates administered by the government, and cuts in subsidies to oil and wheat consumption. All of these inflationary pressures were aggravated by a crop failure in 1983. Add to that the indexation of wages, bonds, and the exchange rate, and it is not surprising how easily the inflationary shocks spread, leading to inflation rates of 200 percent.

A related factor in the acceleration of inflation is the shortening of the interval for adjustment of wages, public sector prices, and the exchange rate. In high inflation economies, institutional arrangements provide for a periodic resetting of real wages to a peak. The peak real wage occurs at the date of the contract immediately after the nominal wage increase. Subsequently, the real wage is eroded by inflation until the next adjustment occurs. Figure 6.10 shows the actual real minimum wage in Brazil between 1976 and 1986. At fixed intervals the real wage increases to a peak and then is eroded over the interval between adjustments, reaching a trough just prior to the next adjustment, a year or six months later.

Escalation of inflation to three or four digits invariably involves a shortening of adjustment periods for wage and price setting. This shortening of the adjustment interval increases inflation; in a context of overlapping contracts, it means that a larger number of contracts are revised on the same date, pushing up costs and, hence,

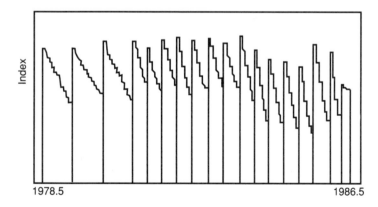

Figure 6.10
Real minimum wage, Brazil, 1976–1986.
Source: Fundação Getúlio Vargas, *Conjunctura Economica*, various issues.
Rio de Janeiro: Fundação Getúlio Vargas.

inflation. In 1979, the annual adjustment of wages in Brazil was accelerated to a biannual basis. This translated into a cost shock for firms and led to a doubling of the inflation process. Higher inflation in turn further shortened intervals, pushing inflation up once more. By the end of 1985, firms and workers were beginning to move into three-month revision cycles. The government was keenly aware that the transition to even shorter periods must have hyperinflationary consequences and hence tried to avoid the shortening of intervals, an effort that culminated with the wage-price freeze of the Cruzado Plan (discussed in the next chapter).

3   CONCLUSION

High inflation in Latin America poses a threat to the region's infant democracies. It erodes the purchasing power of wages, creates intense feelings of insecurity, and undermines popular support for constitutional governments. Even if indexation is widespread, covering wages, prices, interest rates, and taxes, inflation hits hardest the lower classes, whose subsistence is not protected. Escalations of conflict in Brazil and Peru suggest that the mixture of inflation and bad income distribution does not make for a stable combination. Furthermore, inflation tends to result in overvaluation: investors fear the exchange rate risk as well as economic instability. Balance of payments problems are not far behind.

Much has been written about the high costs of stabilization policies; however, the cost of rapid inflation, in terms of lost growth and lower real wages, is not any smaller. Results of a poll in Peru in October 1988 showed that 75 percent of respondents favored adoption of an agreement with the IMF, indicating that inflation is more unpopular than austerity, particularly when the chaos associated with inflation has brought the country to the brink of a coup.[11]

A variety of factors contribute to inflation. Inflation rarely takes off without growth in the money supply. Yet there is no record of pure inflation in which the money supply started to grow at the whim of the monetary authorities. There is always some economic reason that forces governments to turn to inflationary policies. Clearly there are situations where external shocks, pressure to meet popular demands for higher standards of living, and inertia play a relatively larger role than money creation in explaining inflation.

What are the appropriate solutions? The prescriptions for containing inflation vary with the diagnosis. In the following chapter, we discuss orthodox stabilization policies derived from monetarist interpretations, as well as recent heterodox programs derived from theories of inertia and structuralists' recommendations.

FURTHER READING

Dornbusch, R., F. Sturzenegger, and H. Wolf. *Extreme Inflation: Dynamics and Stabilization.* Brookings Papers on Economic Activity 2. Washington, D.C.: Brookings Institution, 1990.

Williamson, J., ed., *Inflation and Indexation.* Washington, D.C: Institute for International Economics, 1985.

World Development. Special Issue: The Resurgence of Inflation in Latin America. August 1987.

Chapter 7

STABILIZATION

Stabilization programs, aimed at reducing inflation and resolving balance of payments disequilibria in countries where problems have already reached crisis proportions, are undeniably the most controversial subject affecting Latin American economies. The debate is not over long-run structural change, which must occur, but over the effectiveness of fast-acting remedies.

Stabilization programs are closely associated with the explanations for inflation described in the preceding chapter. Orthodox programs are derived from the monetarist interpretation of inflation. Among orthodox programs we include IMF programs and the neoconservative experiments in the Southern Cone. Heterodox programs, including the Inti Plan in Peru, the Cruzado Plan in Brazil, and the Austral Plan in Argentina, are based on interpretations of structuralism and inflation inertia. Mexico used a combination of orthodox austerity followed by a heterodox incomes policy with success.

To evaluate the effectiveness of these programs, one needs a clear set of priorities. How much misery is justifiable in pursuit of single-digit inflation? If one considers that inflation itself imposes costs on the poor, the trade-offs involved in stabilization are not so easy to assess. Furthermore, while immediate action is needed in the face of hyperinflation and external imbalance, stabilization programs tend to set the course of policy for several years; efforts to restore stability in the short run must be consistent with long-run development goals.

An orthodox program stopped inflation in Bolivia, for example, but did not improve the prospects for real growth. Until 1985, Bolivia lived with high government deficits and a huge bureaucracy. After August 1985, reforms broke the power of trade unions, deregulated the labor market, eliminated wage indexation, unified the exchange rate, and allowed for foreign currency as a domestic means of exchange. Despite deregulation efforts and the success of stabilization, Bolivia's level of activity remains stagnant. Of course, one might argue that unless one expects policies to have a fast payoff, it is improper to use Bolivia as an example of laissez-faire failure. But it is remarkable that the investment rate in Bolivia continues to be exceptionally low—10 percent of GNP over 1986–1989. This could reflect lack of confidence or lack of opportunity.

Stabilization programs in Bolivia, Chile, and Mexico have succeeded in stopping inflation (table 7.1). However, success did not

Table 7.1
Inflation rates in Latin American countries with successful and failed stabilization in the 1980s (percentage per year)

| | 1960–1979[a] | 1980–1985[a] | December- December | | | | | |
			1985	1986	1987	1988	1989	1990[b]
Successful stabilization								
Bolivia	11	2,252	8,170	66	11	22	17	18
Chile	99	24	26	17	22	13	21	29
Mexico	9	15	64	106	159	52	20	30
Failed stabilization								
Argentina	78	336	385	82	175	388	4,924	1,833
Brazil	38	142	228	58	366	993	1,765	2,360
Peru	18	97	158	63	115	1,723	2,777	8,292
Nicaragua	16[c]	42	334	747	1,347	33,603	1,690	8,500
A recent case								
Venezuela	4	7	6	12	40	36	81	32

a. Average in the period.
b. Preliminary data.
c. 1973-1979.
Source: ECLAC, *Preliminary Overview of the Economy of Latin America and the Caribbean, 1991* (New York: ECLAC, 1991). International Monetary Fund, *International Financial Statistics* (Washington, D.C.: IMF, various issues).

come about without costs, a point discussed at length in the next sections. On the other hand, stabilization programs in Argentina, Brazil, Nicaragua, and Peru have clearly failed.

Venezuela's orthodox plan of late 1989 is an experiment still in progress. Having the fundamentals (fiscal, monetary, and exchange policies) in place and favorable external conditions set the stage for success. In early 1989, the government in Venezuela faced an exploding fiscal deficit and an exchange rate premium of almost 200 percent, following a failed attempt at stabilization in 1988. The government responded by floating the exchange rate, freeing prices and interest rates, reducing the fiscal deficit, and embarking on trade reform. In response to the program, nonoil GDP dropped by almost 10 percent, while inflation increased to 80 percent per year. But in 1990 inflation was on its way down. Success is not yet assured. Most of the fiscal correction came from the real exchange rate depreciation, which favors government oil revenues in Venezuela.[1] A tax reform remains to be undertaken.

One lesson from failed programs is that persistent deficit finance is unsustainable. Stability requires fiscal balance. This proposition might seem too general to be useful, and disagreements quickly appear when the issue of implementation arises. Nonetheless, recent agreement among economists and policymakers on this general statement does represent progress; in 1970, policymakers would have argued that deficit finance was the only way out of underdevelopment and that printing money to finance government investment was a good idea. Even as late as 1985, policymakers promoting the Cruzado Plan in Brazil argued that budget deficits and inflation were unrelated.

Cutting budget deficits is not the complete answer to stopping inflation. Several factors may explain the difference between inflation acceleration and stabilization in Latin American countries. Initial conditions, policy sequencing, a rapid demonetization process, delayed domestic adjustment due to political reasons, lack of mechanisms to compensate for external shocks, and the fragility of domestic financial markets are crucial variables.

More elusive is the credibility factor. By freezing bank assets in 1990, the Collor administration created a major crisis of confidence among investors in Brazil. It takes years to regain the trust that is lost with just one such freeze. The Mexicans learned this in 1982, when all dollar deposits were temporarily blocked. Having once let an economy spin out of control, a regime has difficulty regaining public confidence. For this reason, a change in regime (although not necessarily a coup) may be important for stabilization to succeed. In stepping down early after the 1989 elections in Argentina, Raúl Alfonsín acknowledged this. Even a change in regime may not be enough. Will anyone ever believe that Argentina is about to become a low inflation country?

In this chapter we describe stabilization programs in Latin America during the last twenty years. We start with an analysis of orthodox programs.

1 ORTHODOXY

Although the IMF was created to aid in the management of a stable international exchange rate system, its main activity since 1970 has been to manage foreign exchange crises of Third World countries. With Mexico's near default in 1982, the IMF became the main organizer of international debt agreements. Not only did it lend to countries facing debt crises, it also became the pivot around which negotiations turned. The banks insisted on linking their rescheduling agreements to the fund's seal of approval for a debtor's economic policies. Ironically, as the debt crisis grew, the IMF became a net recipient of capital from developing countries.[2] Its role as adviser and negotiator overtook its role as a source of finance.

The IMF's prescription for balance of payments problems and inflation invariably involves a sharp recession. Only by bringing down spending is it possible to bring prices and the trade balance quickly into line. To many people who have witnessed the consequences of IMF programs on the poor, this cure seems about as sensible as the idea of bleeding a feverish patient.

While the IMF is praised by mainstream economists for containing crises, its most radical critics do not even grant the possibility of good intentions on the part of the IMF. Cheryl Payer, for example, identifies the IMF as an "instrument for imposing imperialist financial discipline upon poor countries."[3]

Whether orthodox measures serve the interests of international capitalists or local peasants, there is wide agreement that the medicine is bitter. The *New York Times* described the rioting in

1989 that led to 300 deaths in Caracas following measures taken to meet IMF guidelines:

The violence began in Caracas on Monday, when the price increases took effect. Crowds took to the streets to protest the economic adjustment programs announced by the Government. . . . Included among the new measures, which were adopted under pressure from international lending institutions, were increases of 30 to 50 percent in fares for public transportation . . . and a sharp increase in gasoline prices. . . . Witnesses said they saw several casualties, including a man in his 20s who was reportedly shot in the head and killed as he looked out of a window to survey the commotion.[4]

Why does the IMF seem so preoccupied with inflation, given its primary goal of resolving external imbalances? The links between the two are strong. Inflation tends to create overvaluation, since nowhere is there a completely free currency float. It also erodes the tax base, making it impossible for governments to pay foreign debts. The instability caused by inflation depresses foreign investment, promotes capital flight, and leads to dollarization of the economy. All of this feeds into external imbalances. In short, it is not possible to fix the external account without addressing inflation and internal policies.

Monetarism supplies the rationale for orthodox stabilization programs: budget deficits and consequent fast money growth cause inflation. The ageless orthodox medicine for stabilization consists of two basic ingredients: a cut in the budget deficit and devaluation. These are usually accompanied by an emphasis on freeing prices. The most widely used policies in IMF-supported adjustment programs are listed in table 7.2. The IMF also recommends liberalization of imports and exchange controls, elimination of price controls, and higher interest rates.

By reducing the fiscal deficit and curtailing money growth, the IMF hopes to attack the roots of inflation directly. The first target is often the government payroll. Because governments are major employers in most Latin American countries, deep cuts in the number of government jobs immediately dampen demand in the economy. A second tourniquet is applied to the flow of fiscal red ink through the privatization of steel, cement, oil, airline, and telephone companies (box 7.1). This is intended both to reduce the cost of government subsidies to these industries and to improve their efficiency.

Table 7.2
Policies employed in IMF-supported adjustment programs

	Percentage of programs adopting the measure
Ceilings on credit expansion	98
Restraint of central government current expenditure	91
Curtailment of investment or delay in new projects	60
Reduction in subsidies	61
Raise in taxes on goods and services	73
Wage guidelines	46
Increase in energy prices	46

Note: From ninety-four programs for sixty-seven countries between 1980 and 1984.
Source: International Monetary Fund, *Fund-supported Programs, Fiscal Policy and Income Distribution*, Occasional Paper, no. 46 (Washington, D.C.: IMF, 1986).

Devaluation improves the current account by raising the cost of imported goods and making exports more profitable, but it can also cause inflationary pressure as the price of imports rises and the domestic cost of debt service increases. Moreover, if exports do not respond quickly to the stimulus, a devaluation can be contractionary. Orthodox economists tend to be optimistic about the elasticity of export supply. Even if there are short-run setbacks, the purpose of devaluation is to set the economy in the direction of greater export orientation over the long run.

Elimination of price controls on consumer goods (such as grains, electricity, transport, and milk) serves three purposes. First, subsidies on imported grains, for instance, encourage consumption of white bread instead of locally grown corn and cassava. Elimination of subsidies and price controls brings consumer choice in line with international prices and cuts food imports. Second, price controls hurt local producers by directly limiting the price received for their output or by forcing them to compete with artificially cheap substitutes. In the long run, a ceiling on the price of corn discourages production and contributes to urban food shortages. Finally, price controls on public goods and subsidies increase fiscal deficits. Elimination of subsidies and increases of public prices help to bring the budget under control.

Box 7.1
Privatization in Latin America

Governments throughout Latin America are eyeing privatization of state-owned enterprises as a means of cutting government deficits. Unprofitable parastatals are jettisoned with the hope that private management will reverse their negative ledger sign. Profitable assets are liquidated to raise funds for current expenditures.

Potential targets for privatization include utilities, food processing operations, and food storage facilities. These companies lose money partly because they serve a redistributional function, albeit with a lot of leakages. Privatization can raise their efficiency, but alternative transfer programs may need to be put in place to avoid regressive consequences.

Labor has resisted privatization, with good reason: the logical first step in cutting losses is to cut the payroll. A small number of worker ownership schemes have been set up in Chile and Costa Rica. The main challenge is financing: few workers can raise substantial capital. Unions have taken the lead in fighting privatization. When Aeromexico was privatized in 1988, the three affected unions managed to obtain substantial severance pay and a 64 billion peso indemnity for their workers. Because public sector workers form an important part of the ruling party's constituency in Mexico, they have been able to negotiate concessions as parastatals are sold off.

In Mexico, the total number of parastatals dropped from 1,155 in 1982 to approximately 700 in 1988. Not all of these enterprises were sold to the private sector, however. Some were merged or transferred to local governments, while others were simply disbanded. The antiquated Funditura Monterrey steel mill was shut down altogether, with a loss of 9,000 jobs.

Chile undertook a major privatization of its national pension fund in 1980. Under the prior system, workers, firms, and the state paid into a common fund administered by the state. Benefits bore little relationship to contributions, and contributions failed to accumulate in value. Under the new system, private firms collect payments, manage funds, and supervise distributions. Pensions have markedly increased. At the same time, payments to the disabled and to widows and orphans are more than twice their previous level.

Source: Peter Accolla, "Privatization in Latin America," in *Foreign Labor Trends* (Washington, D.C.: U.S. Department of Labor, 1989).

Proponents of liberalization rightly argue that the consequences of eliminating price controls and subsidies are not necessarily regressive. At least some programs (such as free universities in Brazil) primarily benefit the middle class. Other programs (such as the tortilla subsidy in Mexico) benefit too broad a spectrum of class interests rather than focusing relief on the poor. Yet orthodox stabilization programs rarely call for more efficient forms of redistribution or international aid to make adjustment less painful.

Wage policies go beyond simply stopping the inflationary spiral caused by nominal wage indexation. Real wages must fall. Is there a sinister intent behind this? In theory, this increases the competitiveness of exports and encourages firms to hire more labor. Unions and minimum wage legislation mainly benefit the workers who have jobs in the formal sector. High real wages in the formal sector may reduce the number of good jobs and push more workers into the informal sector, where incomes are low.[5]

To sum up, most orthodox measures are aimed at one of several core objectives:

• A smaller role for government

• Stable prices through slower monetary growth

• Greater efficiency and competitiveness by bringing prices into line with costs

• Balance of payments stabilization through promotion of exports and foreign investment.

Experience has shown that the first result of orthodox policies is recession. How long the recession lasts depends on whether the cut in real wages sticks and on how fast the economy adjusts to new relative prices. Economists of a more conservative strand tend to believe adjustment costs are short-lived. Once budgets are cut and prices are "right," the economy adjusts quickly, and growth takes off in the traded goods sector. Others emphasize that economies take time to adjust to changes in relative prices. In the meantime, falling standards of living and political unrest often become an unfortunate by-product of such experiments.

Critics argue that IMF programs fail to address structural problems in the economy, that they raise instruments to the status of targets, and that they mandate unsustainable policies. Manuel

Pastor empirically assessed IMF programs in Latin America during the period 1965–1981.[6] His major findings were that fund programs

• Led to significant balance of payments improvements, mainly due to increased capital inflow induced by the IMF's seal of approval rather than to significant current account improvement;

• Had mixed impacts on growth rates;

• Were associated with accelerating inflation, not inflation reduction; and

• Were significantly and consistently associated with declines in the wage share in output.

In short, Pastor argues that IMF programs hurt income distribution, exacerbated social tension, and made no improvement in the inflation and growth fundamentals. Fund economists have challenged criticism with cross-country studies, which show that fund programs have mixed effects on growth rates, coupled with significant success in achieving the IMF's goal of current account improvement.

The Political Implications of Orthodox Stabilization

Stabilization policies are unpopular because they lower standards of living. As such, they pose a problem for governments dependent on consent rather than on coercion. Conventional wisdom maintains that authoritarianism is a necessary condition for successful stabilization in Latin America. The argument is that democratic rulers postpone corrective actions as long as possible because popular groups have greater capacity to disrupt stabilization policies under a democratic regime. By contrast, effective management of economic stabilization is made easier under authoritarianism because of the autonomy given to technocrats.

Thomas Skidmore's analysis of stabilization in Argentina, Brazil, and Mexico concludes that all cases of successful stabilization have been carried out by authoritarian governments.[7] He claims that governments in competitive systems find it extremely difficult to reduce inflation and pay a very high political cost for their efforts. However, Karen Remmer looks at the broader experience of IMF standby agreements in Latin America and argues that authoritarian regimes are not more likely to initiate stabilization programs or to survive their political reverberations.[8] The reason is that democracies enjoy strengths that have been overlooked, such as legitimacy and popular support. The rationality, efficiency, expertise, and coercive capability of authoritarian governments have been grossly exaggerated. Remmer also indicates that regime change may make an important difference in the success of a program, regardless of whether it is democratic or authoritarian, because regime breakdowns that occur during economic crises create unusual space for the implementation of stabilization policies. Having lost the trust of the country, few incumbent regimes can reverse the collapse of an economy.

The distributional consequences of stabilization programs are also fairly complex. Urban workers who produce goods that use imported inputs are likely to lose as devaluation raises the cost of production and cuts sales. They will lose again if they are heavy consumers of imported goods, including food and gasoline. Nor will domestically produced goods be cheap: anything that can be exported, such as fruit, will become more expensive. With the increase in the price of tradables, the loss in real income creates a recession with yet another negative feedback for import-dependent industries: fewer automobiles are now sold not only because of higher cost but because recession has set in. On the other hand, exporters benefit from devaluation. In theory, so do agricultural workers and other producers of import substitutes.

Overvaluation serves the interests of importers but ultimately leads to foreign exchange crises. Devaluation gives exporters the upper hand and helps to restore international liquidity. Rather than being a simple redistribution from workers to capitalists, orthodox stabilization measures generate substantial intraclass redistribution. While mass protests and urban riots can give the impression that austerity is imposed from abroad, there are internal forces pushing for orthodoxy as well.

The political feasibility of imposing austerity without repression undoubtedly depends on how anarchic the economy has become. When inflation hits 1,000 percent, many people are willing to try a radically different approach to economic management. The cost of instability itself can be so high that orthodoxy is not very painful by comparison. It is not surprising, then, that austerity measures have been implemented by very different regime types, including leftists (the Sandinistas), rightists (Pinochet), and moderate democratic regimes (Costa Rica).

Orthodoxy in Use

From the 1950s to the 1980s, numerous orthodox programs were applied to Latin America: Chile (1956–1958, 1973–1978), Argentina (1959–1962, 1976–1978), Bolivia (1956, 1985), Peru (1959, 1975–1978), Uruguay (1959–1962, 1974–1978), Mexico (1983), Venezuela (1988), and Brazil (1964–1973, 1982–1983). In no case was success, or even partial success, achieved without high costs. Temporary reductions in inflation and external deficits were combined with large increases in unemployment and a reduction of the labor share in output. Brazil in the mid-1960s and Mexico in the late-1980s are two examples of successful orthodox programs; however, both countries made use of price and wage controls to achieve stabilization.

Brazil

Following several years of stagnation, high inflation, and political unrest, the military coup of 1964 began a period of rigorous stabilization in Brazil. Initially the budget deficit was drastically curtailed by increasing taxes and reducing current government expenditures. The exchange rate was devalued and restrictions on nominal wage increases were imposed. As a result, the inflation rate fell from 100 percent in 1964 to 20 percent per year, which is modest by Brazilian and Latin American standards. Real growth fell at first, but from 1967 until 1973 it steadied at nearly 10 percent per year. External accounts also improved.

Much of the Brazilian "miracle" can be attributed to the virtual elimination of the fiscal deficit, however, it also depended on tax incentives and subsidized credit (especially for exports and agriculture), elimination of bureaucratic red tape, and increased public investment in infrastructure and heavy industries (electricity, transportation, steel, mining, and petroleum). Far from leading an experiment in laissez-faire, the Brazilian government was involved in directing growth within the economy.

The costs were not minor for the group who paid the bill. Real wages of unskilled workers dropped, and the share of national income accruing to the poorest 40 percent of the population fell from 11.2 percent in 1960 to 9 percent in 1970. The fall in real wages and the negative effects on income distribution were made possible only by massive political repression. (We discuss the distributional effects of this experience in chapter 9.)

Mexico

Inflation rose in Mexico during the late 1970s with the budget deficits of President José López Portillo's government. Although revenues from oil rose by a factor of twelve between 1977 and 1981, government expenditures increased even more rapidly in an attempt to speed up economic development. Public revenues lagged behind. To moderate inflation, deficits were financed by external borrowing.

Pressure built up with the international recession of the early 1980s, the drop in oil revenues, and the increase in foreign debt service resulting from higher world interest rates. Continuing deterioration in Mexico's external account gave rise to expectations that gradual depreciation would be insufficient to correct the imbalances. As a result, capital flight reached unprecedented levels. Reserve losses finally convinced the government to impose exchange controls, close the Mexodollar market, and nationalize the banking system—measures that came at considerable cost to the government's credibility among investors.

Stabilization came with the new Miguel de la Madrid regime. The critical target of the program called for a reduction of the public deficit from 17.6 percent of GDP in 1982 to 8.5 percent in 1983. The costs of adjustment were high: approximately 750,000 jobs were lost. By the end of 1983, fears of financial disaster had ebbed. The program, however, was met with an increase in inflation. Another round of sharp devaluations and fiscal austerity was imposed in 1986 and 1987. Again, inflation accelerated. After five years of orthodoxy, it appeared that Mexico faced a choice between price stability and external equilibrium. Inflation subsided only in 1988 when an agreement among business, labor, and government known as the Economic Solidarity Pact froze the exchange rate, wages, public sector prices, and a range of private prices.

The Neoconservative Approach

A twist on orthodox monetarism, applied in Uruguay, Argentina, and Chile in the mid-1970s, was dubbed global monetarism or neo-conservatism. Based on the ideas of theorists at the University of Chicago, the neoconservative strategy puts a strong emphasis on free markets. While orthodox programs encourage market liberalization, neoconservatives deify the free market. It is not simply fiscal deficits that are at the root of the problem but government activity itself.

In addition to their emphasis on market liberalization, global monetarists call for fixing the exchange rate. A fixed exchange rate forces domestic producers to hold down prices to compete with imports and serves as a central price around which price expectations can be formed. Once committed to maintaining a given exchange rate in an economy without import and capital controls, the government must use fiscal discipline to avoid undermining the program. According to this theory, an exchange rate freeze, coupled with a fiscal package that makes it sustainable, brings inflation down to international levels.

Joseph Ramos offers an excellent guided tour through the ups and downs of the neoconservative experience in Argentina, Chile, and Uruguay.[9] Common to this strategy are the following policies:

• Freeing prices to reflect costs.

• Eliminating import licenses and reducing tariffs while choosing an exchange rate that encourages trade.

• Freeing interest rates and eliminating controls over the allocation of credit.

• Promoting the free entry and exit of capital.

• Preventing all forms of "collusion", including labor unions and professional groups.

• Reducing the participation of the public sector in production.

• Eliminating fiscal deficits and strictly controlling monetary growth.

The approach is similar to orthodoxy except in its emphasis on a fixed exchange rate as a vehicle of disinflation.

Southern Cone countries became the laboratory for testing neoconservative ideas in the 1970s. Dictatorships in the three countries took advice from the "Chicago Boys" to heart. In assessing these experiments, one must pay attention to their global context.

Commodity prices bounced around in the mid-1970s: the price of copper fell by 40 percent from a historically high level and then more than recovered its value over this period; wheat, beef, and wool prices hit similar extremes; and oil shocks affected economic performance. Perhaps most important, international interest rates were low during this period. In all three countries, external indebtedness grew substantially while neoconservative policies were in place.

Before undertaking an evaluation of neoconservative policies in the Southern Cone, we describe their evolution. Table 7.3 shows growth rates and inflation in Argentina, Chile, and Uruguay.

Chile

The neoconservative period in Chile can be divided into three phases: from late 1973 to mid-1976, output declined, while inflation first increased and then declined; from mid-1976 to 1981, inflation declined and output increased; and from mid-1981 to 1983, the financial crisis caused a deep recession (table 7.3).

On taking power in September 1973, the regime of Augusto Pinochet sharply devalued the currency, eliminated price controls, demobilized labor, and restricted monetary growth. This was clearly a case of shock treatment. Financial deregulation increased interest rates from –24 percent to 178 percent. Combined with the effect of import liberalization, businesses were forced into bankruptcy, and unemployment shot up. Inflation was far from under control, however. GDP fell 14 percent in 1975 while prices quadrupled. The only bright note was that nontraditional exports began to grow.

Monetary reform introduced the peso, each worth 1,000 escudos, and in 1976, the government adopted a policy of preannouncing the exchange rate for each month. The monthly devaluations lagged behind inflation, and in 1979, the regime went even further, fixing the exchange at 39 pesos to the dollar, a rate that lasted for three years.

Borrowing was easy in the late 1970s, especially because Chile enjoyed some peculiarly attractive characteristics. By preannouncing the exchange rate, the government assured investors that, at least in the short run, they would not be caught by a sudden drop in the dollar value of their earnings from local investments. Furthermore, the liberalization of financial markets had increased Chilean

Table 7.3
Growth rate of GNP per capita and inflation rate, Argentina, Chile, and Uruguay,
1950–1989 (percentage per year)

	Argentina		Chile		Uruguay	
	Growth	Inflation	Growth	Inflation	Growth	Inflation
1950–1970 average	1.9	24	1.9	30	0.7	29
1971–1973 average	1.0	52	-1.0	192	-0.5	66
1974	4.4	23	-0.7	498	3.1	77
1975	-2.5	183	-14.4	379	5.6	81
1976	-2.1	443	1.8	233	3.5	51
1977	4.7	176	8.0	114	0.7	58
1978	-5.0	176	6.4	51	4.6	45
1979	5.4	160	6.5	33	5.5	67
1980	-0.5	101	6.0	35	5.1	64
1981	-7.4	105	3.9	20	1.2	34
1982	-6.8	210	-14.5	20	-10.6	20
1983	1.2	434	-4.1	24	-6.6	52
1984-1989 average	-1.5	1,100	4.1	20	1.8	73

Sources: Joseph Ramos, *Neoconservative Economics in the Southern Cone of Latin America*
(Baltimore: Johns Hopkins University Press, 1986); and ECLAC, *Preliminary Overview*, 1991.

interest rates well above international rates. This meant that deposits and short-term loans to Chilean firms were both lucrative and
relatively riskless. Finally, bankers' concerns about political instability had ebbed.

Inflation dropped with the implementation of exchange rate
stability. The economy grew rapidly for four and a half years, finally
recovering the level of output it had enjoyed in 1972 by 1978.

Several factors led to the unraveling of this experiment. The fixed
exchange rate resulted in the increasing overvaluation of the peso.
Despite high copper prices, export growth fell off while imports rose
to 1.7 times the level of exports in 1981. Across-the-board tariffs of
only 10 percent (except for automobiles) put local products at a new
disadvantage relative to imports. Combined with overvaluation, the
new openness of the economy stifled production for the domestic

market. Tight monetary policy produced high interest rates. Few firms could match international prices and maintain long-term payments on loans at 30 percent interest. Banks collapsed, and capital flight began.

While other Latin American economies were also hit by the debt crisis, Chile suffered an especially hard blow. GDP fell 14 percent in 1982. Open unemployment rose to 21 percent. Although the Pinochet regime pursued conservative economic policies throughout the 1980s, this marked the end of its neoconservative program. The peso was sharply devalued in 1982, bringing to a close any attempt to achieve disinflation with a fixed rate. In addition, the collapse of the financial sector led to massive government intervention as the government felt compelled to take on nonperforming assets.

Argentina

Beginning in the 1940s, Argentina followed import substitution strategies. By the early 1960s, growth in the consumer goods industries petered out, and overvaluation induced widening external imbalances. Authorities faced the rising expectations of a growing working class and tried to accommodate conflict by using inflationary finance. Eventually policymakers decided that industrialization had to be deepened through the addition of basic industries in order to make growth possible again. Their projects required external financing, and they realized that direct investment would not be attracted to countries wracked by social conflicts and political instability. The solution was bureaucratic authoritarianism. National security doctrine provided the ideological justification for military intervention by claiming that the survival of free societies depended on putting an end to the popular classes' resistance to authority.

When the Perónist regime was overthrown by military coup in 1976, Argentina was on the verge of hyperinflation. The first priority of the new regime was to stabilize prices. The disinflation program relied on wage controls. At the same time, the fiscal deficit was gradually reduced. These policies brought about favorable results on the inflation front. Because inflation failed to decline further once it neared 150 percent, policymakers opted for an "expectations-managed approach." Beginning in 1979, they prefixed the exchange depreciation rate with a *tablita*, announcing gradual depreciation. As in Chile, this policy was expected to lower inflation in three ways: by reducing the rate of import price inflation, by imposing discipline on price setters, who would have to compete with cheaper imports, and by providing a benchmark to which inflationary expectations could converge. Inflation fell below 100 percent, but it continually exceeded depreciation. By 1980, overvaluation had become so extreme that, despite the government's assertion that the policy would continue, speculation led to rising capital flight. The central bank was forced to borrow massively to support the *tablita*. Private speculators in turn bought dollars and deposited them in Miami.

The undoing of the overvaluation started with the 1981 change of presidents. Over the next few years, depreciation and inflation became rampant. The budget deficit increased with growing external interest payments. A deterioration in the terms of trade and the Malvinas war amplified the devastation of the economy. The inflation rate was up to 600 percent by the time Alfonsín came to power in 1983.

Assessment

In Chile and Argentina, inflation was substantially below historical levels by 1980, although it remained very high in Argentina. Successful stabilization in Chile was maintained throughout the 1980s. In Argentina, however, once foreign lending dried up, capital flight became the order of the day. Policies had to be reversed; inflation picked up again.

The neoconservative approach followed in Uruguay was more pragmatic than in Chile. Uruguay never managed to bring inflation under control; however, except for the 1982–1983 crisis, it experienced fast growth, especially compared to historic growth rates (table 7.3).

Uruguay's program first targeted export promotion through highly subsidized credit and tax exemptions. Real wages were also cut by more than 20 percent between 1974 and 1978. Financial markets were widely liberalized, initiating a new role for the country as regional banker. Efforts to trim the size of the state and to reduce tariffs were both more modest and came later than in Chile. Even the process of using a *tablita* turned out to be relatively moderate in the sense that overvaluation was not as extreme as it was in Argentina. As a result, tourism grew rapidly as Argentines crossed the border to shop. The collapse of the economy reflected both global events and the effect of Argentina's massive devaluation in 1981.

All three economies became much more export oriented than they had been. Sharp initial devaluations, the deterioration of domestic markets, lower real wages (which increased the competitiveness of exports), and elimination of export taxes contributed to export growth. At the same time, production of import-competing goods for the internal market collapsed as a result of sharply lower tariff barriers. Overvaluation became a serious problem, particularly in Chile and Argentina, as regimes attempted to maintain the exchange rate despite continued inflation. Foreign borrowing was used to cover growing current account deficits (table 7.4).

In the Southern Cone, the idea of getting prices right was taken to an extreme. Government-owned industries were put up for sale to force them into competitiveness. Subsidies of food and utilities were cut, as much to improve the efficiency of consumer choice as to reduce fiscal deficits. In Chile, the zeal for market allocation of resources was extended to the rural sector, where land expropriations made under Allende were reversed on the grounds that prereform deeds, though largely based on *caudillo* spoils, reflected efficient market allocation.

Table 7.4
External sector indicators, Argentina, Chile, and Uruguay, 1971–1983 (averages during the period)

	Argentina		Chile		Uruguay	
	Current account/ exports (percentage)	Debt/ exports ratio	Current account/ exports (percentage)	Debt/ exports ratio	Current account/ exports (percentage)	Debt/ exports ratio
1971–1975	-8.7	2.1	-25.1	2.5	-14.8	2.0
1976–1980	0.4	2.0	-22.8	2.0	-25.0	1.5
1981–1983	-32.8	4.3	-54.5	3.4	-15.6	2.6

Note: A minus sign indicates a deficit. Source: Ramos, *Neoconservative Economics*.

The most controversial aspect of the neoconservative experiment was its distributive impact. Military regimes put an end to worker activism by crushing strikes. Table 7.5 shows the real wage decline. Even during the few years when the economies enjoyed growth, this expansion did not bring wages above their 1970 level. Compounding the suffering associated with lower real wages was a sharp rise in the unemployment rate in Chile and Uruguay. High unemployment in Chile stubbornly persisted throughout the neoconservative phase.

Political repression by the military is no doubt the single most important reason that popular opposition was not stronger. The disappearances and torture of an estimated 20,000 people in Argentina and 10,000 in Chile eliminated the leadership needed to organize opposition and frightened people from engaging even in mild protest. The economic chaos that preceded the coups also gave the regimes some support even among those who paid dearly during the neoconservative era. Lower real wages were silently accepted by many as a necessary price to pay for stability.

The neoconservative experiment succeeded in stabilizing inflation in Chile and in making Chile more export oriented. By the late 1980s, noncopper exports accounted for more than half of the country's export earnings, and foreign investors eagerly bought Chile's accumulated debt, swapping it for pesos to be used in new projects. Yet workers unambiguously lost during the neoconservative phase, as evident in the long decline in the wages and the high level of sustained unemployment.

Table 7.5
Real wage index, Argentina, Chile, and Uruguay, 1970–1983 (1970 = 100)

	Argentina	Chile	Uruguay
1970	100	100	100
1975	111	62	78
1978	72	76	67
1981	83	98	70
1983	91	87	55

Source: Ibid.

2 HETERODOXY

Programs based on a combination of incomes policy, fiscal correction, and monetary reform are called heterodox programs. In contrast to conventional IMF packages that emphasize tight monetary policy and fiscal correction as the main instruments of stabilization, heterodox programs recognize that aggregate demand discipline is not enough for stability. In order to break the cycle of inertial inflation, active government intervention is necessary to settle the struggle between workers and firms over relative shares of national income.

Rather than liberalizing markets, heterodox programs typically involve wage and price controls. Franklyn Holzman described inflationary expectations as analogous to the behavior of spectators at a football game:

Everyone is seated. Then, in an exciting moment, someone stands up. Moments later, everyone has to stand to see. Then someone stands on his seat, and eventually everyone has to stand on his seat. In the end no one sees any better, everyone is uncomfortable and the short people can't see at all. Fortunately, standing at football games always ends when the action slows down.

Unfortunately, the present economic situation cannot be solved so easily. Nevertheless, as a first step, the economy must be made to 'sit down.'[10]

Wage and price controls stop inertial inflation by 'outlawing standing at football games.' Social consensus is necessary to stop inflationary spirals, and this is possible only if everyone sits down at once.

Conventional analysis argues that price controls will lead to shortages unless there is a recession. Heterodoxy views this as a small price to pay for greater stability and less unemployment.

In addition to an incomes policy, heterodoxy urges a sharp reduction in fiscal deficits. Heterodox programs can work only if fiscal consolidation takes place. Wage and price controls alone have long been proved ineffective in stopping inflation. Unless the underlying causes of inflation are addressed, a price freeze will reduce inflation temporarily, but once removed, inflation will rebound. Persistent fiscal deficits erode any headway made by introducing monetary reforms and ultimately lead to the breakdown of a social consensus to contain inflation.

Another important difference between IMF programs and hetero-doxy is that while the former prescribes monetary restraint, hetero-doxy calls for monetary growth to avoid raising real interest rates. When price stability is achieved, the demand for local currency rises in real terms. This is easy to understand if one remembers that people try to avoid holding local currency in a hyperinflationary environment. With the return of stability, real interest rates will turn sharply positive unless the government engages in a substantial monetization. The big difficulty is to know how much is enough. Being too conservative is problematic because high real interest rates in the presence of a large public debt create a fiscal burden. Being too bold is equally problematic because excessive money growth fuels inflation, and low interest rates favor speculation. In this case, firms will build up stocks waiting for higher prices.

Monetary reform, or the introduction of a new currency, has been associated with heterodox programs.[11] In 1985, the Argentines in-troduced the austral, and the Peruvians converted to the inti. Brazil switched to the cruzado in 1986. There are at least three reasons for a monetary reform: to ease bookkeeping by eliminating zeros, to fight the expectation of inflation by using the new currency as a symbol for policy change and, most important in the context of heterodoxy, to avoid wealth transfers that would take place after stabilization.

Many contracts are not explicitly indexed in a backward-looking way but instead reflect expectations of future inflation. Short-term loans, for example, carry forward-looking inflation adjustments with a maturity of six months or a year. They specify interest rates that reflect inflationary expectations. If inflation disappears, a 10 percent interest rate per month becomes the real interest rate. Similarly, rent contracts specify payments that reflect the assump-tion of rising prices, as do most long-term agreements between firms and their suppliers. A sudden disinflation would result in an arbi-trary redistribution between debtors and creditors. To avoid this, as well as pervasive bankruptcy, contracts have to be revised.

A monetary reform provides a practical way of revising contracts that no longer reflect a fair deal between debtor and creditors. A *tablita* converts the old money into a new one according to a set timetable of depreciation. In Brazil, the cruzado, equal to 1,000 cruzeiros, was introduced to help facilitate stabilization. Starting on

March 3, 1986, the cruzeiro would depreciate at the rate of 0.45 percent per day relative to the cruzado. Thus, a 100,000 cruzeiro debt due for payment on March 13 was converted to a 96 cruzado debt. The *tablita* provides an instrument to align the real value of payments with the expectations implicit at the time contracts were concluded.[12]

Wage contracts pose a problem in designing a freeze. As the government prepares to declare zero inflation, some contracts are coming up for renewal, and workers will ask to be compensated for past inflation. But this would create cost increases and new inflation. Others will have just received their adjustment and find themselves with high real wages relative to the average. Freezing at this level will be perceived as inequitable. Depending on where workers are in this cycle, a sudden freeze can mean high or low real wages relative to the past average. The program will have to include recontracting to avoid conflict and a resurgence of inflation. Those who had recent increases must see their real wages rolled back, and those who are in a low position need upward adjustment.

The first attempts at implementing heterodoxy were made in the summer of 1985 by the Alfonsín regime in Argentina with the Austral Plan and by the García regime in Peru with the Inti Plan. Brazil followed with the Cruzado Plan in March 1986.

The Austral

In June 1985 the annualized inflation rate in Argentina reached almost 6,000 percent. The situation was ripe for the Austral Plan, a program of stabilization based on wage-price controls and a fixed exchange rate.

The price freeze was enforced by a band of forty inspectors. Tough as they appeared, their role was largely symbolic. Without public confidence in the program, prices would have exploded. Indeed, it appeared that Argentines believed Alfonsín's promises to finance the government only with "genuine resources."

The first year proved rather successful: inflation dropped from 30 percent per month to 3 percent; however, austerity measures also accentuated an existing decline in output and real wages. When the price freeze was lifted and growth recovered, prices took off. In February 1987, the government tried to market a sequel to its earlier hit. Again, inflation declined briefly, only to become the central feature of the economy some months later. Along with it, real wages fell. So did real government revenues, and as a result, the budget deficit increased again. By 1989, per capita output was lower than it had been fifteen years earlier. Argentina, which traditionally had a better income distribution than the rest of Latin America, was experiencing growing poverty.

At the time of presidential elections in 1989, the government was weak, isolated, and unable to collect taxes. Revenue from corporate income and value-added taxes had fallen by 24 percent in the first quarter of 1989 relative to a year before, and other indirect taxes had fallen by more than 50 percent. In March and April alone, the real value of the deficit of the treasury was twice the size of the deficit for all of 1988. In May, interest rates hit 150 percent per month. Exchange houses were flooded by small savers trying to protect themselves from the erosion of the austral. Smuggling through Paraguay had increased to avoid export taxes. Rumor had it that the government was forced to declare a bank holiday on the first Friday of May 1989 because it had run out of paper and ink to print money. Paper and ink, imported from Brazil, did not arrive because of a Brazilian dock strike.

A widespread loss of confidence led Alfonsín to step down early after the elections. Few options were left. Devaluation was ordered, but it was clear that this would fail to stimulate investment in the export sector. As the economic minister, Juan Carlos Pugliese, commented, "There are no technical measures we can apply to take fear away from the people."[13]

The Cruzado

When the Cruzado Plan was announced in February 1986, the difficulty of controlling inertial inflation had been widely discussed. Policymakers believed that past inflationary shocks were being perpetuated in a vicious cycle created by indexation and that the freezing of prices, exchange rates, and wages would create a rupture with the past.

The main obstacle was the absence of synchronization in price readjustments. In 1986, the typical wage contract ran for six months, with different wage earners having their wages revised at different times. Rent contracts ran for either one year or six months. Government bonds were readjusted monthly. Simply freezing wages and prices would favor those who had just managed to increase their nominal income immediately before and would drastically punish those who were to have received their new settlements the next day.

The key steps of the Cruzado Plan were the following:

1. Wages were readjusted and frozen. Contracts with several months to readjustment were rolled up, and those that had been adjusted recently were rolled back. As a sweetener, minimum-wage workers received a bonus of 15 percent over the past real average and other workers an 8 percent bonus.

2. Rents and installment payments were converted into cruzados, using their average real value during the last twelve months, and frozen at that level for a year.

3. All prices and the exchange rate were frozen until further notice.

4. A *tablita* was devised to eliminate the expected inflation built into extant contracts and, thus, to avoid arbitrary redistribution between debtors and creditors.

5. Indexation, which had been blamed for the acceleration of inflation, was eliminated. For wages, an *escala movel* (automatic indexation) with a 20 percent threshold was substituted. Wages would not be automatically indexed unless inflation exceeded 20 percent. In financial markets, indexation was maintained only for instruments of more than one year maturity.

6. There was a sharp initial monetization of the economy to avoid exceptionally high real interest rates. In the first three months following stabilization, the monetary base doubled.

External factors favored the program in three respects: world interest rates declined, reducing the debt service burden; oil prices fell sharply; and the drop in the value of the dollar reduced the cost of dollar-denominated debt and imports.

Between February and June, cumulative inflation was zero. Industrial production increased by 12 percent in the first half-year of the program relative to the same period a year before. But between June and November, the program took on a life of its own. Fueled by strong popular support for the price freeze, Finance Minister Dilson Funaro elevated controls to a dogma. The budget was allowed to deteriorate dramatically, the trade surplus disappeared, and shortages and black markets became pervasive. But "zero inflation" remained the ministerial obsession.

Among the factors leading to the failure of the Cruzado Plan, the most prominent was the expansion of demand through wage, monetary, and fiscal policies. The economy was already overheated from the start: accelerating inflation reflected the development of bottlenecks in an economy that grew 8.3 percent in 1985. Inflation was not solely inertial. The increase in real wages, combined with rising employment, sustained a consumers' boom.

On the fiscal side, revenues of state-owned companies were hurt by the price freeze, spending ran higher than anticipated, and subsidies that were cut during 1983–84 came back. The wage bill for government workers increased in line with the economy-wide trend.

Money growth was accelerated after March 1986 as policymakers recognized the need to remonetize the economy following disinflation. With hindsight, one could argue that monetary growth proceeded too fast to warrant price stability. Part of the problem was that low interest rates permitted firms lacking confidence in the program to build up speculative stocks and thus wait for the removal of the price freeze to pocket gains. Low interest rates also fueled consumer purchases of durable goods.

Finally, distortions resulting from the price freeze were increasingly evident. Some sectors of the economy hit bottlenecks earlier than others. Acute shortages, especially of meat and milk, commanded the headlines of all newspapers.

Politicians preferred to deny evidence of repressed inflation rather than to give up their zero inflation fetish for more realistic policies. More cynically, one can argue that policymakers tried to avoid adjustments until after the November elections. The structure of the consumer price index was altered five times to conceal price increases in the year before November 1986. Credibility of the plan dwindled.

The government's promise to maintain the price freeze permitted a landslide election victory, which was followed by a round of excise tax increases. Once again, the government tried to eliminate their effect from the price index but encountered strong resistance. Clearly the government was trying to reenact the 1964 program of real wage cuts to restore the external balance and the budget, but the absence of any austerity and the restraints of a democratic regime put severe limits on the exercise. Having established the *escala movel*, there was no avoiding a return to indexation once inflation hit 20 percent. The freeze was removed, and prices exploded.

New attempts at controlling inflation were made in mid-1987 with the Bresser Plan and in January 1989 with the Summer Plan (figure 7.1). Once again the government froze prices, squeezed credit, and cut zeros off the face value of the currency. Promises to eliminate budget deficits were not kept because President José Sarney lacked the political power to implement fiscal consolidation. He also lacked credibility, determination, and allies in the Congress. With the budget deficit left untouched, all three plans merely amounted to attempts to stop inflation by decree.

Lessons from Heterodoxy

Several lessons from heterodoxy stand out. First, a wage and price freeze that directly deals with the issue of equity through an incomes policy is valuable in achieving disinflation. By itself, however, it is not enough. Without fiscal consolidation, the disinflation is not viable, and with a boom, it does not even last long.

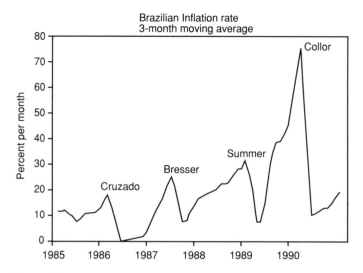

Figure 7.1
Brazil's stabilization plans, 1985–1990.
Source: Fudação Getúlio Vargas, *Conjuntura Economica*, various issues. Rio de Janeiro: Fudação Getúlio Vargas.

Second, the effort to roll back contracts of workers who have just received inflation adjustments involves a reduction in nominal wages. The addition of an across-the-board increase in wages above past averages makes a wage policy more politically palatable but fuels consumer demand. Either some workers must sacrifice wage gains or prices must be allowed to increase by some percentage to hold down an increase in real wages.

The third lesson concerns indexation. Indexation in the presence of supply shocks is a source of inflation propagation, but it also protects the inflation rate against rapid acceleration. An economy with long adjustment periods has an inflation process that is not expected to accelerate rapidly. Indexation of assets reinforces this element of stability. In Brazil, indexation was eliminated in 1986 and replaced by adjustment triggers without caps and financial indexation to the short-term interest rate. This setting led to a highly volatile atmosphere in which inflationary expectations easily became the driving mechanism for an actual inflation.

Finally, it is clear that fiscal consolidation is extraordinarily difficult to sell politically. This is especially true in the presence of a large public debt. Raising taxes to pay debt rather than to provide services is an unmarketable political decision, particularly in economies used to a long inflationary tradition and where distributive conflicts inevitably lead to strong pressures on the budget. The great merit of heterodox programs is that they provide a brief period during which price stability can be achieved without a recession. In doing so, they create political support that can be used to implement the fiscal reforms necessary for stability. Yet this opportunity was lost in Argentina, Brazil, and Peru. In Brazil, the initial honeymoon with the price freeze was mistaken for success, and the fiscal consolidation was avoided.

In the case of Peru under García, which we discuss in chapter 8, mismanagement was even more dramatic. From the start, the Peruvian program was different from our description of a heterodox program. Although the regime used price controls, policymakers diverged strongly from orthodox economics and maintained that in Peru, fiscal deficits bore no relationship to inflation. They claimed that during a stabilization program, it is necessary to spend even at the cost of a fiscal deficit. This constituted the basic premise of economic policy. It did not take long for Peru to learn that rapid demand growth is incompatible with a program to reduce inflation.

3 STABILIZATION À LA CARTE

At the start of the 1990s, charismatic leaders took power promising renewed growth. Fujimori's program of 'Honesty, Technology and Work' promised an efficient, modern economy that would reward hard-working Peruvians. Menem offered a capitalist revolution to restore Argentina's glory. And Collor promised to keep Lula from inaugurating socialism in Brazil. Each devised a shock program and sheathed his fists in velvet gloves during the electoral campaign. Within a year, however, political instability seemed as serious an issue as economic instability.

Fujimori

When Alberto Fujimori took power in August 1990, Peru was broke. Yet his *paquetazo* stunned those who believed matters could get no worse. Price controls and subsidies were eliminated overnight. Food prices skyrocketed. The price of gasoline increased by a factor of twenty-seven. Monthly inflation, which had averaged 38 percent in the preceding seven months, climbed to 400 percent in August.

Fujimori's *paquetazo* reduced import tariffs and eliminated import licenses. The program also abolished multiple exchange rates and freed the exchange rate. It was hoped that the readjustment in fuel prices, as well as a series of taxes on net worth, insurance coverage, and exports, would reduce the fiscal deficit. Inflation also dramatically cut the real cost of the public payroll.

Chaos ensued. The economy came to a standstill in response to lower demand and sheer uncertainty. Middle-class Limeños could no longer buy food in bulk to beat inflation; electricity was so erratic that freezers regularly melted down. Even access to fuel for private generators could not be counted on. Poor Limeños who depended on community kitchens for their meals found that their numbers had swollen to unmanageable levels, while soup kitchen cupboards were bare. The government resorted to tear-gassing a protest by the women who run Vaso de Leche, a food relief program for children.

Menem

In Argentina, Carlos Menem's program, which began in July 1989, emphasized public sector reform, limiting various subsidies and pushing forward the privatization of public enterprises. Although a Perónist in name, Menem embarked on a program involving fiscal restraint, wage repression, and economic liberalization.

Fiscal consolidation was achieved by raising the real price of public services, increasing the value-added tax base, and forcing a conversion of domestic debt into long-term bonds. In order to promote private enterprise, the tax rate on profits was cut, as was the top marginal income tax rate. To support greater openness of the economy, Menem's program called for a reduction of export taxes, import tariffs, and import licenses.

During the first six months of 1990, the public sector deficit in GDP had been brought down to an estimated 4 percent of GDP, and the country recorded an unprecedented trade surplus. In the process of achieving these gains, however, the rate of unemployment in Greater Buenos Aires hit an all-time high, and GDP contracted sharply.

By the end of 1990, inflation had been brought down to a modest 5 percent, although the rate for the year exceeded 1,000 percent. Overvaluation had supported the disinflation. The austral rose against the dollar throughout the year as a result of the trade surplus and real high interest rates. The artificially strong rate was allowed to persist in an attempt to reduce inflation, but exporters were already complaining by the end of the year that the exchange rate hurt output.

Nevertheless, few Argentines could sleep comfortably in early 1991. In January, the austral fell 40 percent against the dollar, Menem appointed his fourth economic minister in nineteen months, and the military continued to threaten a coup.

The Collor Plan

By the end of 1989, the maturity of Brazil's domestic debt was explosively short. The attempt to reduce inflation through high interest rates during 1989 had backfired. As real interest rates rose, so did the cost of servicing the government's debt and the debt itself.

Issuing additional interest-bearing debt to pay interest on the existing debt implies a growing stock of real government interest-bearing debt per capita. Such growth cannot go on forever. Debt maturity shrinks as government avoids paying high risk premiums, giving people illusory liquidity. It follows that fighting current inflation with a tight monetary policy must eventually lead to higher future inflation or debt repudiation. There is also the alternative, applied by Menem, of forcing consolidation of the debt into longer-term bonds or into public enterprise ownership. The Collor Plan chose a third alternative: blocking financial assets for eighteen months. It stressed four areas: monetary reform, fiscal policies, price and wage settlements, and trade liberalization.

Monetary Reform

The Collor government closed the banks for five days, blocked bank accounts, and introduced a new currency using an old name, the cruzeiro, to be exchanged on a one-to-one basis for the cruzado novo. The plan set an eighteen-month freeze on savings accounts of more than 50,000 cruzeiros (U.S. $1,200) and limited withdrawals from bank deposits and money market funds. Frozen assets, yielding 6 percent interest per year, were to be redeemed for the new currency beginning in September 1991. Quasi-money in circulation (M4) was reduced 68 percent.

Monetary regulations were introduced piecemeal, differentially affecting various classes. Withdrawals were allowed for the unemployed and retired, for charities, and for payments of taxes and debts. Using official and unofficial loopholes, most large companies legally emptied their frozen accounts, forcing the adjustment on middle-class savers. An illegal secondary market developed, trading frozen cruzados into cruzeiros, but was cut off by tougher government regulation.

Blocking assets effectively reduced government debt service and thus reduced the budget deficit, at least for a while. It also limited the extent to which money could be traded for goods. From the beginning, production, sales, fuel consumption, and employment plunged. For a month, the economy stopped.

Fiscal Policies

The government reduced ministries from twenty-eight to twelve and announced major cuts in the public work force. Tax administration was tightened by requiring identification on financial investments. The government also collected a one-time tax on stocks, gold, and savings accounts. Expenditures fell with the reduction in debt payments. Beyond the suspension of debt servicing, however, expenditures were only minutely reduced. Plans to cut government subsidies, close state agencies, and privatize the economy were implemented only timidly.

Prices and Wages

The Collor Plan froze prices and wages for one month at March 12 levels and during the following ten months changed the wage legislation six times. Monthly indexation was abolished. By January 1991, real wages reached their lowest levels in ten years.

Foreign Trade

The Collor Plan abolished import quotas, import licenses, and the list of prohibited items. In their place remain tariff barriers. As a consequence of these measures, the monthly inflation rate dropped from 80 percent in March to 10 percent in May 1990 but later began to rise again, reaching 20 percent in December (figure 7.1). GDP per capita fell by 5.5 percent in 1990. With inflation once again running out of control, the government imposed a new wage and price freeze on February 1991 and announced the end of most indexation and monetary correction mechanisms.

Is there a social consensus opposing inflation? A strong proinflation lobby includes debtors, firms that can easily pass on costs (or let prices ride up with inflation even if costs do not), banks that profit from brokering domestic debt, and employees with well-indexed salaries. As these Brazilians find their way around mechanism to control inflation, the credibility of each new stabilization plan sinks.

4 CONCLUSIONS

The goal of stabilization with growth remains elusive. Moreover, neither heterodoxy nor orthodoxy seems to offer a program that advances long-run development goals. Latin American production must become internationally competitive if the region is to enjoy the benefits of development. The ideal way to achieve this goal in the long run is not through wage cuts but through improvements in workers' skills and productivity. This almost certainly calls for greater expenditure on education, more reliable public services, better development of agricultural resources, and investments in industrial plant and equipment.

Stabilization programs have a tendency to be short-sighted and dramatic. Although they can provide the shock necessary to stop inflation, they often only add to the sense that long-run policies have a time horizon of six months. Sharp contraction does not build confidence among private investors, even if relative prices are moving in their favor; nowhere in Latin America have we seen a sudden increase in investment in response to austerity measures. Nor is erratic public spending ideal in terms of development; administrators of schools, libraries, and health clinics need some sense of budget stability in order to plan a rational expansion of services.

Gradual stabilization, realistic exchange rates, rationalization of public expenditures and taxes, and incentives for both export production and import substitution (in industry and agriculture) make more sense in terms of a development strategy. For this to be an option, however, a strong social consensus must develop so that action can be taken before rising prices and foreign exchange shortages become full-blown crises. This advice is like telling a patient on the operating table that his heart attack might have been avoided with more modest diet, exercise, and fewer stressful family spats. Perhaps the next generation will take heed.

FURTHER READING

Bruno, M., and S. Fischer, *The Aftermath of Stabilization*. Cambridge, Mass.: MIT Press, 1991.

Díaz-Alexjandro, C. "Southern Cone Stabilization Plans." In W. Cline and S. Weintraub, eds. *Economic Stabilization in Developing Countries*. Washington, D.C.: Brookings Institution, 1982.

Dornbusch, R., and M. Simonsen, *Inflation Stabilization with Incomes Policy Support*. New York: Group of Thirty, 1987.

Ramos, J. *Neo-Conservative Economics in the Southern Cone of Latin America.* Baltimore: Johns Hopkins University Press, 1986.

Remmer, K. "The Politics of Economic Stabilization: IMF Standby Programs in Latin America, 1954–1984." *Comparative Politics* 18 (October 1986): 1–24.

Chapter 8

ECONOMIC POPULISM

Recent bouts of economic instability have led economists to describe contemporary regimes in Latin America as populist. Sarney, Alfonsín, García, and the Sandinistas have overseen macroeconomic imbalances that show strong similarities with the economic records of Juan Perón, Getúlio Vargas, and João Goulart, three leaders traditionally identified as populists. All bore the trademark of economic populism: hyperinflation caused by budget deficits and balance of payments crises.

This chapter explores the evolution of several episodes of instability in Latin America. Although each regime failed to rein in budget deficits, the economic strategies pursued and their underlying motivations display considerable heterogeneity. Recent leaders should have learned from traditional populists. The most basic lesson is that failure to live within constraints posed by the balance of payments and the internal productive capacity leads to inflation and disaster. Yet the early warning signs, evident in rhetoric and specific policies, have varied widely. Because populism is associated with redistribution (although not toward the poorest), it is important to clarify the role of redistribution in these cases of hyperinflation.

We begin by describing classical populism as it has been viewed by Latin Americanists over the past four decades and use the Argentine experience between 1945 and 1952 to illustrate it. This earlier formulation is distinct from the new economic concept of populism, which stresses the repeated willingness of Latin American regimes to push demand beyond economic bounds. We then examine specific cases of populism and discuss their diversity. There are at least three separate roots of inflationary finance in Latin America:

1. Excessive optimism about the potential for rapid growth through demand stimulation and inward-looking industrialization, as seen in the Peruvian experience under García.

2. Market-based socialism, which causes insecure property rights and triggers intervention from the United States, forcing up defense budgets, as observed in Nicaragua in the 1980s.

3. An inability to impose the burden of contractionary adjustment on various groups, as in Brazil after the oil shock and debt crisis.

Far from providing a compelling indictment of redistributive efforts, the history of populism makes conspicuous the paucity of genuine redistribution programs in Latin American. Most regimes failed to target the poor. Urban workers in the informal sector did not benefit from populist increases in the minimum wage, nor did social programs concentrate resources on the indigent. The rural poor suffered from both a deterioration in agriculture's terms of trade and from populists' failure to implement land reform with adequate credit and technical assistance.

1   CLASSICAL POPULISM

Social scientists traditionally associate populism with the policies pursued by Perón in Argentina between 1946 and 1949, by Getúlio Vargas in Brazil after 1945, by Lázaro Cárdenas in Mexico between 1934 and 1940, and by Juan Velasco in Peru between 1968 and 1975. Classical populism represented an urban political movement that opposed the primary product, export-oriented status quo of the nineteenth century and endorsed accelerated industrial development. It constructed alliances linking the working class to the industrial bourgeoisie and minimized interclass antagonisms through the propagation of a broadly nationalist ideology.

Classical populism favored activist governments committed to a strong role in price determination, protection of workers and wages, policies of cheap food, state ownership of key industries, state allocation of credit at low interest rates, and favors for private industry. It rejected any appeal to the need for overall restraint on spending. The consequences were extensive growth of government relative to the private sector and pervasive corruption in varied forms, including tax evasion. Growing budget deficits resulted in rising external debts. Import substitution associated with trade restrictions resulted in dependence on foreign capital. The urban bias of economic policy and resource allocation accentuated rural poverty.

Economists and political scientists from the right and the left have emphasized the negative sides of populism. The right attacks populists as demagogues who fuel inflation, frighten capital, and provoke political instability. The left accuses them of betraying the masses. But most populist regimes did not intend to carry out a revolution, as in Allende's Chile or Ortega's Nicaragua. Populists hoped to reform the system, not to overthrow it. Their program was designed to deliver economic growth based on industrialization as the path to sustained employment. Overwhelmed by their mistakes, we now tend to forget the successful role played by import substitution industrialization in Latin America, which brought extravagant growth rates of more than 5 percent per year between 1950 and 1980.

The distributive agenda of populism called for an increase in urban incomes at the expense of rural producers, exporters, and foreign capital. Velasco and Cárdenas promoted agrarian reforms in Peru and Mexico, but their credit and price policies favored the urban sectors. Specific policies included higher minimum wages, price controls on food, and protectionist barriers. The urban working class and domestic industrialists together served as the primary constituencies of Perón, Vargas, and Velasco.

The classical populist agenda of redistribution was not sustainable for the same reasons that ISI failed in the end. Protectionism did not raise real productivity enough to create a basis for large gains in urban wages; nor did tax collections grow enough to finance government subsidization of the industrialization process. Inelasticity of supply in the agricultural and export sectors was overestimated; it did not take long for overvalued exchange rates and price controls to cause stagnation in these sectors. Alienation of foreign capital only exacerbated these problems. In the absence of a major boom in export prices, classical populism rapidly self-destructed.

Perón

The most representative populist was Perón, who came to power in 1946 by building a base of support among unions as secretary of labor between 1943 and 1945. He promoted the vision of a rapidly industrializing Argentina, free of foreign influence.

Wages rose rapidly as Perón's government settled strikes in favor of workers: real wages rose 25 percent in 1947 and 24 percent in 1948. Labor's share of income rose from 40 percent in 1946 to 49 percent in 1949.[1] Social security benefits expanded dramatically. What made this rapid redistribution possible without an immediate collapse of the economy was the boom in Argentina's export prices after World War II. Export revenues more than doubled between 1945 and 1948, although volume remained roughly the same.[2] Industry grew markedly faster than agriculture. Control of the state marketing board for agricultural output enabled the government to keep food prices down and reap a surplus from exports. Despite high world prices, agricultural income declined 27 percent between 1946 and 1949. Perón's strong nationalist streak led to expropriation of the railroads, the telephone system, and the dock facilities, although with ample compensation to foreign firms.

Problems emerged in 1949. Argentina's terms of trade deteriorated sharply as adjustment in postwar Europe curtailed the region's ability to import food and agricultural protectionism in the United States excluded Argentine goods. The trade balance turned from surplus to deficit; reserves disappeared. Complicating the situation was the adoption of inconvertible currencies by Argentina's trade partners. As Fodor noted, "Europe could not pay; the United States would not buy."[3] Exchange rate policy and low prices paid by the agricultural marketing board sharpened the consequences of unfavorable shifts in the world economy.

Internal expansion had gone well beyond what could be financed by agricultural surpluses. The money supply was increasing rapidly in order to finance industrialization. Inflation doubled to 31 percent in 1949. In a reversal of policy, Perón launched a stabilization program, tightened credit, cut government spending, and capped wage and price increases. He offered incentives to agriculture and made overtures to foreign capital. A severe drought in 1950–1951 forced further adjustment.

The multiclass, nationalist alliance needed robust economic growth to sustain political legitimacy. After 1952, the state no longer had the luxury of allocating shares of increasing output. Recession meant that its role became more coercively redistributive.[4] The government became increasingly authoritarian to force adjustment on various groups. Growing levels of violence and social tension prompted a military takeover in 1955.

2   ECONOMIC POPULISM

Recent economic literature argues that populist policies like those of Perón were repeated in the 1980s, leading to comparable crises.[5] Unlike political scientists' concept of populism, which stresses charismatic leadership and cross-class alliances, analyses of economic populism focus on poor macroeconomic policies. Latin America's extreme income inequality creates political pressure. In an environment of high social conflict, populist regimes attempt to improve the lot of low-income groups through demand stimulation. The result is a set of unsustainable macroeconomic policies, including government deficits and overvalued exchange rates. Perpetuating the cycle of populism are expansionary policies that yield favorable results at first. Because leaders have insecure tenure in office, they adopt shortsighted policies that bring immediate gains to their constituencies.

Economic populists are marked by a common set of mistakes. Their belief in excess capacity sets up the expectation that government deficits and higher real wages are feasible. Devaluations are avoided because of their distributive consequences. As higher wages go into effect, the economy responds with more rapid growth, but it does so by running down inventories and foreign reserves. Bottlenecks become binding constraints, and inflation takes off. The failure to reverse redistributive efforts leads to growing government deficits, balance of payments problems, and pervasive shortages. The collapse of the economy makes workers worse off than they were at the beginning of the populist period.

In the literature on economic populism, the politics of each regime and their specific policies are less significant than the results. What needs to be learned is a universally applicable lesson: policies must be consistent with the capacity of the economy to generate foreign exchange for imports and savings to finance investment. In the past two decades, several Latin American regimes have failed to manage their economy within these limits. Nowhere is the sense of déjà vu stronger than in the case of Peru's once-charismatic president, Alan García.

García

García took power in 1985 promising growth at 6 percent per year and a weakening of the *Sendero Luminoso* guerrillas. A demand-driven expansion was set in motion. Wages were sharply increased, interest rates cut, and taxes reduced. Old-style structuralism provided the rationale: inadequate demand prevented the economy from reducing costs through economies of scale; low elasticities of supply in the export sector accounted for balance of payments problems; unemployment and unused industrial capacity implied that the economy could grow much faster.

Policies were nationalistic and inward looking. García increased tariff levels, imposed restrictions on capital flows, and announced that Peru would not pay more than 10 percent of its export earnings in debt service. To control inflation, he froze prices and fixed the exchange rate. Like Perón, he intended not only to serve labor through higher wages but to raise profits for local industrialists through stimulation of demand and increased protectionism.

The initial results were fantastic. In 1986, inflation dropped to less than half its level in the preceding year, and growth shot up to 9.5 percent. Strong growth continued in 1987 (at 6.7 percent), but then inflation exploded and the economy moved quickly toward collapse. The public sector deficit had more than doubled, from 4.4 percent of GDP in 1985 to 9.9 percent in 1987.[6] As reserves evaporated, García continued to raise wages, announcing a generous wage package in April 1987. He executed his own *coup de grâce* in late July by nationalizing the banks. Industrialists immediately withdrew their support, and social conflict intensified. By early 1988, inflation was well over 1,000 percent and output was sliding rapidly (table 8.1). For all intents and purposes, García relinquished control to his aides.

Like Perón, García did not aim at the very poor. Urban wage earners (especially unionized workers and public employees) and

Table 8.1

Peruvian economic indicators, 1980–1990

	Average, 1980-84	1985	1986	1987	1988	1989
Real GDP growth[a]	-1.0	2.4	9.5	7.8	-8.8	-10.4
Real per head GDP growth[a]	-3.6	-0.2	6.9	5.2	-11.4	-13.0
Employment growth[a]	2.2	-0.5	4.3	5.7	-0.8	-3.7
Inflation rate[a]	87	158	62	114	1,722	2,775
Tax revenue/GDP[b]	13.5	12.4	10.8	8.2	7.3	4.4
Current account[b] Deficit/GDP[b]	3.9	0.3	6.0	7.2	7.4	1.0
Real wage[c]	95	64	83	90	71	38

a. Percentage per year.
b. Percentage of GDP.
c. Index: 1979 = 100.
Source: Ricardo Lago, "Pursuing Redistribution through Macropolicy: Peru's Heterodox Experience," in R. Dornbusch and S. Edwards, eds. *Macroeconomics of Populism in Latin America* (Chicago: Chicago University Press, 1991).

domestic capitalists were the first to gain. These gains were more distributive than redistributive; growth in the size of the pie can benefit all. Initially the rural sector was hurt by García's exchange rate policies. As shortages of foreign exchange developed, he allowed peasant prices to rise and made credit more readily available, but he never implemented a program to overcome widespread rural poverty. Support for the *Sendero Luminoso* barely wavered.

If Perón served as populism's archetype, the mold fit García fairly well. Neither was serious enough about redistribution to do it without trying to boost growth, and both were more interested in distributive issues affecting the politically powerful than the poor. As the literature on economic populism suggests, lack of consensus about income distribution does indeed cause political tension, and policymakers often try to defuse this with inflationary spending. The poor, however, are neither part of the political conflict nor prominent in the populist solution.

Genuine efforts to mitigate poverty do not necessarily lead to hyperinflation; Costa Rica has done fairly well on this score. At the same time, hyperinflationary experiences are not always the result of failed populism. Few authors would be willing to argue that the neoconservative agenda pursued by José Martínez de Hoz was populist, but his policies also led to a balance of payment crisis and the explosion of inflation in Argentina in the early 1980s. The easy access to foreign capital enjoyed by the military regime in the late 1970s helped sustain poor policies and macroeconomic imbalances. Argentina's neoconservative experience indicates that even without populist rhetoric, governments are quite capable of pursuing policies that fuel inflation and balance of payments crises.

Allende and Ortega: Populists?

Two socialist experiences, Allende's regime in Chile (1970-1973) and the Sandinista era in Nicaragua (1979–1990), have been placed under the broad rubric of economic populism. Both regimes collapsed as hyperinflation created increasingly chaotic economies. Moreover, both governments promoted redistribution and ran deficits that were the proximate cause of inflation. In the case of Allende, there was also excessive optimism about the potential for economic growth through demand stimulation. Nonetheless, the socialist nature of these regimes sets them apart; their challenge to capitalism vitiated any possibility of building a multiclass alliance and set up strong internal and external forces determined to overthrow the regime. The instability caused by uncertain property rights and U.S. hostility figured strongly in the development of macroeconomic imbalances in both countries.

Allende

When Allende took power in 1970, Chile was already a highly urbanized, industrial economy. Chileans enjoyed the third highest per capita income in Latin America. An extensive social welfare system kept extreme poverty to low levels compared to the rest of Latin America. In contrast to Perón and Vargas, who introduced an import substitution industrialization strategy and social welfare legislation, Allende came to power after this had already occurred in Chile. The economy depended on imported parts and materials for its heavily protected industry, and agriculture had been neglected for decades. Whereas Perón tried to set up a successful and profitable industrial sector, Allende's Popular Unity program targeted redistribution. The multiclass base of Perón's regime in Argentina was not evident under Allende in Chile. Instead, he took power despite strong opposition from capitalists.

Allende's first step in early 1971 was to increase real minimum wages by 37 to 41 percent for blue-collar workers and by 8 to 10 percent for white-collar workers. He expanded housing, food, and educational assistance; public housing starts went up twelvefold, and eligibility for free milk was extended from age 6 to age 15. The government deficit rose from 3 percent to 10 percent of GDP.[7]

Initially, idle capacity, high copper prices, and large reserves of foreign exchange helped. Real GDP rose 7.7 percent, and unemployment in Santiago fell from 8 to 4 percent in 1971. Industrial output rose sharply as consumer demand expanded. The hard currency needed for this expansion came from ample foreign reserves, a drawing down of inventories, and reduced capital imports (the last reflected industrialists' concerns about potential expropriation).

Allende attempted to repeat his early success with a new round of wage increases in 1972. Real blue-collar wages were increased by 27 percent, and white-collar wages were fully indexed. But shortages of foreign exchange became serious, and it was impossible to increase Chileans' consumption without sustained copper earnings and commercial lending. Working-class consumption in Chile was very import intensive, as both manufactured goods and food imports required foreign exchange. The country's backward agricultural sector was in no position to absorb growing demand for food. Eduardo Frei's gradual process of land reform was accelerated: takeovers increased eightfold in Allende's first year. Despite rising real food prices, both the area planted and output fell.

Compounding Allende's problems was a steep decline in foreign exchange receipts. Copper prices fell by a sharp 23 percent in 1971 and did not recover until mid-1973, a few months before the coup. At the time, copper accounted for two-thirds of the country's export earnings. Although volume did not change markedly, export earnings fell 24 percent between 1970 and 1972. The U.S. government, opposing Allende from the start, contributed to his downfall by withdrawing aid, placing an embargo on exports to Chile, and financing his opponents. Allende's refusal to compensate foreign firms after their nationalization provided a specific basis for opposition, though Allende's socialist ideals were the general cause of U.S. antagonism. Net official capital flows from the United States dropped from $172 million in 1969 to –$198 million in 1971. Lack of debt repayment later restored capital flows to a negligible positive amount. Commercial lenders also eliminated their short-term credits. Over the course of his tenure, Allende was offered more aid from communist countries than he lost from Western creditors; however, almost all of this aid was granted for purchases of industrial plants and technical assistance, which Chile did not need. It did not provide spare parts for existing equipment or necessary intermediate materials and food. By June 1973, the Chileans had taken up only 21 percent of the credits offered by the East Bloc.

Was Allende a populist? In terms of the new economic definition of populism, three criteria are met: he pursued redistribution through wage increases, government deficits rose dramatically, and a balance of payments crisis figured prominently in the economy's collapse. By more traditional notions of populism, the case is not clear. The Popular Unity program never aimed at satisfying both capitalists and workers. From the start, it was expected that capitalists would gradually lose. The regime's socialist agenda brought property rights into question. Workers increasingly demanded that the state take over plants, and social tension over property rights turned to near anarchy by the end. The Allende constituency was distinctly not a multiclass coalition, as political scientists so often describe populist regimes. Nor was Allende's long-term strategy to promote capitalist growth with the help of selective state intervention. The Popular Unity platform explicitly rejected the power of industrial monopolists who had gained power during Chile's import substitution period.

The Popular Unity agenda violated basic rules of good macroeconomic management. Allende's problems, however, derived also from his willingness to step into the conflict between superpowers and his challenge to private property rights, two significant factors that cannot be dismissed. And one can debate just how socialist the Allende regime was; it never controlled the legislature enough to implement a dramatic change in the nature of production or the structure of social classes.

The Sandinistas

The Sandinistas' downfall also resulted from weak economic performance, but they followed a different path from the one chosen by Allende. The Sandinistas put no stake on demand-driven growth. They counted the beans in their bag and knew that none were magic. Yet pursuit of a redistributive program (as distinct from distribution with growth) caused an unmanageable political backlash.

When the Sandinistas took power in 1979, the rural sector represented roughly half of the economy. The industrial sector employed a smaller proportion of the labor force than in other Latin American countries. Although some basic industries were in place (food processing, cement, fertilizer, and petroleum-refining industries), there were virtually no sophisticated assembly operations. The Sandinista strategy did not have to cater to a highly protected industrial sector, nor did the program call for import substitution industrialization.

The first years of the revolution brought an energetic attack on urban and rural poverty. During Anastasio Somoza's last years, Nicaragua had the highest child mortality rate in Latin America, and 47 percent of the population was illiterate. The Somoza regime itself estimated that 60 percent of rural Nicaraguans were undernourished. The Sandinistas embarked on a massive literacy campaign, construction of health clinics and schools, extension of water services, and agrarian reform.

Initially there were resources to finance these revolutionary programs. Foreign aid was extraordinarily generous during the regime's first three years. Moreover, the government took over land owned by Anastasio Somoza and his close associates (23 percent of the country's cultivated land) to initiate its land reform program. Taxes increased from an average of 13 percent of GDP in the period 1974 to 1978 to 22 percent in 1980 and peaked at 35 percent in 1984. The government deficit, at 8.9 percent of GDP in 1978, stayed at that level through 1981 and then jumped when contra activity began in 1982; however, extensive foreign aid mitigated repercussions from this deficit in the regime's first years.

The Sandinistas were careful to avoid across-the-board wage increases. The right to strike was tightly controlled, and wage increases were strongly discouraged as early as 1979 in an effort to contain inflation. The hope was that a tight lid on wages would help the private sector to recover slowly from the destruction caused by the war. Inflation was modest in the regime's first years (table 8.2). From 37 percent in 1980, it dropped to 12 percent in 1981, 17 percent in 1982, and 11 percent in 1983. It did not top 100 percent until 1985.

What went wrong? Four factors contributed to the Sandinistas' problems. First, socialist rhetoric and threats to expropriate property created enormous uncertainty for private producers, who were expected to generate the most output. Second, world prices of cotton and coffee, which account for about 60 percent of the country's export earnings, fell after 1980. Third, the currency was grossly overvalued as early as 1980. Finally, the war with the contras, which started in 1982, must take most of the blame.

Table 8.2
Nicaragua's economic indicators, 1978–1990

Year	Real GDP per head (1977=100)	Private consumption per head (1977=100)	Exports (millions of dollars)	Real wages (1985=100)	Inflation rate[a] (percentage per year)
1978	89.4	93.2	459	140	4
1979	65.0	67.9	449	127	70
1980	64.9	80.0	354	119	25
1981	66.2	68.7	419	121	23
1982	63.6	59.9	340	117	22
1983	64.3	56.5	388	115	36
1984	61.2	53.6	355	112	47
1985	56.7	49.3	269	100	334
1986	54.3	45.3	218	101	747
1987	52.1	42.9	255	74	1,347
1988	44.9	33.8	201	51	33,603
1989	41.8	41.7	233	33	1,690
1990	38.6	n.a.	260	67	8,500[b]

a. December–December.
b. Preliminary.
Sources: J. A. Ocampo, "Recent Hyperinflation and Stabilization in Nicaragua," Mimeo. (1991); and ECLAC, *Preliminary Overview of the Latin American Economy, 1991* (New York: United Nations, 1991).

As a result of the civil war, the government deficit soared to 30 percent of GDP in 1983 and stayed in the 15 to 25 percent range thereafter. Half of the government's budget was devoted to the military, squeezing out social spending. The war effort drew scarce resources from the rest of the economy. The draft exacerbated labor shortages while export earnings were diverted toward weapons, forcing industry and agriculture to get along without imported parts and fertilizers. Rebel attacks destroyed Nicaragua's transportation infrastructure and prevented harvests in the most important agricultural areas of the country.

The war made distributive issues more critical. Rural peasants could not be alienated for fear they would support the contras. Both in pursuit of socialist goals and for defense reasons, the government continued to give peasants title to land and to build schools and health clinics even as budget deficits became unmanageable.

It became increasingly important to maintain the presence of large private producers. They not only brought in most of the country's hard currency, but they legitimated the government's claim of respect for private property, blunting European support for a full-scale invasion by the United States. The government paid dearly for their support. Subsidies to this group included a multiple exchange rate system that enabled large producers to buy pesticides and fertilizers at low rates while selling export dollars back to the government at the parallel rate. Credit was also heavily subsidized.

Urban workers were the easiest to control. Although the government courted urban workers with rhetoric, their real wages fell every year after 1981 (and they had increased only minimally before that). Shortages of basic goods were pervasive in urban areas early on and became worse as the economy deteriorated.

Unable to impose the full burden of defense expenditures on any group, the government increasingly used the printing press. By 1986, private consumption had fallen to roughly a third of its prerevolution level. For the next three years, Nicaraguans scrambled to outwit inflation by hoarding and speculating, making matters worse. By 1988, inflation had reached 11,500 percent, and output had fallen back to levels of the late 1960s.

Populism was not the problem in Nicaragua; socialism was. It caused too much hostility from the United States and uncertainty about property rights, and it triggered a war that could not be afforded. Although the Sandinistas ran deficits, the reasons for these deficits differed from those common in classical populist experiences.

Brazil: Cyclical Populism?

The year 1945 provides a good starting point for discussing politics in Brazil. Getúlio Vargas's populist reputation is based on the last ten years of his political career. Having relied on a ruling coalition of military elites, coffee exporters, and industrialists throughout the 1930s, Vargas began to bid for the support of workers in the mid-1940s. In 1942, he instituted a minimum wage and in 1943 a labor code. In 1945, a group of radicals in the Brazilian Workers Party, Partido Trabalhista Brasileiro (PTB), called for reform socialism and for special development banks that would provide massive injections of capital to broaden the internal market for domestic manufactures. This more radical program greatly influenced the PTB after Vargas's reelection in 1950. Vargas moved to the left within the framework of restrained militancy of organized labor and state control over union financing. With unions extensively supervised, Brazilian industrialists and exporters did not feel threatened and acquired a vested interest in the government's subsidies and investment policies. During the decades to come, Brazil was to operate under the legacy of its most notorious populist leader. Continuing expansionist policies attenuated distributional conflicts and blended the interests of business and bureaucracy.

By 1950, the easy phase of populist import substitution industrialization was over. Adjustment was avoided by violating budget constraints and engendering inflation. Such problems encumbered Vargas in 1954, Kubitschek in 1958, and Goulart in 1964. When Goulart, trapped in deep economic crisis, tried to undertake radical reforms, the military stepped in. The doctrine of national security provided the ideological justification for intervention by claiming that the survival of a free society depended on putting an end to the popular classes' resistance to authority.

The new military government announced a series of policies aimed at reducing the public sector deficit, raising taxes, cutting import tariffs, establishing wage controls, and allowing foreign investors easier access. The limits of the import substitution strategy were recognized, and important modifications to commercial policy were introduced in the late 1960s. A crawling-peg exchange rate avoided the overvaluation so predominant earlier. Explicit concern for promoting nontraditional exports produced special export subsidy programs. In the context of a buoyant international market, these policies produced positive results as exports grew rapidly and diversified.

The commitment to industrialization nevertheless remained, and that meant an intrusive role for the public sector even under the "orthodox" policies pursued by military governments. Their administrations were clear descendants of import substitution, not of outward orientation. Brazil's large domestic market still dominated production decisions. Economic austerity did not last long. By 1974, the populist tradition of accommodation staged a comeback.

Mounting indebtedness and the deterioration of domestic policy in a more difficult external environment marked the postoil shock experience. Brazil chose a strategy of accommodation: it borrowed heavily to finance investment and large current account deficits, postponing the negative real income effects of the shock. The strategy succeeded in sustaining high rates of growth, but the debt/export ratio almost doubled. At the same time, fiscal disequilibrium increased as the government pursued its ambitious investment plan. Even on the eve of the second oil shock, Brazil faced the need for a midterm modification of strategy. But the "recessionist" proposal of Finance Minister Mário Simonsen yielded to a more ambitious supply side plan undertaken by Antonio Delfim Netto in 1979. Priority was given to credit expansion in order to finance investment in the agricultural and energy sectors. Low interest rates were rationalized as a means to contain inflation.

Delfim's "populist" strategy did not work. The weakness of the economy became fully apparent only when a new oil price rise, an abrupt increase in real interest rates, and an OECD recession coincided in the early 1980s. The balance of payments registered a record current account deficit in 1980. The inflation rate reached the three-digit level, reflecting excess demand, supply shocks, and the consequences of a new wage law mandating a shorter adjustment lag. In October 1980, a more orthodox package of fiscal and monetary restraint was fashioned, and subsequently Brazil entered into a recession that lasted until 1983.

Transition to democracy in 1985 opened the way for popular resistance to austerity measures. Sarney brought in a new populist experiment, the Cruzado Plan. The goal was to stop inflation without imposing contraction. With prices frozen, the budget was allowed to deteriorate while monetary policy turned expansionist. Inflation disappeared temporarily, but new stabilization programs were necessary in 1987 and in 1989. Once again, the government froze prices and cut zeros off the face value of the currency. Promises to eliminate the budget deficit were made but not kept. President Sarney lacked the political will to implement measures of fiscal consolidation.

Was Sarney a populist? He certainly meets all the criteria of the new economic concept of populism, yet according to more traditional views, he fell far short of the customary charisma of the populist leader. The heterodox Cruzado Plan reflected his inability to impose contraction on any constituency, for he lacked popular support and allies in the Congress.

The threat of hyperinflation at the end of 1989 coincided with the presidential election that brought Fernando Collor de Mello to power in March 1990. During his campaign, Collor spoke to the poorer sectors of society against the existing institutions of the state. His rhetoric had no precise or logically consistent ideology; it appealed to alienated or deprived members of a mass society and directed its energy against existing elites. He attacked traditional symbols of prestige in the name of popular equality. His populist rhetoric was a collection of strands of both left- and right-wing thought, with heavy stress placed on his charismatic leadership, often with a highly illiberal and intolerant stand on traditional civic liberties.

His economic program, however, did not fit the new paradigm of economic populism. The plan mixed free marketeering and authoritarian intervention. It created a major recession. The businessmen who in 1989 had hustled to fill Collor's campaign coffer grieved, moaned, and whined in 1990. The trade unions protested mass unemployment. Was Collor a populist?

3 POPULISM, POVERTY, AND DISTRIBUTION

Redistributive efforts based on government deficits and overvaluation will melt in an inflationary pyre. Despite ample experience from the past, this is a lesson that bears repeating. There is, however, an important distinction to be made between policies of excessive spending and programs aimed at overcoming poverty.

Far from providing an indictment of redistributive efforts, the history of populism makes conspicuous the paucity of genuine redistribution programs in Latin American. (We return to this in chapter 9.) Despite compelling criticism, changing relative prices was the most common strategy of classical populism. The costs of this policy included significant leakages as well as large government and efficiency costs. Organized, vocal, and visible groups of the modern sector used their political power to press for increases in the minimum wage, as well as food and transport subsidies. Governments, held directly responsible for the earnings of workers in the modern sector, chose to impose losses on the rural and informal sectors where political clout was nil.

Classical populists distributed the gains from growth among the politically enfranchised. Latin American reformism in the 1960s was based on the alliance of the national bourgeoisie, the middle classes, and urban workers, aiming at the development of an internal market. The favored groups were urban labor and the middle classes. Industrial workers gained union recognition, electoral power, and welfare benefits. The middle classes received more public jobs, better educational facilities, and decision-making authority in the bureaucracy. *Desarrollo hacia adentro* (inward-looking development) involved a pattern of growth based on higher levels of consumption by the urban population included in the *pacto social*. But strengthening the labor movement and increasing real wages soon would face their own limits. The *pacto social* supported policies that favored the urban middle class at the expense of the rural population. Thus, its nature was contradictory: the demand for increased food production by a growing urban population clashed with policies that channeled the bulk of public investment funds to industry.

Regardless of populist promises to serve all the people, some sectors were denied access, ignored, or excluded. Although populism favored the urban sector, it barely touched the urban poor. As the cornerstone of populist redistribution, minimum wage increases promoted the welfare of relatively small groups at the expense of larger groups. When effectively enforced (and often they were not), such laws made wages higher for those fortunate enough to get jobs in the modern, formal sector. In the urban areas, the poorest are self-employed (rather than wage earners), workers in construction (the most likely entry point for immigrants), and people working in public make-work programs, such as those in Chile. Because the poor also tend to have larger families, programs to alleviate urban poverty could have included improvements in access to birth control and prenatal care, nutrition and sanitation programs, child care programs for working mothers, and better primary school education. Classical populists expanded the welfare state, but the emphasis was not on poverty. Broad-based social security programs and state support for universities served the middle class and absorbed resources that could have targeted the poor.

The group most seriously neglected by populists—and nonpopulists—is the rural poor. The extent of poverty is markedly higher in rural than in urban areas in all Latin American countries. Where landownership is concentrated in the hands of a few and large estates are farmed carelessly, agrarian reform can promote economic growth and greater equity. But of the regimes that might be considered populist by economists, only a handful implemented major agrarian reform: Velasco, Allende, and the Sandinistas. Land reform requires broad social acceptance of its inevitable costs. The consequences fall not only on large landowners but also on urban consumers, who will face higher food prices in the short run, and taxpayers, who must be willing to support credit and technical assistance. Unfortunately, populists have generally not been willing to commit resources to land reform.

The need for genuine redistribution and economic growth in Latin America is acute. Attempts to accelerate growth through government deficits fail, as economic populism has amply demonstrated. Redistribution must carry the ball. Even where most prices are indexed, including wages, inflation has a profound impact on those classes whose subsistence is not protected. Stop-and-go policies, whether populist or not, hurt the poor. Stability, on the other hand, might help them.

4 CONCLUSION

In Latin America, a variety of different political agendas have led to economic crisis. Classical populists put too much faith in the possibility of demand-driven growth, inward-looking industrialization, and unrealistic expectations. Perón, García, and Allende, to a large extent, failed to realize that Keynesian stimulus falters on foreign exchange constraints.

Attempts at developing market-based socialism are also to blame for failed economic policy. Insecure property rights make it difficult to sustain private production, and socialist rhetoric triggers costly intervention by the United States. The Sandinistas may have been overly ambitious in their initial plans to redistribute and their early budget deficits were indeed high, but their downfall is more the result of contra activity and uncertainty about property rights than of populism.

Lack of social cohesion and strong political parties make it difficult to impose the burden of contractionary adjustment on various classes. Sarney and Alfonsín could never decide how to distribute the burden of adjustment to the debt shock. As fragile elected regimes without the strong political support of any particular group, they were unable to impose contraction on anyone. The result of this failure to live within the economy's constraints was hyperinflation.

Although redistribution marks populism, the poorest have not benefited from it. Classical populism redistributed income from the agricultural and export sectors to capitalists and workers in the formal urban sector. Rural peasants and the urban poor remained marginalized, both politically and economically. Modern populists did not serve them better.

Solutions to poverty in Latin America lie in a concerted effort to tax and redistribute revenue for support of agrarian reform and programs that aim specifically at the poor. This is possible only if the rest of society accepts redistribution. Experiences with hyperinflation show that the politically enfranchised cannot agree on a distribution of income among themselves, much less on redistribution toward an increase in the share of the poor.

FURTHER READING

Coniff, M., ed. *Latin American Populism in Comparative Perspective.* Albuquerque: University of New Mexico Press, 1982.

Dornbusch, R., and S. Edwards. *Economic Populism in Latin America.* Chicago: University of Chicago Press, 1991.

Harberger, A. "Economic Policy Problems in Latin America." *Journal of Political Economy* 78 (1970): 1007–1016.

Rock, D., ed. "The Survival and Restoration of Perónism." In *Argentina in the Twentieth Century.* Pittsburgh: University of Pittsburgh Press, 1971.

Sachs, J. *Social Conflict and Populist Policies in Latin America.* Working Paper, no. 2897. Cambridge, Mass.: National Bureau of Economic Research, 1989.

Chapter 9

POVERTY

Economic poverty reflects political poverty: the poor lack the means to voice their demands because they possess neither capital nor trade union power. Growth during the 1960s and 1970s in Latin America did not reduce their numbers, and stagnation in the 1980s only reversed progress in many areas.[1]

This chapter provides an overview of research on poverty in Latin America and considers policies for overcoming poverty. It also discusses the relationship of growth, inequality, and poverty. Given the inequality of income distribution in Latin America and the slow growth of output, policies to overcome poverty must involve more efficient allocation of government resources, redistribution, and foreign aid.

Table 9.1 shows the evolution of basic indicators such as infant mortality, population per physician, and literacy ratios between 1960 and 1987.[2] Despite the gains during this period, infant mortality in Latin America is still six times that of the industrial market economies, and life expectancy is a decade short of that enjoyed in the developed capitalist world. Table 9.2 compares poverty in Latin America in 1985 with poverty in other developing regions.

Although the effect of growth on the poor in Latin America during the postwar period is nothing to boast about, the experience of the 1980s makes it clear that in the absence of economic growth, the lot of the poor will be much harder to maintain, let alone improve. The social effects of the 1980s crisis are slowly emerging. Although cuts in wages have been substantial (table 9.3), they tell the story only for those who managed to keep their jobs. There are reports of serious deterioration of physical infrastructure in the education,

Table 9.1
Economic and social indicators in Latin America, 1960–1987

GDP per head, 1980[a]	Life expectancy (years) 1987	Infant mortality (per thousand) 1965	1987	Population per physician (thousands) 1965	1984	Literacy ratio 1960	1978
More than $2,000							
Venezuela	70	67	36	1.21	0.70	63	82
Uruguay	71	48	27	0.88	0.51		94
Argentina	71	58	32	0.60	0.37	91	93
Mexico	69	82	47	2.08	1.24	65	83[b]
Chile	72	103	20	2.12	1.23	84	89[c]
Costa Rica	74	72	18	2.01	0.96		90[b]
Panama	72	58	23	2.13	0.98	73	82
Brazil	65	105	63	2.50	1.08	61	76
Cuba	74	38	15	1.15	0.53[e]		96[e]
More than $1,000							
Colombia	66	99	46	2.50	1.19	63	81[b]
Paraguay	67	74	42	1.85	1.46	75	84
Peru	61	131	82	1.65	1.04	61	80
Dominican Republic	66	111	65	1.70	1.76	65	67
Ecuador	65	113	63	3.00	0.83	68	77
Guatemala	62	114	59	3.69	2.18	32	46[d]
Nicaragua	63	123	62	2.56	1.50	49	90
Bolivia	53	161	110	3.30	1.54	39	63[b]
Honduras	64	130	69	5.37	1.51	45	60
Less than $1,000							
El Salvador	62	122	59	n.a.	2.83	49	62
Haiti	55	180	117	14.00	7.18	15	23[b]

a. Except Cuba, countries are ordered by size of GDP per capita in 1980.
b. 1980.
c. 1970.
d. 1975.
e. 1985.
Sources: World Bank, *World Tables* and *World Development Report* (Washington, D.C.: World Bank, various issues); and United Nations, *Human Development Report* (New York: United Nations, 1990).

Table 9.2
Poverty in Latin America compared to all developing countries, 1985

	Extremely poor		Poor		Social indicators		
	Number (millions)	Percentage of population	Number (millions)	Percentage of population	Under 5 mortality rate (per thousand)	Life expectancy (years)	Net primary enrollment rate (percentage)
Latin America and the Caribbean	50	12	70	19	75	66	92
All developing countries	633	18	1,116	33	121	62	83

Source: World Bank, *World Development Report*, 1990.

Table 9.3
Real wages in Latin American countries, 1980–1989

	Real urban minimum wages		Average wages
	Average percentage variation per year between 1981 and 1989	1989 index (1980 = 100)	1989 index (1980 = 100)
Argentina	-0.6	77	89
Brazil	-3.5	71	
Colombia	1.2	111	119
Costa Rica	2.2	117	88[a]
Chile	-1.9	80	103
Ecuador	-8.7	42	
Mexico	-7.1	51	72[a]
Paraguay	4.0	140	
Peru	-11.2	27	37
Uruguay	-2.4	79	99
Venezuela	-2.7	69	

a. 1988.

Source: ECLAC, *Preliminary Overview of the Latin American Economy, 1989* (New York: United Nations, 1990).

health, sanitation, and housing sectors; increasing incidence of nutrition-related ailments; fewer facilities providing health and nutrition services to pregnant women and nursing mothers, as well as scattered evidence of lower birth weights, increased child abandonment, and youth delinquency. Social service expenditures have also declined as a percentage of total government expenditure, at a time when government expenditures themselves were declining in real terms (table 9.4).

In a few countries, there is evidence that the basic welfare indicators have deteriorated. In Peru, Panama, and Haiti, for example, the infant mortality rate rose between 1980 and 1986.[3] By and large, however, there has been an improvement in life expectancy, infant mortality, and literacy rates since the debt crisis began. The most common explanation for this is that progress in these areas has strong positive inertia. Parents who learn to save a sick child with a simple solution of salt, sugar, and water pass on this information to their children and neighbors. Those who know how to read realize that the skill is worth instilling in their children. Technical progress and the self-perpetuating nature of these gains combine to improve welfare indicators even when monetary resources dry up.

Although death by starvation is rare among Latin Americans, millions suffer from malnutrition, hunger, an inability to afford medical care, and cramped housing. The plunge of real wages and the stagnation of employment in the 1980s amplified poverty in the region.

1   THE DIMENSIONS OF POVERTY

A widely used definition of poverty was developed by Oscar Altimir for ten Latin American countries, based on household surveys from the 1970s.[4] He followed the "absolute" approach of choosing a level of income consistent with "subsistence" and defining poverty as any income level below that amount.[5] Later work done with data from the mid-1980s by the ECLAC follows the same approach.[6]

Construction of absolute indicators of poverty involves hard conceptual problems: how to define needs, what weight to assign to each basic need, whether to measure income or consumption, whether the appropriate income-sharing unit is the individual or the

Table 9.4
Education and health spending participation in total spending of the central government, Latin American countries, 1970–1985

	Education			Health		
	1970	1979	1985	1970	1979	1985
Argentina	11.1	11.3	8.5	3.7	3.4	2.4
Bolivia	32.3	32.1	19.8	9.1	9.1	3.1
Brazil	11.5	4.2	2.2[c]	12.5	5.7	3.3
Colombia	16.9[a]	26.3	24.4[c]	7.9[a]	9.5	5.7[c]
Costa Rica	26.8	32.4	22.5	3.1	5.7	2.6
Ecuador	n.a.	37.1	24.5	n.a.	15.6	7.3
El Salvador	23.6	19.3	16.2	10.5	8.6	6.8
Guatemala	16.6[b]	12.1	12.9	8.1[b]	8.7	7.4
Haiti	6.9	4.9	4.5	7.9	6.9	4.2
Honduras	20.3	14.8	19.1	9.1	6.7	8.1
Mexico	16.9[a]	20.0	10.6	3.1[a]	3.1	1.1
Nicaragua	19.2	12.8	12.0	5.9	10.7	9.1
Panama	20.6	16.0	21.3	9.3	5.4	8.0
Paraguay	13.9	14.1	12.2	3.4	4.1	7.8
Peru	21.4	15.3	16.1	6.3	6.0	6.0
Dominican Republic	14.4[a]	12.5	11.5	10.6[a]	11.4	7.6
Uruguay	15.8[b]	13.4	8.4	3.3[b]	6.2	5.3
Venezuela	16.2	20.3	18.6	7.6	5.8	4.8

a. 1971.
b. 1972.
c. 1984.
Source: Inter-American Development Bank, *Report on Economic and Social Progress in Latin America, 1988* (Washington, D.C.: IDB, 1989).

household, and whether the appropriate period for measuring income is a year or a lifetime. In defining needs, measures of poverty are inevitably determined by cultural values. What North Americans view as an intolerably low standard of living can be luxurious by Bolivian standards.

To define poverty, Altimir and the ECLAC team first estimated the cost of a basic basket of necessities. The minimum food basket,

drawn from World Health Organization recommendations, is based
on a diet with adequate diversity to prevent most nutritionally
caused diseases. In applying it to Latin America, they took into
account the fact that consumption patterns vary dramatically across
countries. For example, cassava, a staple in Brazil, is rarely eaten by
Chileans, no matter how poor they are. Furthermore, food needs
depend on demographics; 2 year olds do not have the same nutritional needs as 20 year olds. They studied specific food consumed
by the poor and defined each country's basic food basket in terms
of minimal nutrition given demographic data and local dietary
customs.

To estimate the cost of a minimum food budget, they also
accounted for differences in the price of necessities among Latin
American countries. Not only does the availability of certain grains
depend on climate and agricultural productivity, but many foods are
subsidized (tortillas in Mexico, wheat in Peru). Urban and rural
households also face different costs. A minimum food basket represents a weighted average of the cheapest adequate urban and rural
diets in each country.

This is perhaps as far as one can go in objectively defining a
subsistence income. However, the cost of a basic food basket does
not cover important basic needs. Nor does it account for the fact that
poor people often do not know what the cheapest, nutritionally
adequate food basket is and would not stop buying Coke even if they
did. The poverty line must also allow for housing and expenditure
on education and health care where it is not provided by the
government. Setting a standard for adequate access to medical help
is difficult. Surgical removal of a lung tumor is not basic health care
in a poor country like Bolivia, but is access to antibiotics? And how
should the fact that the rural poor lack access to doctors as much
because of distance and lack of transportation as inadequate money
for the health care itself be dealt with?

Estimates of basic housing costs are hard to assess. In some Latin
American cities, a third of the population lives in squatter settlements without running water, electricity, or adequate protection
from the weather. Shacks made of scrap wood, plastic, and tin are
the first to fall in the mud slides of Rio or to float down the Mapucho
in Santiago's floods. If this housing is considered inadequate to meet
basic needs, then poverty affects a very large percentage of the

population. Estimating the smallest budget needed to obtain conventional housing in low-income housing projects is futile since there is not enough of it to go around. When markets do not clear, prices are not helpful in assessing minimum budgets.

Access to basic services, especially sewerage, water, and education, is also hard to price. Residents of squatter communities do not pay taxes and consequently are often not entitled to these services from the government. Officials try to avoid providing the service for fear that they will encourage expansion of these communities.

Poverty has many dimensions. Our notions of adequate housing demand protection from the elements, sewerage, and enough room for each occupant. Our concept of literacy goes beyond the ability to sign one's name to contracts that cannot be read. Nonetheless, any single direct measure of these problems is inevitably too rigid in the weight it puts on specific needs. Defining poverty according to income would leave room for substitution among basic needs but poses problems in treating nonmonetary income. Altimir's approach is straightforward. He found that urban Latin Americans who barely met their nutritional needs spent roughly half of their cash income on food; in rural areas, the proportion was about 25 percent. Rather than attempt to nail down the exact cost of housing and services, he set the poverty level at approximately twice the cost of a basic food basket.[7] His poverty lines are thus country specific based on the cost of a nutritionally adequate diet multiplied by two.[8]

Altimir estimated that 40 percent of Latin American households were poor in 1970 (table 9.5). The poor as a group had an average purchasing power from 40 to 55 percent below the poverty line in Altimir's sample. Only in Argentina was the income gap (the percentage shortfall of the average income of the poor from the poverty line) less than 37 percent. Among Altimir's sample, the incidence of poverty was highest in Honduras, Peru, Brazil, and Colombia. Altimir's analysis does not include some of the poorest countries in the region. Three years after Altimir's results were published, Couriel reported that poverty affected more than half of the population in Peru, El Salvador, Guatemala, Honduras, Nicaragua, Haiti, Ecuador, the Dominican Republic, and Bolivia.[9] ECLAC data show that in 1986, more than 70 percent of the population of Guatemala lived below the poverty line.[10]

Table 9.5
Population living under the poverty line, Latin America, 1970–1986
(percentage)

	1970	1981		1986
	Altimir[a]	Molina[b]	ECLAC[c]	ECLAC[d]
Argentina	8.0	8.0		
Brazil	49.0	43.0		
Chile	17.0	16.0		
Colombia	45.0	43.0		
Costa Rica	24.0	22.0	24.8	
Honduras	65.0	64.0	68.2	
Mexico	34.0	29.0		51
Panama	39.0	37.0	53.9	41
Peru	50.0	49.0		59
Venezuela	25.0	24.0		37
All ten countries	39.0	35.0		

a. The national averages of Altimir's poverty line vary between $162 (1970) for Honduras and $296 for Argentina.
b. Molina updated Altimir's work, assuming that each country's poverty line rose by an amount equivalent to one-quarter of its increase in real per capita income.
c. ECLAC direct estimates follow Altimir's methodology.
d. ECLAC direct estimates.
Sources: Oscar Altimir, *The Extent of Poverty in Latin America*, World Bank Staff Working Paper, No. 522 (Washington, D.C.: World Bank, 1982); Sérgio Molina, "Poverty: Description and Analysis of Policies for Overcoming It," *CEPAL Review*, no. 18 (December 1982); and ECLAC, "Magnitud de la Pobreza en Ocho Países de America Latina en 1986," mimeo., for the Proyeto Regional para la Superación de la Pobreza (1989).

For countries with comparable data, the progress of the 1970s was lost in the 1980s as a consequence of adjustment policies in the aftermath of the debt crisis. The most extreme case is Mexico, where the poverty rate increased from 34 percent in 1970 to 51 percent in 1984. There are a few exceptions. In Colombia, for example, higher household income allowed for a further step in the alleviation of poverty. As four-digit rates of inflation become more common throughout Latin America, measures of poverty become less reliable.

Who Are the Poor?

Because the poor have larger families, the incidence of poverty among children is higher than among adults: 27 percent of children live in the poorest quintile of households.[11] There are also more children in poverty among those belonging to households whose heads are female or have little education. Colombian women with the highest education had four fewer children than the women who had completed only their primary education.[12]

The extent of poverty was markedly higher in rural than in urban areas in all Latin American countries. Whereas 26 percent of urban Latin Americans were poor in 1970, 60 percent of rural households were poor. In Mexico, the poorest 30 percent of the population was almost entirely rural. Even in Argentina, Chile, and Uruguay, the most heavily urbanized countries in the region, the extent of rural poverty was not less than 20 percent of rural households. In 1986, the extent of poverty continued to be markedly higher in rural areas (table 9.6). Other indicators confirm this. In the mid-1980s, urban Peruvians and Argentines were at least three times as likely as their rural counterparts to enjoy access to uncontaminated water.[13]

Most of the rural poor in Brazil are landless laborers who subsist on temporary employment. In contrast, most of the rural poor in Peru are subsistence farmers. In Colombia, about half of poor rural households are small producers; the rest are landless labor. Landowners who are poor typically own too little land to subsist and earn a large share of their cash income as laborers on larger farms.

An important mechanism of advancement among the landless is migration to urban manual employment, especially in construction. The economic slump of the 1980s trapped would-be migrants in rural areas, where the effect of the debt crisis has been less severe. For the rural poor, the urban informal sector represents the land of opportunity.

The Informal Sector

De Soto's book *The Other Path* advertised a new way to make poor countries rich: the informal sector can create wealth if policymakers eliminate state intervention and give free rein to business.[14] Unhap-

Table 9.6
Population living in poverty, Latin American countries, 1986

| | Percentage of population below: | | | | | |
| | Poverty line | | | Destitution line | | |
	Urban area	Rural area	Total	Urban area	Rural area	Total
Argentina[a]	11			3		
Colombia	39			16		
Guatemala	60	80	73	31	57	49
Mexico[b]	47	61	51	19	30	22
Panama	36	52	41	16	28	20
Peru[c]	51	71	59	23	53	34
Uruguay		21		5		
Venezuela	34	48	37	11	22	13

a. Metropolitan area.
b. 1984 data.
c. Preliminary.
Source: Comisión Económica Para America Latina y El Caribe (CEPAL), "Magnitud de la Pobreza en Ocho Países de America Latina" mimeo (Santiago: CEPAL, June 1989).

pily, the informal sector has always been around; it is a manifestation of poverty, not an outbreak of free enterprise.

A good criterion for distinguishing between formal activities and informal or underground activities is whether they adhere to the established rules of the game. Four types of underground activities are distinguished according to the institutional rules that they violate:[15]

1. The illegal economy consists of income produced by activities pursued in violation of criminal law, such as drug trafficking and prostitution.

2. The unreported economy consists of activities that evade taxes. Workers in the service sector who receive payment in cash and do not report their incomes are part of the unreported economy.

3. The unrecorded economy consists of activities that do not meet the reporting requirements of governmental statistical agencies. The most obvious example of unrecorded activity is domestic work.

4. The informal sector violates some or even all of these rules of the game. Unreported, untaxed, and—when the police decide to crack

down—even criminal, the informal economy has eluded clear definition. The term is used so frequently and inconsistently that it requires special attention.

Some authors identify the informal sector with all activities outside the legal system. For example, dentists in Rio de Janeiro offer clients the option of paying a lower price for services if paid in cash so they can avoid income taxes. Should they be counted among the informals? Most social scientists would say no; these dentists are part of the unreported economy, not the informal sector.

Informal markets have always existed in poor countries that grow too slowly to create good jobs for their rapidly increasing and ill-educated labor force. Shops and curbside establishments compete with larger enterprises and fill market niches that larger formal firms consider unprofitable. Migrants can enter the informal sector easily. Even if they lack the twenty dollars of capital needed for self-employment, they can work for others as domestic servants or hired hands.

The International Labour Office and its Latin American Program (PREALC) characterize the informal sector as the large number of small-scale production and service activities that are individually or family owned and use simple, labor-intensive technology. Informal workers have little education and lack capital resources. As a result, their labor productivity and income are lower than those of workers in the formal sector. Moreover, informals do not enjoy the measure of protection afforded by the formal sector in terms of job security, decent working conditions, and old-age pensions. Most informals work for survival rather than for profit, relying on their personal creativity to invent jobs. The whole household, including young children, is involved in income-generating activities. Many live in slums where tuberculosis is rampant or in squatter settlements built with their own labor and lacking minimal public services.

Organization in the informal sector varies widely. On the one hand, there are abandoned children who pull dead roses out of the dump to sell at traffic intersections. Only with a long stretch of terminology can they be called anything but beggars. On the other hand, migrants to Lima have established a tradition of joining together to invade land. They establish new neighborhoods, *pueblos jovenes*, where they are better off, especially after the government legalizes the settlement and provides water, electricity, and sewage disposal. Social structures are very tight in some of these neighborhoods, as seen in the important role of community kitchens.

The modern urban sector depends on the informal sector for cheap inputs and goods for its workers. Informals depend on the growth of the formal sector for a good portion of their income. They also subsidize the modern sector by providing materials and services at very low prices. Large firms in clothing, plastics, and cosmetics often subcontract to smaller firms, which in turn farm out work to family-run sweatshops, where neither the minimum wage nor other regulations are enforced. These connections are the reason that many social scientists view the informal sector as a dependent appendage of the modern sector, in contrast to De Soto's interpretation of the informal sector as a dynamic, self-sustaining, capsule economy. The informal sector also absorbs the unemployed during recessions. A traveler to Rio de Janeiro in 1983, during the first Brazilian adjustment to the debt crisis, would have noticed that Avenida Rio Branco, the major downtown artery, had been invaded by street vendors. They disappeared in 1986, when the economy recovered and better jobs were created.

How Big Is the Informal Market?

Estimates of the underground economy range widely. By their nature, these are difficult data to estimate. In 1985, PREALC estimated that almost one-fourth of the Latin American labor force was involved in the urban informal economy (table 9.7).

Should We Promote the Informal Sector?

The informal sector plays an important role in providing income opportunities for the poor. But the question must be asked whether the informal sector is just a holding ground for those who are waiting to join the formal sector. If that is the case, it should be made more productive but not bigger. Some, however, believe that informal markets are vital segments of the economy and should be promoted as a major source of employment. There are good arguments to support this view. The formal sector will not grow fast enough to

Table 9.7
Urban informal economy, Latin American countries, 1950–1980

	Urban informal underemployment as a percentage of total economically active population		Growth rate of urban informal underemployment (cumulative annual rate)
	1950	1980	1980–1985
Argentina	15.2	21.4	3.2
Bolivia	15.0	23.2	
Brazil	10.7	16.5	9.3
Chile	22.1	21.7	1.2
Colombia	15.3	22.3	5.4
Costa Rica	12.3	15.3	2.2
Ecuador	11.7	28.6	
El Salvador	13.7	18.9	
Guatemala	14.0	18.9	1.6
Mexico	12.9	22.0	8.4
Panama	11.8	14.8	
Peru	16.9	19.8	6.5
Venezuela	16.4	18.5	2.2
Uruguay	14.5	19.0	
Latin America (fourteen countries)	13.5	19.4	

Source: PREALC, *Mercado de Trabajo en Cifras, 1950–1980* (Santiago de Chile: International Labor Office, 1982).

absorb the growing labor force in developing countries, and the informal sector has shown its ability to generate employment with low capital requirements. The informal sector also provides inexpensive goods and services to lower-income populations.

Promotion of the informal sector is not without problems, however. One reason for the sector's growth is that it enables firms to skirt minimum wages and other regulations. Many informal activities cause pollution and congestion. Moreover, they threaten the health and safety of the workers themselves.

What should be done? Latin American governments and international agencies have increasingly directed credit and technical assistance to microenterprises. The single most important policy initiative in raising worker productivity is education. Most informal workers are young and unskilled and, hence, require training—measures that use scarce resources. Childcare responsibilites also drive women into the informal sector (box 9.1). Given the limited international and domestic resources directed toward poverty, should financing small businesses be a high priority?

2   GROWTH, INEQUALITY, AND POVERTY

Studies of Latin American countries demonstrate increasing inequality in income distribution as measured by Gini coefficients in Argentina, Brazil, El Salvador, Mexico, Panama, Peru, and Puerto Rico.[16] All of the evidence points to persistent, even growing inequality in the distribution of income.

Table 9.8 presents the share of the richest quintile as a multiple of the poorest quintile as well as Gini indices for fourteen Latin American countries. Relative shares of income are relevant not only to issues of equality but to the assessment of policies designed to overcome absolute poverty. Average incomes in most Latin American countries exceed those in African and Asian countries, yet extreme poverty persists as a result of unequal income distribution. The region has more than enough resources to feed, house, and clothe its people.

Table 9.9 shows that the percentage of GDP needed to eliminate poverty is small in most countries, implying that better tax administration would go far to reduce poverty in the relatively rich Latin American countries. In Honduras and Peru, the problem is stickier. Honduras, for example, would have to more than double its tax rate to eliminate poverty. A few caveats are worth remembering. First, the administrative costs of targeting the poor will increase the share of GDP that needs to be transferred from the rich to the poor. Second, these transfers will have to take place every year unless the ability of the poor to generate their own income changes concretely. Finally, and most daunting, is the difficulty of achieving a social consensus to redistribute.

Box 9.1
Women and Poverty

To no one's surprise, a study by the ILO found that household work is not equally distributed among family members. Latin American women not only do most housework but increasingly work in the market. In 1985, women earned between 58 percent of male incomes (São Paulo) and 84 percent of male incomes (Panama City). In the region as a whole, 65 percent of women worked in services, compared to 34 percent of men in 1980. Among low-income occupations, paid domestics are almost exclusively female. Women in the informal sector also subcontract for work that enables them to care for family members while preparing food, sewing, and doing piecework assembly jobs. Low-income working women desperately need better day care services, programs for elderly relatives, and an equal footing in access to credit for small businesses.

In rural areas, women have little access to ownership of land, although there is ample evidence that they carry out heavy manual labor. In many Latin American countries, women cannot legally inherit land.

Women are taking a lead in organizing neighborhood associations and other grass-root movements to pressure governments for resources and to carry out self-help projects. Since 1983, for instance, an organization directed toward raising rural women's productivity, the Capacitación de la Mujer Campesina, has promoted social change in Oruro, a desolate region 13,000 feet above sea level in Bolivia. In Peru, women organized communal dining halls that have buffered the negative nutritional consequences of economic crises. Many poverty problems cannot be effectively addressed by grass-roots techniques alone and require broader financial commitments, but the grass-roots approach has proved itself a constructive path in some circumstances.

Alternative Models

According to some economists, inequality is necessary for growth; it ensures that the most able occupy the most important jobs and that they continue to be motivated to do their jobs. Without the mechanism of unequal pay, incentives to work hard and save would be undermined. Without the savings of the rich, investment would decline. Samuel Morley goes so far as to argue, "Rising inequality

Table 9.8
Income shares and Gini indexes, Latin American countries, circa 1970

	Income share of top 20% as a multiple of bottom 20%			Gini index		
	Kakwani	Lecaillon et al.	Zimbalist and Brundenius	Kakwani	Lecaillon et al.	Zimbalist and Brundenius
Brazil	21	15		.574		
Mexico	15	16		.524	.567	
Argentina	7	7		.437	.425	
Venezuela	24	18		.622	.531	
Colombia	17	15		.557	.520	
Peru		26			.591	
Chile	12	14		.506	.503	
Ecuador	16	24		.526	.625	
Dominican Republic	13			.493		
El Salvador	18	11		.539	.532	
Costa Rica	11	9		.416	.466	
Panama	20	24		.557	.558	
Uruguay		13			.449	
Honduras		21			.612	
Cuba			3			0.25

Note: For comparison, the average of developed countries Gini index is .380.
Sources: Manek Kakwani, *Income Inequality and Poverty: Methods of Estimation and Policy Implications* (New York: Oxford University Press, 1980); Jacques Lecaillon et al., *Income Distribution and Economic Development: An Analytical Survey* (Geneva: International Labour Office, 1984); Andrew Zimbalist and Claes Brundenius, *The Cuban Economy* (Baltimore: Johns Hopkins University Press, 1989).

Table 9.9
Shortfall of the average income of the poor from the poverty line as a
proportion of GDP, Latin American countries, 1981 (percentage)

Argentina	0.5	Honduras	21.8
Brazil	4.2	Mexico	2.6
Chile	1.6	Panama	5.7
Colombia	5.3	Peru	12.8
Costa Rica	2.7	Venezuela	3.6
All ten	3.6		

Source: Molina, "Poverty."

is the short run cost that society must pay for the long run improvement in the well being of the poor."[17]

But empirical evidence indicates that economic growth is not closely associated with inequality. The experiences of South Korea and Taiwan (where World War II is largely credited with having brought about an initial asset-ownership equalization) support the proposition that a more equitable distribution of assets at the start of the growth process is the best solution to poverty.

Serious methodological problems with the available data fuel controversies about growth, distribution, and poverty in Latin America. The basic survey data from which indexes of poverty and distribution are drawn, disproportionately undercount poor groups such as the homeless and the indigenous populations separated by linguistic barriers. Those in surveys underreport their incomes, as shown by comparisons with independent sources of data. Consequently, even for the same country, the same year, and the same income recipients, estimated shares of quintiles can be very different. Some of the differences derive from different assumptions made to correct for underreporting of incomes. Cross-country comparisons of Gini indices are even more controversial. (Appendix C contains rankings of Gini coefficients from different studies.) When the data are controversial, interpretations will be even more so.

Rather than making cross-section comparisons, we will base our discussion on two case studies, Brazil and Colombia. Before we turn to these examples, it is worth noting that Costa Rica stands out as an exception in the region.

With its democratic institutions and social harmony, Costa Rica has enjoyed relatively stable growth and equality. Although its per capita income level is roughly a third less than that of Venezuela, its infant mortality rate is only half as high. Costa Rica's per capita income is almost exactly equal to Brazil's, but its infant mortality rate is one-third of Brazil's. While its efforts in education, health, and social security are important and worth emulating, several factors have worked to the country's advantage. It has a tiny indigenous population and none of the racial tension common to Peru, for instance. The inequities of colonial Spanish America bypassed the country, and it has received a large amount of aid.

Brazil

For no other country has the academic debate over growth versus equality been sharper than for Brazil. The core of the discussion has been whether the poor benefited from growth during the 1965–1974 "miracle" and whether they might have done better under different policies.

Table 9.10 shows the evolution of Gini coefficients and poverty measures over time. The Gini index jumped from 0.5 in 1960 to 0.6 in 1970, an unusually large deterioration in only ten years. In 1960, the wealthiest 10 percent of the economically active population earned 28 percent of total income. By 1970, they earned 48 percent. At the same time, the bottom half of the population saw its share drop from 18 percent to 15 percent.[18] The consensus is that the benefits from Brazil's growth disproportionately went to the rich. Supporters of Brazilian policies during this period argue that rising inequality was the result of skill-intensive growth in a labor-surplus economy. Job creation more than kept pace with growth of the labor force, and most jobs created were good ones.

An increase in inequality is not necessarily an indicator of decline in welfare. Arguing that redistribution itself undermines growth and would leave the poor no better off, apologists for the Brazilian "miracle" rely on census data showing that nearly every income class in Brazil experienced an increase in real incomes. Yet the piece of the new pie served to the richest was vastly bigger than that received by the poor.

The inequality observed in Brazil cannot be justified as necessary for growth. Consider the data: if the earnings of the richest 1 percent

Table 9.10
Evolution of poverty among families in Brazil, 1960–1985

Year and data source	Average income[a]	Gini index	Poverty rate	Percentage of total income necessary to overcome poverty
Census 1960		0.500		
Census 1970	2.56	0.608	0.422	7.7
Census 1980	4.83	0.597	0.219	1.9
PNAD[b] 1981	4.60	0.584	0.208	2.1
PNAD 1982	4.68	0.587	0.211	2.0
PNAD 1983	3.82	0.589	0.265	3.3
PNAD 1984	4.04	0.588	0.243	2.8
PNAD 1985	4.51	0.592	0.211	2.2

Note: The poverty line is defined as the equivalent to one minimum wage of August 1980.
a. In multiples of the minimum wage.
b. PNAD (Pequisa Nacional de Amostra de Domicilios).
Source: Helga Hoffmann, "Poverty and Prosperity: What Is Changing?"in E. Bacha and H. Klein, eds., *Social Change in Brazil: The Incomplete Transition* (Albuquerque: University of New Mexico Press, 1989).

of Brazilians were distributed to the poorest 50 percent in 1980, the average income of half the population would have doubled. It is hard to imagine that there was no way to implement more progressive taxes and employment policies without destroying the incentives for investment. Certainly it has been possible to achieve rapid growth with more equality in Asia and with no more repression.

One explanation for widening inequality during this period is the stabilization program adopted between 1964 and 1967. The concentration of income resulted not from growth but from policies restraining nominal wages and adjusting government-administered prices. Real wages fell dramatically between 1964 and 1969. There is some controversy as to whether income distribution deterioration can be attributed to the government's wage policies. Minimum wage policies are arguably ineffective in modifying Brazil's income distribution, for two reasons: low-income groups do not receive the official minimum wage, and, the evidence does not point to a clear positive correlation between the official minimum wage and the wages below it.

If policies restraining wages did not favor equality, neither did credit policies. Despite a rising flow of credit to agriculture, its allocation remained highly concentrated and selective. Only 20 to 25 percent of producers had access to credit in 1978. Even within this small minority there is high inequality in the distribution of credit by size of establishment. The volume of credit allocated to large concerns rose tenfold between 1969 and 1975, whereas the flow to small concerns did not quite double.[19]

The Brazilian share of social service expenditure by government in GDP is as high as or higher than that of other middle-income developing countries, but Brazilian social welfare indicators are strikingly low. Infant mortality is well above the average for countries in its income group, and in the northeast part of the country it is higher than in much of sub-Saharan Africa. Brazilian children complete fewer years in school than in any other country of Latin America except El Salvador and Nicaragua. The country is characterized by low literacy rates and a high incidence of chronic diseases.

The reasons for poor Brazilian social performance are twofold: public resources are poorly managed, and they are not efficiently targeted. The poorest 19 percent of the population (with less than one-quarter of a minimum wage per household member) receives 6 percent of social benefits. An estimated 78 percent of all spending on health is devoted to high-cost curative hospital services and only 22 percent to basic preventive health care, such as immunization programs, malaria control, and maternal and child health. In education, the government supports free tuition in universities despite the fact that the cost of educating each university student is eighteen times higher than the government expenditure per student at the primary and secondary level combined.

Colombia

There is considerable controversy regarding Colombia's success in reducing inequality. Some data show that income distribution did not worsen in the 1970s and that the real incomes of the poor improved significantly, especially later in the decade.[20] A recent survey by the Colombian Ministries of Planning and Agriculture shows that the incidence of "critical poverty" among rural families fell from 52 percent to 32 percent between 1978 and 1988.[21] The eclectic Colombian system used exchange controls but avoided the extreme protectionism of other Latin American countries; its crawling peg kept the exchange rate at reasonable levels, and the government avoided inflationary finance. By stimulating housing construction and exports other than coffee, Colombia experienced sustained growth and avoided the spectacular crises found in other Latin American countries.

Evidence from the 1970s indicates that the wages of agricultural workers increased faster than national income, while wages of lower-income urban workers grew faster than wages of higher-income urban workers and salaries of white-collar employees. At the same time, the tax system was slightly progressive in the 1960s, and it was more so after the reforms of 1974–1975. The income of the first decile was twice as high after taxes and government transfers, while the income share of the top decile was reduced. Nevertheless, some evidence indicates that Colombia's income distribution actually deteriorated in the 1970s. The contradiction derives in part from a concentration of analyses on urban wages and extreme volatility in the Gini coefficient during the mid-1970s.

In both the 1970s and the 1980s, education, health, and public services such as water, electricity, and welfare programs substantially raised standards of living among low-income families. From 1973 to 1985, the share of rural households with access to electricity rose from 15 percent to 41 percent, and rural illiteracy fell from 29 percent to 23 percent. Although rural income distribution remained strikingly unequal as of 1988, the productivity gap between small farmers and large producers had dramatically decreased as a result of government efforts to channel resources for modernization into the campesino sector.

Long-run data from the turn of the century to 1988 show a Kuznets-type of U-shaped curve for Colombia, with a sharp deterioration in income inequality up to the 1960s and improvement since then.[22] The dominant factors at work have been a shift of the labor force from agriculture to industry, broader access to formal education, and demographic changes. Education is especially important in explaining trends in inequality. Two implications seem evident. First, the distributional effects of short-run macroeconomic policy cannot be assessed without looking at long-run structural changes, which are a powerful determinant of equality. Second, formal education determines who can best take advantage of rapid growth.

Educational policy may ultimately be as important as macroeconomic policy in determining the distribution of income.

Growth

The examples of Brazil and Colombia are suggestive, but they do not provide systematic empirical work on the effects of economic growth on poverty in Latin America. In the case of Brazil, growth helped many poor people but left 20 percent of the population with only $1.30 in income per day in 1988. As a solution to poverty, inequitable growth works too slowly and for the poorest of the poor, it does not work at all.

If growth-oriented policies help the rich more than the poor, one must also ask whether there are alternatives that would substantially improve the lot of the poor over the long term. Are taxes progressive? Are education, public services, and social security biased toward urban workers with jobs? Are rural property rights equitably distributed?

More important, the issue of whether rapid free market growth is effective in alleviating poverty is moot in the current context. Per capita GDP fell in the 1980s, and the prospects for rapid macroeconomic recovery in the 1990s are dim. It is unlikely that macroeconomic expansion will alleviate poverty in the next decade. Trickle down, after all, presumes that new resources flow into the system. After eight years of stagnation, it is disingenuous to claim concern for the poor while relying on growth as a solution.

Cuba: A Radical Alternative

Much of the literature on Cuba is marked by ideological dogmatism from both ends of the political spectrum. A dispassionate evaluation of Cuba's development is difficult because even estimating Cuban growth or comparing it to data from market economies is not a simple matter. The main problem comes from the Cuban system of national income accounting, which is quite different from the system used in the United States. Despite this difficulty, we believe that until 1985, Cuba succeeded in achieving substantial economic growth along with distributional equity (table 9.11). Cuban health performance in Latin America is unparalleled. Moreover, all Cubans

Table 9.11
Economic and social indicators, Cuba, 1950–1990

	1960–1970	1971–1980	1981–1985	1986–1988	1989	1990[a]
Population growth	2.0	1.2	1.0	1.0	1.0	1.0
Real growth per capita[b]	1.6	4.0	5.7	-1.5	0.0	0.4

	1950s	1980s
Percentage of total income received by 30% of the population with lowest salary	5 (1953)	18 (1986)
Illiteracy rate (percentage)	24 (1953)	2 (1981)
Life expectancy (in years)	63 (1955–60)	74 (1984)
Infant mortality rate (per thousand live births)	79 (1953)	12 (1988)
Persons per doctor	1,076 (1958)	344 (1988)

a. Preliminary.
b. Measured in terms of total material production at a constant price.
Sources: José Luiz Rodriguez, "The Cuban Economy," in S. Halebsky and J. Kirk,eds., *Transformation and Struggle: Cuba Faces the 1990s* (New York: Praeger, 1990); ECLAC, *Cuba, Estudio Economico de America Latina, 1989* (New York: ECLAC, November 1990).

can read and write. Unhappily, the press is so restricted that Cubans have good reason not to believe what they read.

By 1991, Fidel Castro's revolution entered its thirty-third year beset by shortages of food and consumer goods. The decline in Soviet trade forced Cuba into an extreme form of adjustment comparable to that which other Latin American countries faced after the debt crisis. Cuba's task was made harder because its economy is particularly ill equipped to compete in world trade; its productive capacity had been geared largely to sugar. The price of sugar has been depressed for years, and the U.S. trade embargo has excluded Cuba from its potential market.

Since 1986, Cuba has followed a "Rectification Process," reducing the market-oriented mechanisms tested between 1976 and 1985. Between 1986 and 1990, Cuban economic performance deteriorated. Output per capita and labor productivity declined, the government's budget deficit increased almost nine times, average annual wages stagnated, and housing construction declined, despite the revival of cooperative construction brigades. In 1991, the economy was undergoing a deep crisis that required drastic measures to cut the use of energy and materials. Factories were shut, and 750,000 Chinese bicycles were on order. Workers who lost their jobs were sent to farm camps alongside bureaucrats drafted to contribute two weeks of manual labor.

Unlike Eastern Europe's fallen leaders, Fidel was once a genuine revolutionary leader. Many Cubans still respect him, others do not, although they value their education and health services. But patience with food shortages is limited. An economy going nowhere, infighting in ruling circles, desertion by the brightest, restless youth, and an aging leader make for a potentially explosive political time bomb.

3   SOLUTIONS?

Between the 1950s and 1980s, Latin America's poor increased as fast as the population. Which policies will improve their lot? Reducing poverty involves both the creation of income-earning opportunities for the poor (through a pattern of growth that encourages labor intensive technology) and the provision of social services that increase the poor's capacity to respond to new opportunities.

In the long run, changing the characteristics of the poor remains the winning strategy because it removes the cause of poverty. The most important characteristic of the poor is their inferior education, not only in formal schooling but also in skills. Education explains as much as 50 percent of wage and salary inequality in Brazil's urban areas.

There are significant externalities for growth itself from expenditures on publicly provided education and health services. Primary education is an important means for raising productivity and, hence, growth. This also holds true for health expenditures. Fairly sophisticated simultaneous estimations have shown that caloric intake, literacy rates, and primary school enrollments have a significant impact on economic growth rates.

The question is how to finance programs that raise the productivity of the poor. Inflationary finance of public services is self-defeating. In the current environment, hyperinflation is easily sparked, and the poor are hurt. More efficient allocation of government revenues, income redistribution, and foreign aid remain critical to the process of eliminating poverty.

One of the most progressive steps toward reallocating government revenues is the elimination of free university education. Ten primary school pupils can be trained for the cost of one university student, and in some countries (Brazil and Colombia) the ratio is thirty to one. The resources saved through the introduction of realistic changes in priorities could improve and expand primary education considerably, especially in the rural areas.

More radical ideas include the reallocation of funds from the military to education. Guatemala has more soldiers than teachers. Is asking for change unrealistic? If soldiers are averse to lining up in employment offices with their civilian counterparts, they might be convinced to work on literacy campaigns and health projects. Their image and internal security would both benefit.

The difficulty of reordering fiscal priorities reflects underlying social and political barriers to overcoming poverty. Not only do those with political power lack the will to redistribute income, but substantial resources are devoted to ensuring that the poor do not gain enough control to force redistribution.

Redistribution

Redistributive policies fall into two types: relative price changes and direct transfers. Despite compelling criticism, changing relative prices remains the most common strategy. For example, the tortilla subsidy in Mexico has been criticized as providing cheap food for the middle class. The costs of this policy include significant leakages, as well as large administrative and efficiency costs.

Transfers have a big advantage: they directly benefit the poor. This advantage, of course, applies only to the subset of transfers that can be and are targeted directly to the poor. Limitations derive from the expense of collecting data for direct targeting. Because it is difficult to ascertain incomes, targeted programs tend to work on a de facto basis: public schools are so poor that the middle class will not send its children to them, and health clinics provide inferior treatment. Efforts to improve these programs are expensive in part because they draw in more people as their quality rises. Transfers intended to make housing, education, and health accessible to the poor have often ended up subsidizing more favored groups of society. Partly for this reason, the World Bank has increasingly emphasized ways of charging users and hence recovering costs in social expenditure areas.

Some programs that specifically target the poor, such as the UNICEF strategy for infant survival, are low cost and achieve extremely favorable results. Popular educational techniques that make use of mass media—television soap operas have proved very effective—offset the shortcomings of limited infrastructure.

Effective targeted programs are not difficult to define. They include better access to birth control and prenatal care, sanitation programs, child care programs for working mothers, and good primary school education. The difficulty lies in creating the political momentum to shift resources from broad-based programs to those that serve the poor, whose political voice is weak.

International Aid

The basic needs approach of multilateral agencies in the 1970s helped to build irrigation systems, health clinics, and basic education programs. The decision to shift away from these programs was not so much the consequence of perceived failure as the urgency of avoiding international financial collapse with the onslaught of the debt crisis. As this threat has ebbed, these agencies should turn their attention back to their basic mandate: overcoming poverty.

A concentration of resources on balance of payments issues primarily serves the interests of the banks. The need for bailing them out has passed. Loans aimed at macroeconomic expansion quell dissent in the middle class. In some countries, this is the strategically important constituency. But as guerrilla movements throughout the region prove, the poor are not to be ignored. Poverty programs serve both the selfish and charitable interests of the developed capitalist world.

If the goal of international aid is to eliminate poverty, international agencies might follow their own advice and target their aid to the poor. The poor gain too little from policies that simply promote growth.

FURTHER READING

Altimir, O. *The Extent of Poverty in Latin America*. World Bank Staff Working Paper, no. 522. Washington, D.C.: World Bank, 1982.

Berry, A. "Poverty and Inequality in Latin America." *Latin American Research Review* 22, 2 (1987): 202–214.

Hoffmann, H. "Poverty and Prosperity: What Is Changing?" In E. Bacha and H. Klein, eds. *Social Change in Brazil: The Incomplete Transition*. Albuquerque: University of New Mexico Press, 1989.

Lustig, N. "The Impact of the Economic Crisis on Living Standards in Mexico: 1982–1985," *World Development*, forthcoming (1991).

Urrutia, M. *Winners and Losers in Colombia's Economic Growth of the 1970s*. New York: Oxford University Press, 1985.

Chapter 10

AGRARIAN REFORM

"Talk about land reform can get you killed."[1] Hyperbole? A check through Amnesty International reports will confirm the extensiveness of political violence tied to issues of land reform in Latin America. In Brazil, the National Landless Workers Movement (Movimento dos Sem Terra, MST) and the church-related Pastoral Land Commission (Comissão Pastoral da Terra, CPT) blame the violence on gunmen hired by large landowners determined to stop any movement for land reform. Hired gunmen killed 142 landless laborers and rural activists in Brazil in 1985, 137 in 1986, and 154 in 1987 (table 10.1). Although the Brazilian legislature has shelved the subject, peasants continue to demand land reform as a solution to poverty and inequality in the rural areas.

"Five hundred years of oppression, five hundred years of resistance," is a popular slogan among Native Americans in Ecuador, for whom the 1992 anniversary of Columbus' initial voyage has become a catalyst for redressing centuries of European colonization. In June 1990, up and down Ecuador's Andean region, a million Native Americans rose up in protest; they barricaded highways with trees and occupied churches and estates. They unnerved Ecuador's farmers by rallying under banners reading, "Not one plantation left by 1992."

The Indians' movements are related to different factors: Ecuador's economic stagnation in the 1980s, which dried up job prospects in the cities, growing demographic pressure, and the pro-Indian stand of the local Catholic church. But at the heart of Ecuador's clash is real estate. Although Ecuador, an oil-exporting country, earned extra income from higher oil prices in the second half of 1990, the

Table 10.1
Rural conflicts, Brazil, 1985–1988

Year	Conflicts	Number of people involved	Number of people killed
1985	738	566,041	142
1986	744	810,573	137
1987	782	1,363,729	154
1988	621	403,733	n.a.

Source: Instituto de Estudos Socio-Economicos, *Reforma Agraria: Por Que?* (Brasilia, 1988).

government does not want to use the oil windfall to buy farmland for Native Americans. By 1991, Indian communities were threatening to take over "unused" land on about sixty estates, and landowners were starting to hire private guards.

The Lorenz curves represented in figure 10.1 provide a tenuous measure of inequality. They do not inform us about how many agricultural workers are landless or about the conditions in which they live. They also do not show the relative weight of the agricultural sector within society. But they do give some notion of the extreme concentration of land tenure in Latin America in comparison to Asian and European countries (see also appendix D).

What do we know about the success of land reform in Latin America? What costs does it carry? This chapter studies land reform in Bolivia, Mexico, and Peru to assess its accomplishments and failures. It also questions whether land reform might be a helpful development instrument in Brazil and elsewhere.

1 BASIC ISSUES

Traditional land tenure can contribute to poverty, political unrest, and economic stagnation. Under these circumstances, land reform is an instrument of development.

Market Failure?

Market failure in Latin American agriculture results from labor market dualism caused by extreme inequality of wealth and

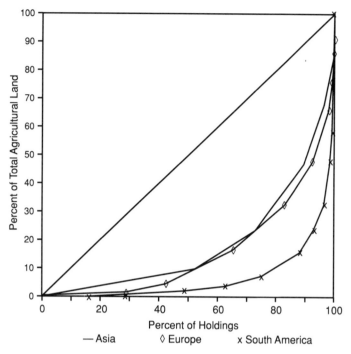

Figure 10.1
Lorenz curves for Asia, Europe, and Latin America, circa 1970.
Source: Food and Agricultural Organization of the United Nations, *1970 Census of Agriculture* (Rome: FAO, 1981).

landownership. Economies in which wealth is very unequally distributed face serious incentive problems. Sharecropping, for instance, may be an efficient system of land tenure given the great inequality of landholdings, but national output would be increased if workers received all of their marginal product rather than half of it. Thus, even a few free marketeers favor land reform despite the threat to private property. Both market failure and an objectionable distribution of income justify government intervention. However, the question arises about the impact of land reform on productivity. It is indeed difficult to predict results when institutional, organizational, and incentive structures change.

The most common argument made in favor of land reform is that it can improve the productivity of agricultural land and bring idle land into use. Both the tendency among the wealthy to hold land as a hedge against inflation without concern for its immediate productivity and the apparent underutilization of potential cropland for grazing lend credence to claims that land redistribution will raise output.

If land is already in use, the argument is made that there is an inverse relationship between farm size and productivity because small units in labor-surplus economies use more labor per hectare than do large farms. Small farmers use unpaid family workers, press all arable land into production, use farm-produced inputs to reduce costs, and extract as many crops per year as they can. But very small plots seem to be less productive than larger plots. The extent to which this is attributable to genuine scale economies rather than access to technology and credit is difficult to establish.

Antireformists predict that radical alteration of the production structure will reduce output. They claim that Latin America's institutional background does not allow for the results of productivity-enhancing reforms such as those instituted in Taiwan, South Korea, and Japan, for the following reason. In East Asia, managerial tenants made the bulk of economic decisions before reform. Reform simply cut the ownership ties to the landlord. In contrast, Latin America's administrators, foremen, and landlords make the key decisions, while uneducated campesinos simply follow orders. Also weighing against reform is the concern that land expropriation will discourage investment in agriculture. Peasants have few resources for investment in irrigation, tractors, and modern processing equipment. Irrigation, in particular, is a key determinant of land productivity. If the state is to provide this capital as part of land reform, the costs can run high. Further, there is the fear that peasants will shift land from cash crops, which feed urban workers directly or provide the cash for importing food, to subsistence farming. Land reform may improve the welfare of the rural poor, but at what cost to urban workers, who hold a stronger set of political cards?

Politics

Any assessment of the prospects for land reform has to address the political context realistically. One argument in favor of reform has been that it will lead to political stabilization. The degree of rural landlessness relative to the whole society may reflect the potential for this sector to destabilize society.[2] For developed countries, this percentage is below 5 percent. Northeast Brazil has a ratio close to the one observed in prerevolutionary settings (more than 30 percent). In fact, however, there is far less guerrilla activity than in Peru and Colombia, which have lower relative landlessness. An accumulated history of racial and class tension can create more instability than relative landlessness.

As a political issue, land reform is riddled with contradictions. History shows that land reform succeeded politically when imposed by revolutionary governments committed to breaking the power of the landed oligarchy. Gradualist approaches usually fizzled out as landowners succeeded in obtaining exemptions or changing regimes. But the difficulty of implementing land reform is not purely a matter of succumbing to objections raised by the landed aristocracy. Policymakers also fear a loss of output for urban food and export markets. Plagued by foreign exchange crises and afraid to alienate urban workers sensitive to food prices, they drag their heels on land reform. The image of land reform is marketable to urban Latin Americans as a concept of social justice, but disruptions in the food supply clearly are unpopular. If anything, politicians in power tend to put their efforts into modernizing agriculture, a process seen as incompatible with the goal of turning land over to peasants.

Pressure for actual implementation of a land reform program tends to come from three different sources: intact indigenous communities seeking control over local land, *minifundistas* or small tenant farmers eking out a marginal existence on too little soil, and wage laborers discontent with the distribution of income in a plantation setting. Each movement for land reform has its own vision of how change should proceed.

Implementation Issues

The first step is to choose the area subject to reform. "Idle land" is the obvious target, but rarely is land entirely idle; most is at least used for pasture. Often the criterion applied is whether the land is actively cultivated for crops. Implicit in this criterion is the judgment that food for direct human consumption is more important than grazing land for animals consumed by the wealthy. However, the extent of tillage does not necessarily measure productive use of the land.[3] The threat of expropriation has been known to create a rush to plant crops without producing much increase in output in the end because other efforts were not made to ensure a successful harvest. In any case, the actual amount of idle land is often inadequate to satisfy peasant needs, and thus other land becomes the target of reform.

The most common criterion in taking over land in use is the size of the owner's landholdings; land in excess of a given amount is taken over for redistribution. A few problems arise with this approach. Landowners usually can choose to keep the most productive irrigated portion of their land while turning over land that is difficult, if not impossible, to farm. Artificial divisions of land among relatives often enable landowners to evade expropriation under the size rule, effectively increasing their reserve area. The peasants themselves do not necessarily want the land expropriated by this criterion; often the pressure for land reform is strongest in one densely populated portion of the country, whereas the size criterion affects larger, more remote farms.

Perhaps most important is that using a size criterion alone may jeopardize well-run farms that produce needed output. The size rule arbitrarily leaves untouched small, idle farms but dismantles large, productive farms. Typically a host of exceptions crop up to accommodate this; for example, dairy farms may be excluded on the grounds that milk is needed for the nation's children. Similarly, certain provinces characterized by commercial farming are exempt, while more traditional areas are affected. Case-by-case appeals can allow landowners to convince authorities of their merits for special exemption. This arbitrary process creates tensions and corruption. By increasing the uncertainty of property owners, it also extends the disruptive effect of land reform on output.

No landowner eagerly turns property over to the state. There is good reason for landowners' resistance: they are virtually never compensated at the full value of their land. The beneficiaries of land reform obviously do not pay market value for their land; if they could, land reform by the government would be unnecessary. Most of the cost of compensation must be covered by taxation or government borrowing. Governments usually try to avoid full compensation by questioning the historical roots of ownership or by referring to delinquent tax payments of landowners. Even where the government seems willing to acknowledge market value, compensation is often in the form of long-term bonds that fail to hold their value against inflation.

Rarely does the decision to implement land reform take effect immediately. The transition period enables landowners to subdivide their land and sell parcels commercially; this reduces the concentration of landholdings but does not meet the goal of turning land over to peasants. Delay in implementation also makes it possible for farmers to liquidate their investments (for example, by slaughtering livestock and selling equipment) and to shift assets to their reserve area. If the transition is dragged out, several years may pass during which no new investments are made and capital on the land (irrigation networks, buildings) is run down.

The decision to target certain areas for land reform generally has spillover effects in the nonreform area where farmers fear an expansion of the program to their land. Depending on the situation, this can have a beneficial effect if farmers try to raise their productivity to avoid a takeover, or it may discourage new investment in the nonreform area. Often governments try to encourage long-run investment in the nonreform sector by guaranteeing protection from reform, but credibility is hard to generate in this context.

Expropriation itself is only the beginning of the story. Once it is accomplished, two models of land reform prevail: division of large holdings into smaller individual plots and the establishment of cooperative farms. When land is allocated to individual peasants, plots tend to be small, and peasants lack access to credit. The result is marginal subsistence production and limited progress in modernizing agriculture. Attempts at setting up collectives have been stymied by problems of management and conflict over revenue/cost sharing between government and growers.

Land Tenure after Reform: Cooperatives or Individual Holdings?

In Latin America, the Bolivian experience is more typical of the subdivision approach, while Peruvian collectives exemplify the cooperative approach. Not all land reform programs fit neatly into either category. For example, the Mexican *ejido* system established individual plots of land under public title. This conceptual division is helpful here, however, since it sets up an outline for many of the dilemmas faced in devising new land tenure schemes.

A central issue in deciding whether to subdivide land is the existence of economies of scale. Economies of scale are hard to nail down empirically. Can small farms use resources as efficiently as large farms? The answer depends on the type of crop grown and the physical characteristics of the land. Some of the factors relevant in considering economies of scale are the efficient use of equipment, marketing, and access to credit and new technology. Mechanical cultivation of soybeans and sugar is easier on relatively large tracts of flat land. This equipment is expensive and is not designed for tiny plots of land. The costs of storage facilities, irrigation pumps, and onsite processing plants (for sugar cane, for example, which must be crushed immediately) also do not rise in proportion to capacity.

In theory, it is possible to get around some of these problems by having farmers rent equipment together and work abutting plots at the same time. However, the closer the cooperation that is necessary to take advantage of large-scale equipment, the more incentive there is to design land reform with a collective structure.

Collectives enable the government to retain the integrity of large-scale operations while redistributing wealth. Sugar plantations are particularly hard to break up, which helps to explain why the collective model was implemented on sugar plantations in Cuba, Nicaragua, and Peru. Subdivision may do more than destroy a productive operation, it may lead to ever tinier plots as property is divided among future generations. At some point, postage-stamp plots undoubtedly do run into cost inefficiencies. The advantage of a collective is that it avoids this fragmentation, even if it leaves issues of inheritance unresolved.

In addition, large farms may be in a better position to market their output due to economies of scale in transportation and the gain of knowledge about export markets. Diffusion of information about new seeds and farming methods is also arguably easier if land is not subdivided since fewer people need to learn about the new technique to implement it. The fact that large-scale farmers are usually the first to use modern methods contributes to the view that absorption of technology is hurt by subdivision. A fair challenge to this view comes from evidence that small farmers quickly learn about new technology if it is profitable but are held back by lack of access to credit, which may itself be a function of size.

From the perspective of the government, which provides the bulk of agricultural credit to the reform sector, subdivision requires an extra layer of bureaucratic coordination. Allocation of credit is simpler if only one farm is involved rather than several. (This is also true of agricultural extension programs designed to diffuse new farming methods.)

Weighing against the claim that economies of scale are necessary for efficient modernization of agriculture are some strong arguments in favor of subdivision. Perhaps most important, collective operations tend to be more heavily controlled by the government. They put the burden of losses on the government and thus are undesirable in countries already plagued by large budget deficits and inefficient public enterprises. If the government is not to wind up as the sole supplier of credit, individual ownership has an advantage in private credit markets: private title serves as collateral and clearly identifies responsibility for repayment of loans. Moreover, the arguments for collectives may be overly optimistic about the availability of funds for modernizing agriculture. Analyses based on overvalued exchange rates and government-controlled interest rates underestimate the true costs of capital-intensive, large-scale farming relative to labor-intensive micro farming.

Collectives also require too much coordination; it is easier for people to take the initiative on private plots than for a collective to reach decisions about farm management. Even if the individual cooperative member finds a low-effort, low-income position inferior to a high-effort, high-income position, the preferred position cannot be maintained in the absence of effective institutional devices to control opportunistic behavior because individuals face incentives to free-ride. By contrast, individual ownership provides a strong incentive to work intensely since the reward structure is direct.

From the perspective of absorbing rural labor, the extreme labor intensity of small farms, though "backward," takes better advantage of abundant labor resources. If land reform is intended as a welfare system for the rural poor, family farms find work for idle hands and ensure that relatives do not go hungry. Cooperatives tend to avoid incorporating new members and instead hire low-wage temporary labor, which is dismissed at the end of a season.

The most important factor in favor of subdivision is the strong desire among peasants to own a plot of land. In 1986, parcelation of Peruvian cooperatives had already extended to three-fourths of coastal cooperatives. In Chile, where cooperatives were set up with an option for subdivision among participants after five years, most participants chose subdivision. In Nicaragua, most large-scale collectives were disbanded within a few years.

2   LAND REFORMS IN LATIN AMERICA

Land reform has yielded both orderly transitions and chaotic disruptions of output in Latin America. By definition, land reform redistributes rights to land away from large-scale owners to rural workers, however, the nature of redistribution has varied considerably within the region. New rights to land have taken the form of individual ownership titles (as in Bolivia), communally organized production (as in Peru), or the allocation of lands to individuals for family farms on a semipermanent basis (*ejidos* in Mexico). It also has involved distribution of unused public or private lands to new settlers, varying levels of compensation for expropriation, and diverse degrees of protection for the nonreform sector.

For the most part, it has been the military and revolutionaries who have reformed landownership. Where landownership is concentrated in the hands of a few, and large estates are farmed carelessly, redistribution will promote economic growth. But democratic regimes with a tenuous hold on power fail to implement change for two reasons: large landowners still influence government, and policymakers fear reform will improve rural diets at the expense of output for urban food and export markets. The fact that military regimes have also reversed or prevented land reform, as in Chile and Guatemala, reflects the difficulty of achieving social consensus on rural property rights.

Among the most ambitious reforms, the Mexican revolution redistributed 43 percent of the country's agricultural land, and the Bolivian revolution shared out about 80 percent of the land. Peru's military government redistributed 40 percent of the country's farming area (table 10.2). A more recent example of radical reform is found in Nicaragua, following the 1979 overthrow of the Somoza dynasty.

Table 10.2
Latin American agrarian reforms

Country	Year initiated and modified	Beneficiaries as percentage of rural households[a]		Percentage of affected forest and agricultural surface[b]	Organization of production[c]
Cuba	1959, 1963	70 (1963)			SF, IH, CO
Mexico	1917, 1971	69 (1971)	42.9 (1970)	43.4 (1970)	Ejidos
Peru	1963, 1969	37 (1975)	30.4 (1982)	39.3 (1982)	CO and some IH
Bolivia	1952	33 (1970)	74.5 (1977)	83.4 (1977)	IH
Nicaragua	1979, 1981	30 (1983)			SF, IH, CO
Chile	1962, 1970	20 (1973)	9.2 (1982)	10.2 (1982)	Asentamientos
Venezuela	1960	17 (1970)	30.6 (1979)	19.3 (1979)	IH, CO
El Salvador	1980	12 (1983)	22.7 (1985)	21.8 (1985)	IH, CO
Colombia	1961, 1973	10 (1975)			IH, CO
Costa Rica	1961	9 (1975)	5.4 (1980)	7.1 (1980)	IH, CO
Honduras	1962, 1975	8 (1978)			IH, CO
Ecuador	1964, 1973	7 (1972)	10.4 (1983)	9.0 (1983)	IH, CO
Dominican Republic	1962	3 (1970)	8.5 (1983)	14.0 (1983)	IH, CO
Panama	1968		13.3 (1977)	21.9 (1977)	IH, CO

a. Total number of beneficiaries until the year in parentheses divided by number of rural households in that year.
b. Affected area until year in parentheses.
c. SF, state farms; IH, Individual holdings; CO, cooperatives.
Sources: C. D. Deere, "Rural Women and State Policy: The Latin American Agrarian Reform Experience," *World Development* 13, 9 (1985); W. Thiesenhusen, ed., *Searching for Agrarian Reform in Latin America* (Winchester, Mass.: Unwin Hyman, 1989).

The Sandinista regime turned the Somoza family's holdings, covering more than a fifth of the country's arable land, into state farms and gave peasants access to idle land.

Throughout the twentieth century, populist regimes in Latin America have used the land reform issue as a means of building a constituency, but few have delivered on their promises. In the 1960s, the Alliance for Progress preached land reform as an alternative to revolution, partly out of fear that Castro's rural guerrilla base might be duplicated elsewhere.

In recent years, reform programs in Latin America seem to have lost momentum. Chilean president Eduardo Frei's reform picked up when Salvador Allende came into office. After 1973, the military regime put an end to expropriations, returned a third of expropriated land to former owners, and privately auctioned another third. In Peru, land expropriations were suspended after 1975, and beginning in 1981, the cooperatives were subdivided into individual holdings. In Colombia, a political agreement between the Conservative and Liberal parties officially ended land expropriations and initiated programs of rural development. In Honduras, the military government increasingly backed away from implementing the land reform law and used repression to control land invasions.

Venezuela provides an example of land reform that involved very little conflict, mainly because there were few economic constraints. The bulk of redistributed land came from fertile but undeveloped frontier land held by the government. Some large estates were taken over by peasants in the late 1950s and redistributed to them, but tension between estate owners and peasants was mitigated by the Venezuelan government's ability to compensate landowners for expropriated land. The upper limit on the amount of land that can be held in one estate remains high, and productive farms are rarely disturbed. In effect, land reform has mainly been a program of colonization. Land reform served as a welfare program for the poor who would have otherwise missed out entirely on the oil boom.

So far, Brazilian policymakers have sought an easy solution to the land reform issue by promoting colonization of the Amazon. Development of the Amazon region in the 1970s, aided by the construction of the Transamazon highway network, was initially intended to help relocate landless peasants from the northeast and *minifundistas* from the south. The intent in 1972 was to provide smallholders with access to land, housing, credit, transportation, warehouses, technical assistance, and education. In implementation, small farmers did not have clear priority over large, commercial operations. The land reform agency failed to establish title to new plots efficiently, making it difficult for colonists to obtain credit. Those who did obtain credit planted rice, beans, or corn, but the soil of the region could not sustain continuous tillage of these crops. Erosion of roads and long distances made marketing the output difficult. By 1973, the government was already shifting priorities toward large commercial farming. By heavily subsidizing livestock operations, the government created a situation in which the most profitable activity for peasants was to deforest land and sell it to ranchers (box 10.1).

There are examples of successful colonization in other parts of Brazil, especially in the northwest region of the state of Paraná. Although government intervention in the agricultural frontier was inefficient, where it was absent, conflicts multiplied and occupation took place in the form of large *latifundia*.

The Sarney government's land reform envisioned the expropriation of 67.2 million acres between 1985 and 1988, to benefit 900,000 families. Only 4.7 million acres were expropriated, benefiting 40,395 families. In 1988, after going through six administrators in three years, the reform agency was closed. The 1988 constitution made land reform more difficult, requiring full payment in bonds protected from inflation and limiting expropriation to "nonproductive" land. The definition of productive land will be the subject of future legislation.

While most Latin American countries have had nominal land reform programs, very little land in the region has actually been affected by it. With rapid urbanization in the past three decades, promises of land reform have become less central to political campaigns than they once were. From the perspective of peasants who remain in the countryside, the issue has not been resolved. Roughly 60 percent of Latin America's poorest people still live in rural areas. Land reform may be the most effective tool in helping these people to survive because it distributes assets that outlive government jobs programs and inflation-prone minimum wage fiats. The experiences of Bolivia, Mexico, and Peru are outlined.

Box 10.1
Deforestation

As everyone with a taste for Rainforest Crunch ice cream knows, the forests of Latin America are disappearing fast. The main culprits are livestock ranching, small-scale slash-and-burn agriculture, fuelwood gathering, logging, mining, road building (which makes other destructive activities possible), dams, and other large projects.

In Central America, deforestation is proceeding at an extraordinary pace as high population growth rates in these rural societies collide with limited resources. A burgeoning peasant population is relegated to small plots on hillsides, where erosion quickly washes away soil nutrients. Flat, fertile lands are the province of large-scale ranchers and commercial farmers. Forests are also tapped for fuelwood in these poor countries. Even Costa Rica, known for its success in creating national parks, has had one of the highest rates of deforestation in the region.

Amazonian deforestation has been more complex: goldminers descend on indigenous lands like locusts, hydroelectric dams must flood huge tracts because of the flat terrain, heavy subsidies have made cattle ranching economically feasible, and the extreme concentration of land tenure in the rest of Brazil has pushed landless peasants onto the marginal land of the Amazon.

Among the solutions, environmental economists suggest the following:

• Improved titling, making deforestation unnecessary to secure property rights.

• The development of markets for exotic woods and rainforest products to create an incentive for forest management.

• An expansion of nature tourism.

• The promotion of debt-for-nature swaps.

Land reform and the creation of urban jobs are the key steps toward saving the forest, but both require financing. If the rest of the world wants the Amazon as its botanical gardens, it will have to pay for preservation.

Bolivia

Land reform in Bolivia followed the revolution of 1952. Urban political organization in the late 1940s spilled over into the countryside, where peasant revolts erupted under the leadership of rural unions. Before the revolution, most haciendas were inefficient semifeudal operations encompassing an entire indigenous community. Part of the hacienda land was assigned to peasants for their own use in exchange for work on the main estate. In most cases, capitalization was minimal. With the revolution, haciendas were expropriated and redistributed to peasants. An attempt was made to keep some of the estate land in communal hands alongside separate smallholdings, but cooperative production did not function long. Land reform largely involved the allocation of title to peasants who had already operated as small-scale producers.

Land reform had an important impact on income distribution but did not dramatically change the structure of agricultural production. What did change was the extent of marketed agricultural output reaching urban areas. Free to consume their own output and unaccustomed to market transactions, peasants engaged in subsistence farming. The 1950s were characterized by food shortages throughout urban areas. Shortages also may have been the consequence of government policies during these hyperinflationary years. Within a decade, however, strong gains in output were already evident. By 1970, the output of potatoes, the main crop of the Altiplano, had more than tripled. Nonetheless, the agricultural sector in Bolivia still lags behind the rest of the continent, as does the rest of its economy.

By 1970, 80 percent of farmland in Bolivia had been affected by reform, providing benefits to a third of the rural population (table 10.3). In fact, in the early 1950s, half of the rural population benefited from land reform, but population growth has since reduced this proportion. In addition to freeing peasants to increase their own harvests in place of fulfilling their obligation to the *hacenderos*, land reform opened the rural area to opportunities for modernization. Reform made it possible to introduce education in rural communities where *hacenderos* had prohibited it. Land title provided an incentive for land improvement that was lacking under the more tenuous land assignments of the hacienda.

Table 10.3
Changes in size distribution of landholdings, Bolivia, 1923–1970
(percentage of total)

	Prereform, 1923		Postreform, 1970	
	Holdings	Area	Holdings	Area
Private farms				
Less than 5 hectares	60	0.2	14	0.2
5–100 hectares	26	1.4	6	1
100–1,000 hectares	7	6.0	1	3
Over 1,000 hectares	6	92.0	1	65
Land reform beneficiaries			78	30

Source: Shlomo Eckstein, Gordon Donald, Douglas Horton, and Thomas Carroll, *Land Reform in Latin America: Bolivia, Chile, Mexico, Peru and Venezuela*, Staff Working Paper, no. 275 (Washington, D.C.: World Bank, 1978).

The Bolivian government provided little assistance in the form of credit or capital improvements. To the extent that the central government has directed resources into improving the domestic food supply, the bulk of it has gone into opening up new lands in the tropical lowlands where large estates have reemerged along with an expansion of peasant-held smallholdings.[4]

One interesting consequence of land reform in Bolivia is that peasants have a vested interest in cocaine policy. Historically, coca was produced both by haciendas and indigenous *ayllus*, though not quite on an equal footing. With land reform, the coca plots of the haciendas were redistributed to small producers. The crop had never benefited from large-scale production but from the ability of hacienda owners to finance construction of terraces for new plots. Small-scale cultivation was the rule. Land reform fostered the distribution of relatively small plots to the peasants.

Although the bulk of the revenues from cocaine accrue to middlemen in the smuggling chain, small coca leaf producers earn more than they would producing most other agricultural goods. The unions, organized to initiate demands for land reform in the 1950s, have since become centers of peasant activism on the drug issue. Thousands of small coca producers protest any effort to restrict coca production.

The interaction between land reform and cocaine production in Bolivia shows that poorly educated peasants, given access to markets and the right financial incentives, rationally choose marketable crops over subsistence crops. In recent years, however, Bolivian peasants have experienced a sudden drop in the price of the cash crop. With a glut of cocaine in world markets, Bolivian peasants were earning $20 per hundred pounds of coca in 1988, compared to $350 in 1984, a drop in income of more than 90 percent.

Mexico

Mexico's land reform program has been the most extensive in the region. It is also the oldest. The strength of Zapata's movement during the revolution forced urban leaders to incorporate land reform into the 1917 Constitution, but implementation of substantial reform did not actually occur until the Cárdenas administration came to power in the 1930s. Close to half of the cropland in the country was affected by reform under Cárdenas. Following his administration, the pace of land reform slowed and even suffered some reversal in the 1940s. Peasant activism spurred a renewal of land reform in the early 1960s, and the Echeverria administration made a short-lived attempt at reviving it again in the mid-1970s. As campaign rhetoric, the imagery of revolutionary momentum in the countryside still seems to work.

The Mexican system of land reform is based on the constitutional recognition of community rights to land. These had been torn from indigenous communities by the Conquest and, more specifically, by a 1856 law that made a dramatic increase in land concentration possible. Land reform established *ejidos*, communal property rights on land expropriated from large estates. Depending on government decree, this land was to be farmed collectively or by individual members of the community. Under no circumstances were collective property rights to be alienated by assigning title to private individuals.

For the most part, the result was de facto subdivision of expropriated land among *ejido* members. Access to the land is passed between generations (an *ejiditario's* children can inherit his access to land), but actual title remains in the community. Some *ejidos* were set up for collective farming by the Cárdenas administration and still survive, but these are exceptions rather than the rule. For the most part, plots are farmed individually. The communal nature of most *ejidos* has been limited to shared pastures and occasional efforts by *ejiditarios* to pool their resources in using equipment.

The land subject to reform was first selected on the basis of community petitions to recognize historical rights to land within a 7-kilometer radius of their town. Hacienda owners were permitted to keep up to 300 hectares of cropland, depending on its use, with a 100-hectare limit on irrigated land. Since in principle the land was not rightfully theirs, estate owners were not compensated, a fact that helps to explain the backlash against land reform in the 1940s. Even under Cárdenas, however, landowners did at least benefit from generous credit subsidies intended to promote modernization on large estates.

As land reform progressed, it became apparent that expropriated land close to towns could not sustain large peasant populations unless the productivity of existing farms was sacrificed. Land reform was extended to areas farther from towns and efforts were made to bring uncultivated land into the *ejido* system. Government investment in irrigation was especially important in bringing new regions into production, although not all of this land was devoted to the reform sector.

Particularly after the Cárdenas administration left power, legislation was introduced to make it easier for large landowners to secure guaranteed property rights. Land already in use was increasingly left untouched by reform. This meant that except where the government brought new land into production through irrigation, much of the land incorporated into the reform sector was of relatively low productivity. Between 1952 and 1982, 85 percent of the land distributed to the peasantry was said to be unsuitable for crop farming.[5] This may be an exaggeration, but it does imply that low productivity in the reform sector may be as much a problem of land quality as of land tenure.

The issue of what land is subject to reform is still unsettled. As late as 1981, a new law was put into effect providing for the seizure of idle land, although the definition of idle land was not clearly defined, and *amparos agrarios* (injunctions that indefinitely postpone expropriation) are widely used to spare politically savvy landowners. The same law provided cattlemen with immunity from land reform, although again the terminology was somewhat vague, since it exempted farmers even if cattle ranching accounted for only a small portion of their activity. In practice, there was very little redistribution of land in the 1980s.

Despite the slowdown in reform, the extent of land reform is evident in the fact that 51 percent of the cropland in the country was held in *ejidos* by 1971. Moreover, *ejiditarios* constituted two-thirds of the rural population. Reform was far more extensive than anywhere else in Latin America (table 10.4).

In spite of—or perhaps because of—land reform, dualism in Mexican agriculture is striking. Large farms continue to comprise roughly half of the irrigated land in the country and produce 70 percent of the country's marketable food. They also account for almost all agricultural exports, including tomatoes, strawberries, melons, and flowers, although these are not inherently large-scale crops. By contrast, the *ejido* sector and *non-ejido* peasant farming have generally remained backward. *Ejidatarios* tend to sow their land with corn and beans; some 85 percent of peasant farmers grow corn. While most sell a portion of their harvest for cash, they depend directly on their milpas for food.

Government policy has contributed to this dualism. The prerevolution trend toward commercial farming was barely affected by land reform in the 1930s, and government policy since then has actively promoted modernization. After World War II, agricultural exports were seen as an important source of foreign exchange to

Table 10.4

Changes in size distribution of landholdings, Mexico, 1923–1970 (percentage of total)

	Prereform, 1923		Postreform, 1970	
	Holdings	Area	Holdings	Area
Private farms				
Less than 5 hectares	59	1	18	1
5–100 hectares	32	5	11	6
100–1,000 hectares	7	12	2	15
Over 1,000 hectares	2	82	0.3	32
Ejidatarios	0	0	69	46

Source: Ibid.

finance import substitution industrialization. Although macro-economic policies ran counter to agricultural expansion, public investment in the sector stimulated export production. The United States provided a large market for winter vegetables, citrus crops, cotton, soy, oil seeds, and sorghum, all of which depend on irrigation. A massive irrigation effort started in 1946, leading to a ninefold increase in agricultural exports within a decade. Although *ejiditarios* also benefited from irrigation, government credit and price supports favored large commercial farmers.

On the *ejido* side, several factors have worked against rapid growth. First, the absence of title to the land has prevented *ejiditarios* from using private credit markets since they are unable to collateralize their loans. The government is the exclusive source of credit for the reform sector. As such, it exercises a surprisingly active control over the type of crops grown by *ejiditarios*. It also influences the technology employed by favoring credit for seed over financing for capital improvements. While the bureaucracy established to provide credit to *ejiditarios* is immense, the actual funding for credit does not adequately meet the needs of the reform sector. Credit rationing is evident in the large proportion of applicants for credit who are turned away.

Many *ejido* producers are not well integrated into the market-place, which further cuts into their land productivity. Not only are they poorly connected to international networks for marketing strawberries or tomatoes, but many are quite isolated from urban markets. A major problem in getting small producers to use hybrid corn was their inability to buy seed annually. Because hybrid versions do not yield productive seeds whereas traditional strains retain their quality, the latter were more reliable.

Size has also been a factor; most *ejido* plots are less than 10 hectares, and some are only 1 hectare. This small size precludes investment that might not only save labor but raise yields. Coop-erative pooling of land could conceivably help *ejidatarios* take advantage of scale economies, but the difficulty of obtaining credit undermines this. Since the law prohibits the sale of *ejido* plots, commercial farmers have not swallowed up the reform sector. Illegal rental of land is common among peasants who supplement their income with urban jobs, but this has not led to de facto consolidation of *ejido* land.

While output in the reform sector has grown slowly, land reform has been the cornerstone of the government's rural welfare policies. Government subsidization of corn production provides an important injection of income into the peasant community. Mexican land reform has been accused of doing little more than keeping the poor out of the cities. Yet to the extent that the program has given some 2 million peasants an option preferable to a marginal existence in the cities, it has helped them.

In general, land reform did not retard Mexican agricultural growth. After the bulk of reform in the 1930s, value-added in agriculture grew at 4.6 percent per year between 1940 and 1960, compared to an average growth rate of 2.7 percent for Latin America. The slowdown in growth rates of Mexican agriculture in the 1960s and 1970s (3.9 percent and 3.4 percent, respectively) was more attributable to macroeconomic policy than to problems arising from land reform. Exchange rate policies, credit allocation, and the government's emphasis on industrialization undercut agricultural producers. Growth was also undercut by the rapidly increasing costs of extending irrigated land in the north for vegetables and Green Revolution wheat.

Both the political power of the peasantry and the need to address the fact that some 4 million rural Mexicans still seek land force the government to pay lip-service to expansion of land reform. Yet with a limited amount of land to distribute, there is little chance that the government will be able to satisfy the demands of this growing population. As the urban population grows too, pressure mounts to modernize the reform sector and increase its output of marketable food. For now, there are few resources available for the irrigation and credit necessary to raise peasant productivity.

Peru

The Peruvian land reform provides an example of collective farming in a nonsocialist context.[6] Implemented in 1969 by the military government of Juan Velasco Alvarado, the program incorporated a surprisingly radical emphasis on cooperatives.

For two decades prior to the reform, tension had been building in the peasant community. On political grounds, reform was motivated by a desire to quell an incipient guerrilla movement and to reduce the rural oligarchy's political power. From an economic perspective, reform was adopted in an attempt to reverse deteriorating conditions in the agricultural sector. Per capita agricultural output had been dropping at a rate of 2 percent per year between 1962 and 1969, and agricultural exports, which had provided half of the country's foreign exchange after World War II, no longer exceeded agricultural imports.

Peru has the lowest arable land per capita ratio in Latin America. It has three distinct geographical regions: the coast, the highlands, and the jungle. Land reform affected the coast and the highlands.[7]

In the highlands, which contained three-quarters of the country's agricultural land and two-thirds of the agrarian population at the time of reform, traditional haciendas existed alongside *minifundios*. Haciendas tended to concentrate in livestock or in crop cultivation. The dominant crops were potatoes, barley, wheat, and corn. Idle land on large estates was common, while *minifundistas* overworked their land. Within the haciendas, workers received access to land or rights to graze individually owned livestock in exchange for labor on the main estate.

The coast, less densely populated, produced nearly half of agricultural value-added. Large commercial plantations employing wage labor had been the norm. Sugar, cotton, rice, and corn were the dominant crops. Most coastal land was irrigated and considerable private investment had been attracted to the area.

The military government started by expropriating the most profitable corporate plantations in the coastal area, thus demonstrating their determination to liquidate the rural oligarchy. Expropriations in the highlands came later but followed the same pattern.

The massive land redistribution that the government had hoped to complete by 1975 fell somewhat behind schedule, but by mid-1979 the reform was broadly completed (table 10.5). Despite the reform, the land tenure situation in 1972 looked very similar to that in 1961 (table 10.6), for two reasons. First, the expropriated estates were not subdivided but reorganized as Cooperativas Agrárias de Producción (CAPs), functioning as large-scale, integrated cooperatives. Second, sharecropping and renting were forbidden. Peasants who rented land were given the legal title to the land they worked, but for census purposes, these units remained intact.

Table 10.5
Targets and accomplishments of land reform, Peru, 1975–1979

	Expropriation		Adjudication	
	Area (hectares)	Farm units	Area (hectares)	Families
Target	10,150	14,494	10,150	400,000
Accomplished December 1975	7,426	9,740	6,210	254,000
Mid-1979	10,500	15,826	7,800	337,662

Sources: Tom Alberts, *Agrarian Reform and Rural Poverty: A Case Study of Peru* (Boulder, Colo.: Westview Press, 1983); Cristobal Kay, "Achievements and Contradictions of the Peruvian Agrarian Reform," *Journal of Development Studies* 18, no. 1 (January 1982): 141–170.

Table 10.6
Land tenure, Peru, 1961–1972

	Production units		Area	
Size (hectares)	1961	1972	1961	1972
	(percent of total)		(percent)	
Less than 1	34.7	34.8	0.7	0.8
1–5	48.2	43.2	5.1	5.8
5–20	12.8	16.7	5.0	8.6
20–100	2.9	4.3	5.4	9.3
More than 100	13.0	11.0	60.1	54.3

Source: Alberts, *Agrarian Reform.*

In the coastal area, the government expropriated corporate plantations in their entirety and turned them over to workers for collective management. Production techniques—determined mainly by the existing capital structure—remained in place. Workers gained nominal control over management, which substantially reduced the harsh discipline that had been in place before reform. The extent of self-management is subject to debate, however. The state played an important role in providing administrative oversight and, when deemed necessary, intervened militarily to bring striking workers back into line. Furthermore, the state controlled the prices of sugar, cotton, and rice and monopolized their marketing. Between 1969 and 1977, wages rose considerably as workers appropriated profits from the plantation and output increased. However, a combination of drought, mismanagement, and a steep drop in international sugar, cotton, and rice prices has debilitated the cooperatives since then.

Beginning in 1981, the CAPs in the coastal region began to subdivide into individual holdings. By 1986, parcelation had extended to three-fourths of coastal CAPs (table 10.7 illustrates this process in two valleys). Significant economic changes took place: clearer work incentives, loss of insurance implicit in joint ownership, and a scale of operation smaller than optimal for some indivisible inputs.[8] CAP members' evaluation of the process has been positive. Social evaluation is ambiguous, however. Proponents of the change say a more productive and still egalitarian agricultural sector is appearing. Opponents doubt the feasibility of small-scale agriculture and believe that the process will lead in the end to inequitable land reconcentration or to a proliferation of low-produc-

Table 10.7
Change in agrarian structure with parcelations in Peru, 1980–1986 (percentages)

Farm size	1980		1986	
(hectares)	Farm units	Area	Farm units	Area
Valley of Canete				
Less than 3 hectares	84.2	13.2	63.2	13.2
3–10 hectares	11.7	19.2	33.9	63.8
10–50 hectares	3.4	15.4	2.5	15.4
More than 50 hectares	0.4	7.6	0.3	7.6
CAPs	0.3	44.6	0.0	0.0
Valley of Chincha				
Less than 3 hectares	86.5	14.0	74.5	14.0
3–10 hectares	11.6	17.5	24.0	52.0
10–50 hectares	1.4	10.5	1.2	10.5
More than 50 hectares	0.3	10.5	0.3	10.5
CAPs	0.2	47.5	0.04	13.0

Source: Michael Carter and Elena Alvarez, "Changing Paths: The Decollectivization of Agrarian Reform Agriculture in Coastal Peru," in Thiesenhusen, *Searching for Agrarian Reform.*

tivity *minifundios*. Currently the impact of parcelation on productivity and on income distribution is unclear.

In the highlands, the long-run goal was also to establish collective farms, but in fact reform quickly turned toward subdivision. Peasants resisted losing the small plots that they had tilled on the haciendas and on livestock ranches and balked at the idea of losing their right to own livestock individually. The result was an attempt to maintain individual plots and herding rights while developing cooperative production on the main estates. Even this was not very successful, although the livestock cooperatives fared better than crop-oriented haciendas. Whereas there were economies of scale to be sustained by cooperative production on the coast, the terrain of the highlands offered few efficiency benefits from centralization. Any effort performed for the highland cooperative came at the expense of productivity on one's own plot. The tension between private and community goals made collective production untenable. Postreform growth rates were considerably lower in the highlands than along the coast, attributable partly to government policy, which favored the coast for its production of exports and food for urban markets over subsistence farming in the sierra.

Peruvian agricultural performance since the reform cannot be called a success. In the postreform period, agricultural value-added continued to grow at the same low rates as before. Yet reform alone does not seem to account for the stagnation. Prices of most agricultural goods have been so closely linked to government pricing schemes that is hard to separate the impact of land reform from other agricultural policies. The military's import substitution industrialization strategy discriminated against the agricultural sector by penalizing agricultural exports through the exchange rate policy, imposing price controls, and subsidizing food imports, thereby reducing profitability and investment in the agricultural sector.

The distributional effects of this reform effort are interesting. Landowners unambiguously lost; they were paid for expropriated land, but the military cleverly based the value of the land on assessments made by the landowners themselves in paying 1968 land taxes. Compensation was made partly in cash and partly in bonds that quickly lost their value through inflation.

The main beneficiaries were the members of cooperatives on the coast, who enjoyed higher wages, and the peasants, who received access to more land in the highlands. Two groups of poor Peruvians gained little or even lost: highland workers who had not been tenants on haciendas received little land and temporary workers on the coast found it harder to get work because cooperative members resisted paying outside labor or paid low wages. The nonbeneficiaries actually account for a large proportion of the rural population. About 40 percent of the country's land was adjudicated to 35 percent of agrarian families; land reform did not ameliorate poverty among the remaining two-thirds of the rural population.

3 LESSONS

Land reform schemes in Latin America have not been unqualified successes. Policymakers and researchers quickly pronounced them a failure or, at least, passé. Their assessment is questionable, however. In economic terms, land reform was lackluster. Farmers had few means to increase production; limited access to credit and research, as well as unfavorable prices, reduced whatever stimulus emerged from access to land. In political terms, however, land reform has been relatively successful. In Bolivia and Mexico, land reform pacified the countryside and clearly contributed to political stability in Mexico. Peru is the exception.

Peru failed in both economic and political terms. Land reform not only failed to stimulate production and eradicate rural poverty, but it also failed to pacify the countryside. Its failure can be blamed in part on the weaknesses of the reform program, but mostly it reflects the bad economic policies of the military regime and their successors. The cooperative model also contributed to the poor results. The large-scale cooperatives met with opposition from the peasantry. Imposed from above, they were perceived as a constraint by those they were supposed to benefit. Giving land to tenants and peasant communities would have removed a source of rural conflict. The Peruvian experience is a reminder that land reform is not sufficient for rural development unless it is accompanied by proper price, marketing, credit, and investment policies.

Three lessons stand out in assessing land reform. First, in most countries the amount of underutilized land is in short supply. Reallocating land in use carries a cost: less food is likely to be marketed to urban areas and fewer export crops grown. This price may be worth paying but not without preparing for the consequences. Generally land reform has been most successful from an efficiency perspective when it has involved the takeover of traditional, inefficient haciendas or the colonization of undeveloped land. There is not much sacrificed in this situation, and peasants eager for land are quick to put it into use. Where the land has not been aggressively developed by its owners, reform has catalyzed a move toward greater efficiency on reserve acreage as large farmers look for ways to justify their claim to the land. The takeover of commercial farms is most difficult; the transition period is damaging due to decapitalization, and existing managerial efficiency is difficult to duplicate. Even in Nicaragua, where political conditions were ripe for radical land reform in the early 1980s, many commercial farms were left untouched as long as they continued to operate efficiently.

Second, redistribution of land tends to help the better off among the poor. The most destitute often lack the social connections to get an individual plot of land or are not employed to qualify as members of a collective. While land reform is often motivated by welfare concerns for the rural poor (as well as a desire to quell peasant activism), the very poorest campesinos are often not its beneficiaries. Land tends to be distributed to those who know how to work with the authorities, who can get their name on the right list and who have some influence in the community. At the same time, in the process of consolidating their estates, landowners lay off workers, creating a class of unemployed workers who are in a weak position to get land. As a welfare measure, land reform should be accompanied by programs that target the very poor.[9]

Finally, land reform works best when it is accompanied by generous credit and technical assistance from the government. It is not a cost-free solution to rural poverty. Often expectations for land reform go far beyond what is possible. Governments can proclaim a change in ownership at little fiscal cost (except a loss of political support among landowners), but credit and technical assistance to help land reform succeed are expensive. Past experience with land reform programs has demonstrated that capitalization and market stability are important if small farmers are to participate in the modernization of agriculture. Without credit, adequate irrigation and transportation networks, and reliable markets, access to a small piece of land may be only marginally better than the alternatives open to the rural poor.

Even under the best circumstances, land reform usually fails to absorb the rapidly growing rural population common to most developing countries. A long-run solution to rural poverty must include an expansion of job opportunities in the cities.

What role can land reform play in Latin America? History shows that massive land reform is unlikely except in periods of extreme upheaval. Even then, revolutionaries are increasingly hesitant about promoting sweeping changes in rural property rights. Realistic discussion of land reform in Latin America's countries must presume that the scope of reform is likely to be narrow. In Brazil, there is certainly room for regulating the occupation of the agricultural frontier by setting a limit on the size of future land sales by the government to private enterprises, and even a limited land reform can serve as an important mechanism for easing rural poverty.

What model? Collectives have proved themselves too unwieldy despite their theoretical advantages. Subdivision provides gains that are more sustainable in the long run. Allocation of title to individuals helps establish a more stable division of responsibilities and property rights between the state and peasant. As we have seen, land reform does not necessarily bring long-run agricultural stagnation. Yet if beneficiaries are to participate in modernization, they must have access to credit and markets. A successful land reform program thus requires financing for both the initial compensation of landowners and long-run provision of credit and assistance to beneficiaries.

Where will the money come from? Land taxation should be enforced through better administration, and tax evaders should suffer penalties, including suspension of banking credit and jail. International agencies with an antipoverty agenda can perhaps use debt-for-nature swaps as a model to set up debt-for-land-reform swaps. Latin Americans themselves must take on responsibility for the bulk of the cost. In a region that has made only limited efforts to redistribute income in times of both plenty and want, a few steps forward in land reform is not asking too much. Even a limited land reform could reduce poverty.

FURTHER READING

Eckstein, S., G. Donald, D. Horton, and T. Carroll. *Land Reform in Latin America: Bolivia, Chile, Mexico, Peru and Venezuela.* Staff Working Paper, no. 275. Washington, D.C.: World Bank, 1978.

Redclift, M. "Sustainability and the Market: Survival Strategies on the Bolivian Frontier." *Journal of Development Studies* 23 (October 1986): 93–105.

Sanderson, S. *The Transformation of Mexican Agriculture.* Princeton: Princeton University Press, 1986.

Thiesenhusen, W., ed. *Searching for Agrarian Reform in Latin America.* Winchester, Mass.: Unwin Hyman, 1989.

Appendix A

GROWTH AND COMPOSITION OF EXPORTS AND IMPORTS

Table A.1
Growth rate of exports, Latin America compared to other regions
(annual percentage change in dollar value)

	1955–1960	1961–1965	1966–1970	1971–1975	1976–1980	1981–1985
Latin America[a]	1.6	4.7	7.1	20.4	20.0	-1.0
Asia[b]	4.4	2.3	6.1	25.7	24.1	4.3
Industrial countries	7.5	8.4	11.8	20.9	16.9	0.3
World	6.3	7.6	10.9	23.1	18.1	-1.0

a. Includes Caribbean countries.
b. Includes India and China.
Source: International Monetary Fund, *International Financial Statistics, Supplement on Trade* (Washington, D.C.: IMF, 1988).

Table A.2
Growth rate of imports, Latin America compared to other regions
(annual percentage change in dollar value)

	1955–1960	1961–1965	1966–1970	1971–1975	1976–1980	1981–1985
Latin America[a]	2.2	2.9	9.5	24.9	16.5	-8.5
Asia[b]	6.7	3.2	6.6	24.5	21.6	4.7
Industrial countries	6.7	9.0	11.6	21.0	18.4	-0.2
World	6.2	7.6	10.8	22.5	18.4	-0.6

a. Includes Caribbean countries.
b. Includes India and China.
Source: Ibid.

Table A.3
Composition of Latin American exports, 1960–1989

	1960–1965	1974–1979
Foodstuffs and raw materials	63.0	44.6
Fuels	26.5	36.5
Manufactures	10.0	18.5
Others	0.5	0.4

Note: Includes Caribbean countries.
Source: Economic Commission for Latin America, *Statistical Yearbook for Latin America* (Santiago: United Nations, various issues).

Table A.4
Composition of Latin American imports, 1960–1989

	1960–1965	1974–1979
Foodstuffs and raw materials	18.2	13.4
Fuels	7.0	23.6
Manufactures	73.0	61.2
Machinery and Transportation Equipment	(37.8)	(32.3)
Others	1.8	1.8

Note: Includes Caribbean countries.
Source: Ibid.

Table A.5
Regional groupings in Latin America

	Members
LAIA (Latin American Integration Association; Latin American Free Trade Association, 1960–1980)	Argentina, Bolivia, Brazil, Chile, Colombia, Ecuador, Mexico, Paraguay, Peru, Uruguay, Venezuela
AG (Cartagena Agreement, Andean Group)	Bolivia, Chile,[a] Colombia, Ecuador, Peru, Venezuela
CACM (Central American Common Market)	Costa Rica, El Salvador, Guatemala, Honduras,[b] Nicaragua

a. Withdrew October 1976.
b. Withdrew January 1971.

Appendix B
DEBT RATIOS

Table B.1
Share of 1988 debt in total debt of developing countries (percentage)

	Sub-Saharan Africa	East Asia and the Pacific	South Asia	Europe and the Mediter-ranean	Middle East and North Africa	Latin America and the Caribbean
1988	12	18	8	14	10	37

Source: World Bank, *World Debt Tables* (Washington, D.C.: World Bank, 1990).

Table B.2
Ratio of debt service to exports, Latin America and developing regions, 1980–1989 (percentage)

	Sub-Saharan Africa	East Asia and the Pacific	South Asia	Europe and the Mediter-ranean	Middle East and North Africa	Latin America and the Caribbean
1980	11	14	12	18	20	37
1982	19	18	15	20	21	48
1985	31	25	23	26	24	43
1988	27	20	27	27	38	41
1989[a]	28	17	28	28	38	40

a. Preliminary data
Source: Ibid.

Table B.3
Ratio of debt to exports, Latin America and developing regions, 1980–1989 (percent)

	Sub-Saharan Africa	East Asia and the Pacific	South Asia	Europe and the Mediter-ranean	Middle East and North Africa	Latin America and the Caribbean
1980	98	90	160	102	137	195
1982	182	115	207	120	146	269
1985	240	193	265	159	188	308
1988	361	109	276	139	286	311
1989[a]	369	94	270	153	259	297

a. Preliminary data
Source: Ibid.

Appendix C

RANKING COUNTRIES BY THEIR GINI INDEXES

Table C.1
Ranking of Latin American countries by size of Gini index

	Kakwani	Lecaillon
Costa Rica	1	2
Argentina	2	1
Chile	3	3
Mexico	4	8
Ecuador	5	9
El Salvador	6	6
Colombia	7	4
Panama	8	7
Venezuela	9	5

Note: Only countries appearing in both Kakwani and Lecaillon.
Source: Table 9.8.

Appendix D

LAND DISTRIBUTION

Table D.1
Percentage distribution of holdings and size of holdings, by share of total area, Asia and Latin America, circa 1970

	Asia[a]	South America[b]	Korea	Brazil	Colombia	El Salvador
Under 1 hectare						
% of holdings	52.6	15.7	66.9	8.0	22.9	56.6
% of area	9.9	0.2	53.1	0.1	0.4	4.8
1–10 hectares						
% of holdings	43.9	46.7	33.1	43.3	50.2	37.1
% of area	58.3	3.8	46.9	3.0	6.8	22.3
10–50 hectares						
% of holdings	3.4	25.3		32.4	18.5	5.0
% of area	25.8	11.7		12.4	15.1	23.6
50–100 hectares						
% of holdings	0.1	5.3		7.0	4.1	0.6
% of area	4.4	7.7		7.9	10.3	10.6
100–1,000 hectares						
% of holdings		6.3		8.4	4.0	0.6
% of area	0.6	34.3		37.0	37.0	30.2
Over 1,000 hectares						
% of holdings		0.6		0.9	0.3	
% of area	1.0	42.3		39.6	30.4	8.5

a. Asia: India, Indonesia, Iraq, Israel, Japan, Korea, Pakistan, Philippines, and Sri Lanka.
b. South America: Brazil, Colombia, Ecuador, Peru, Suriname, Uruguay, Venezuela.
Source: Food and Agriculture Organization of the United Nations, *1970 World Census of Agriculture* (Rome: FAO, 1981).

NOTES

CHAPTER 1

1. Mercantilism and the economics of the colonial period are explored in chapter 2.

2. Gross domestic product, (GDP) accounts for all final goods and services produced in a region during a period of time. The word *real* in front of GDP means that output is being measured at the prices of a base year. Changes in real GDP thus measure changes in quantities of goods and services produced in the period under consideration. Rising GDP also means rising incomes.

3. A nation's currency is overvalued if its goods cannot compete abroad with foreign goods and imports are inexpensive compared to domestic products. This usually leads to a deficit in the external accounts.

CHAPTER 2

1. Evangelism also motivated many of the conquistadors. The Catholic church had a profound effect on social values in the region and played an important but ambiguous role in the region's economic development. It protected indigenous groups from slavery but razed local religious temples to make room for costly churches. It encouraged passivity among the masses, but it also daringly criticized inequity.

2. Agriculture played an important role in early colonial exports as well, though less attention was paid to this sector by the crown.

3. Carlos Díaz-Alejandro, *Essays on the Economic History of the Argentine Republic* (New Haven: Yale University Press, 1970), estimated that GDP grew at an average annual rate of at least 5 percent during the half-century preceding 1914.

4. Warren Dean, *The Industrialization of S. Paulo* (Austin: University of Texas Press 1967), challenges this view, arguing that the war interrupted a period of strong growth in Brazil. Nonetheless, later work shows that during the war there was growth, based on fuller capacity utilization, in Brazil.

5. We provide a fuller discussion of exchange rates in chapter 4.

CHAPTER 3

1. The analysis of the enclave economy according to ECLA is very different from the neoclassical and dualistic representation of Latin American development exemplified by Jonathan Levin's *The Export Economies; Their Patterns of Development in Historical Perspective* (Cambridge, Mass.: Harvard University Press, 1960). In the dualistic interpretation, the external sector appears as a protuberance set off against an archaic or traditional sector. But given more time and a continuation of the market development, the system would become more uniform and modern. Dependency theory strongly criticized this view, showing that the relation between the modern and the traditional sectors was not one of separation but of complementarity. Social stratification and segmentation served to channel the economic surplus to the favored classes. They also contributed to reduce labor reproduction costs.

2. The typical mechanism used to capture part of the foreign firms' rent is a licensing fee. There is also the possibility of an increase in factor prices in the export industry (as foreign investors bid up factor costs over and above the level that can be sustained by a smaller-scale domestic export industry).

3. H. W. Singer, "The Distribution of Gains between Investing and Borrowing Countries," *American Economic Review* 40 (May 1950): 473–480.

4. Demand stimulation is not the primary motivation for most aid. It is typically justified in donor countries on the grounds of strategic interests and in recipient countries on the basis of resource needs, but economists who view demand stimulation as an important step toward growth also call for aid as a means of raising incomes and demand.

5. The decline in private investment and growth in debt-ridden countries does not come from austerity alone. The need to carry out an external transfer to creditors represents a source of uncertainty: carrying out the transfer in the future may require tax increases and changes in relative prices. Firms are cautious in their decisions to expand capacity under uncertainty, because investment today can lead to excess capacity tomorrow if circumstances change.

6. These programs can also be justified on the grounds of equity rather than productivity growth.

7. We discuss the related monetarist/structuralist debate in chapter 6.

8. Radical theories of Latin American dependency can also be classified as a distinct school.

9. See Hernando de Soto, *The Other Path: The Invisible Revolution in the Third World* (New York: Harper & Row, 1989).

CHAPTER 4

1. Figure 4.1 shows the ratio of exports and imports of goods to GDP. Table 4.1 shows the ratio of exports and imports of goods and services to GDP.

2. Unfortunately, almost as many sources measure exchange rates in peso/dollar terms as dollar/peso terms. When real exchange rates are measured in peso/dollar terms, the definition above is inverted, and real depreciation is measured by a rise in the real exchange rate.

3. Overvaluation, a separate concept, implies that the current exchange rate leads to unsustainable trade deficits. Real depreciation is an important mechanism in restoring external balance.

4. In contrast, a pragmatic exchange rate policy has prevented any comparable episodes in Brazil until recently.

5. The current account measures total receipts of domestic residents from other countries, less total payments by residents to other countries, for goods and services, including unilateral transfers. Current account deficits reflect an excess of expenditure over income.

6. Nontariff barriers and extensive bureaucratic intervention, with considerable opportunities for abuse, have also been part of the Japanese success story. Why they have been so much more debilitating in Latin America is an unanswered question.

7. C. Díaz-Alejandro, *Essays on the Economic History of the Argentine Republic* (New Haven: Yale University Press, 1970), 128.

8. World Bank, *Chile: An Economy in Transition* (Washington, D.C.: World Bank, 1979).

9. Were economies of scale the only barrier to international competitiveness, firms might have been expected to take the risk of expansion and export, but several factors intervened: overvaluation of exchange rates prevented competitiveness in international markets; high tariffs made domestic consumers a much more attractive market to target than the world market; access to imported inputs was controlled by governments and often subject to delays, preventing firms from meeting scheduled deliveries; Latin America did not achieve internationally competitive levels of quality control, perhaps due to lack of management skills; protectionism in indus-

trialized markets limited or threatened to limit Latin American access to wealthy countries, and ISI elsewhere in Latin America closed off neighboring markets; governments failed to provide assistance in identifying and reaching potential foreign markets (an important ingredient in the success of Asian exporters); and minimum wage rates raised labor costs, compounding the problems of excessive average fixed costs.

10. W., Baer, "Import Substitution and Industrialization in Latin America," *Latin American Research Review* 7, no. 1 (Spring 1972): 95–121.

11. Table A.5 shows regional groupings in Latin America.

CHAPTER 5

1. In their defense, it should be noted that developed countries like the United States also borrow to finance interest payments.

2. In terms of the identity above, this is equivalent to "involuntary interest capitalization."

3. Between 1873 and 1876, Honduras, Santo Domingo, Costa Rica, Paraguay, and Uruguay defaulted. Mexico, Ecuador, and Venezuela had already defaulted in the late 1860s. After a spectacular boom in guano, sugar, nitrates, and cotton, Peru's finances abruptly collapsed in 1876.

4. Chapter 2 offers more details on the crisis of the 1930s.

5. Between 1929 and 1932, Latin American exports had declined by 75 percent.

6. Since 1982, Mexico has had a dual exchange rate regime, with separate rates for commercial and capital transactions.

7. See J. Cuddington, "Capital Flight: Estimates, Issues and Explanations," *International Studies in International Finance*, no. 58 (1986).

8. Capital flight is a response to mismanagement, but it is also true that without the threat of capital flight, a government may be able to pursue policies that capital flight makes impossible.

9. The outlook was for real interest rates to average only 2 percent between 1984 and 1986 (using the U.S. GNP deflator to measure inflation). In fact, however, real rates averaged 5.4 percent through 1986.

10. The situation described in this paragraph is called debt overhang.

CHAPTER 6

1. The relationship is stronger for the high inflation countries. Monetarism also works better for averages taken over a long period. To explain inflation in the short run, we have to be much more eclectic.

2. Bond financing is not a problem-free alternative to the printing press. When real interest rates exceed domestic growth rates for a prolonged period of time, the increasing stock of domestic debt becomes a major cause of spending. In the end, the government might be forced to repudiate the debt or to create more inflation. One of the most important components of government spending in Latin America during the 1980s was interest payments on debt contracted during the 1970s. The large debts made fiscal consolidation very difficult, and thus most stabilization programs during the 1980s were condemned to fail.

3. Briefly, the Prebisch hypothesis is that primary product prices fail to keep up with prices of manufactured goods in the long run, implying that Latin America must industrialize to break the simplistic law of comparative advantage that restricts it to exporting primary goods.

4. Structuralists challenged monetarism by claiming that the high correlation between inflation and money growth does not imply that the direction of causality runs from money to prices. On the contrary, they would argue, it is inflation that makes for fast money growth. In the past, structuralists have been identified as the "money is passive" school. The assumption that monetary authorities accommodate shocks is different from endogeneity of money in orthodox models that comes either from the fact that the exchange rate is fixed or from the recognition of the interdependence of monetary and fiscal policies.

5. Dudley Seers, "Inflation and Growth: the Heart of the Controversy," in Werner Baer (Ed.), *Inflation and Growth in Latin America* (New Haven: Yale University Press, 1964), 89.

6. To be a bit more accurate, the seigniorage received by the government is the increase in the stock of high-powered money. In fact, however, the public also uses bank deposits as money. Thus, part of the increase in the public's holdings of money does not go to the government to finance the deficit. Commerical banks do not reap "seigniorage" if the banking system is perfectly competitive; in practice, however, they do benefit from inflation whenever interest rates on deposits lag the inflation rate.

7. If public sector prices are adjusted with delays, the budget deficit also increases. Latin American governments own telephone and electric companies, as well as a host of basic industries. For political reasons and in an attempt to reduce inflation, public firms are slow to raise prices.

8. Chapter 8 examines the Nicaraguan economy under the Sandinista rule.

9. But avoiding devaluation may also cause capital flight if the exchange rate is widely perceived as unsustainable.

10. *Wall Street Journal*, August 13, 1985.

11. Chapter 8 explores Peru's recent economic experience.

CHAPTER 7

1. Where governments own the main export sector, as in Venezuela, Chile (copper), Ecuador (oil), and Mexico (oil), a real devaluation increases government revenues in domestic currency.

2. Net transfers from official creditors to Latin America and the Caribbean were negative in 1987 and 1988. World Bank, *World Debt Tables 1989-90* (Washington, D.C.: World Bank, 1990), 96.

3. Cheryl Payer, *The Debt Trap* (New York: Monthly Review Press, 1975).

4. *New York Times*, March 2 and 3, 1989.

5. A discussion of formal and informal markets is found in chapter 9.

6. See Manuel Pastor, "The Effects of IMF Programs in the Third World: Debate and Evidence from Latin America," *World Development* 15 (February 1987): 249–262.

7. See Thomas Skidmore, "The Politics of Economic Stabilization in Postwar Latin America," in James Malloy, ed., *Authoritarianism and Corporatism in Latin America* (Pittsburgh: University of Pittsburgh Press, 1977).

8. See Karen Remmer, "The Politics of Economic Stabilization: IMF Standby Programs in Latin America, 1954–1984," *Comparative Politics* 18 (October 1986): 1–24.

9. See Joseph Ramos, *Neo-Conservative Economics in the Southern Cone of Latin America* (Baltimore: Johns Hopkins University Press, 1986).

10. Letter to the *New York Times*, April 14, 1980.

11. Monetary reforms in Europe in the 1940s also reduced the stock of money outstanding. The Latin American reforms of the 1980s did not go that far. In 1990, the Collor program (discussed at the end of this section) froze deposits temporarily.

12. Monetary reforms in Latin America prior to 1985 did not make use of *tablitas*, often because they did not involve price freezes. Among the earlier monetary reforms in Latin America were Brazil's introduction of the new cruzeiro in 1964, Chile's replacement of the escudo with the peso in 1975, and Argentina's conversion to new pesos in June 1983.

13. *Boston Globe*, April 27, 1989.

CHAPTER 8

1. T. Skidmore, and P. Smith, *Modern Latin America* (New York: Oxford University Press, 1984), 91.

2. D. Rock, "The Survival and Restoration of Perónism," in *Argentina in the Twentieth Century*, ed. D. Rock (Pittsburgh: University of Pittsburgh Press, 1975), 186.

3. J. Fodor, "Perón's Policies for Agricultural Exports, 1946–48: Dogmatism or Commonsense?" in *Argentina in the Twentieth Century*, 150.

4. Rock, "Survival and Restoration," 191.

5. See R. Dornbusch and S. Edwards, *Economic Populism in Latin America* (Chicago: Chicago University Press, 1991), and J. Sachs, *Social Conflict and Populist Policies in Latin America*, Working Paper, no. 2897 (Cambridge, Mass.: National Bureau of Economic Research, 1989).

6. R. Dornbusch, "Peru on the Brink," *Challenge* 31 (November–December 1988): 31–37.

7. World Bank, *Chile: An Economy in Transition* (Washington, D.C.: World Bank, 1979), 61-92.

CHAPTER 9

1. The absolute number of poor individuals in Latin America increased between 1970 and 1981 according to Sergio Molina, "Poverty: Description and Analysis of Policies for Overcoming It," *CEPAL Review*, no. 18 (December 1982). Brazil is certainly an exception. Despite its extremely unequal distribution, fast growth reduced the number of Brazilian poor significantly between 1960 and 1980. But Brazil saw their numbers increase again in the 1980s. The World Bank, *The World Development Report* 1990 (New York: Oxford University Press, 1990) contains information about changes in poverty in Brazil, Colombia and Costa Rica. Colombia and Costa Rica (together accounting for 8 percent of the population of Latin America) have made more progress in redistributing income and improving the lot of the poor than other countries in the region. In the two countries combined, the number of poor declined by 1.6 million people between 1971 and 1988. The number of poor in Latin America in 1985 was 70 million people (table 9.2).

2. In some countries, Brazil among them, it is enough to be able to write one's own name to be considered literate.

3. The Economic Commission for Latin America and the Caribbean reported in 1988 other indicators of rising hardship among the poor. In Brazil, the frequency of anemia among children of poor families increased in 1985 in

comparison with 1973–74. In Argentina, the need has arisen for a large-scale national food program administered by the Ministry of Health and Social Affairs. It consists of periodic distribution of food packages and social services. By 1985 it covered 5.5 million of the 30 million Argentines. In Mexico between 1982 and 1985, a sharp deterioration of real wages and drastic cuts in social expenditure impoverished the middle class and increased poverty. Illness and infant mortality were increasingly related to poor nutrition.

4. O. Altimir, *The Extent of Poverty in Latin America*, World Bank Staff Working Paper, no. 522 (Washington, D.C.: World Bank, 1982).

5. The alternative, relative poverty, is commonly measured by the percentage of the population living on less than half the median income. Relative poverty is clearly a measure of income distribution. In contrast, absolute indicators of poverty try to measure access to food, housing and education.

6. ECLAC, "Magnitud de la Pobreza en Ocho Paises de America Latina en 1986," document for the Proyecto Regional para la Superación de la Pobreza, mimeo. (June 1989).

7. Destitution or indigence is set at the cost of the food basket itself. Destitution provides no room for expenditure on nonfood items and does not allow for inefficient food purchases. In 1970, about one-fifth of all households in Latin America had incomes insufficient to pay for an adequate diet. In 1970, the extent of destitution (risk of severe nutritional deficiency) varied from 1 percent of the population in Argentina to 45 percent in Honduras. In 1986, the extent of destitution varied from 3 percent in Argentina to 49 percent in Guatemala.

8. In 1986 dollars, these poverty lines range from $393 per year in Honduras to $718 for Argentina. Multiplying this per capita income by four, Altimir's 1970 poverty line for a four-person family in Honduras would be $1,572 (1986 dollars). In the United States, the offical poverty line for a four-person family in 1986 was $11,203.

9. See A. Couriel, "Poverty and Underemployment in Latin America," *CEPAL Review*, no. 24 (1984): 39–62.

10. See ECLAC, "Magnitud de la Pobreza en Ocho Paises de America Latina en 1986."

11. M. Selowsky, *Balancing Trickle Down and Basic Needs Stategies: Income Distribution Issues in Large Middle-Income Countries with Special Reference to Latin America*, World Bank Staff Working Papers, no. 335 (Washington, D.C.: World Bank,1985).

12. United Nations, *Human Development Report 1990* (New York: Oxford University Press, 1990), 32.

13. Ibid., p. 143.

14. Hernando de Soto, *The Other Path: The Invisible Revolution in the Third World* (New York: Harper Row, 1989).

15. See Edgar Feige, "Defining and Estimating Underground and Informal Economies: The New Institutional Approach," *World Development* 18, no. 7 (1990).

16. Gini coefficients measure the extent to which income distribution deviates from equality. Higher Gini coefficients indicate greater inequality.

17. Samuel Morley, *Labor Markets and Inequitable Growth* (Cambridge: Cambridge University Press, 1982).

18. Different sources report different quintile shares and different Gini indices, but all of them are consistent with the assertion that there was a marked increase in inequality between 1960 and 1970 and that between 1970 and 1980 there was no significant change in inequality. An increase in concentration and Gini indices, between 1984 and 1987 is attributed to a redistribution from the middle classes to the upper classes.

19. See David Goodman, "Rural Economy and Society," in Edmar Bacha and Herbert Klein, eds., *Social Change in Brazil: The Incomplete Transition* (Albuquerque: University of New Mexico Press, 1989).

20. Miguel Urrutia, *Winners and Losers in Colombia's Economic Growth of the 1970s* (New York: Oxford University Press, 1985).

21. Ministerio de Agricultura y Departamento Nacional de Planeación, *El Desarrollo Agropecuário en Colombia, Informe Final: Misión de Estudios del Sector Agropecuário* (Bogotá: Editorial Presencia, 1990), cited by R. Albert Berry, "Colombian Agriculture in the 1980s," mimeo. (1990).

22. J. L. Londono, "Income Distribution in Colombia: Turning Points, Catching Up and Other Kuznetsian Ideas," mimeo. (Harvard University, 1989).

CHAPTER 10

1. Farmhand in Pernambuco, Brazil, *New York Times*, May 3, 1988.

2. See Roy Prosterman and Jeffrey Riedinger, *Land Reform and Democratic Development* (Baltimore: Johns Hopkins University Press, 1987).

3. From a pure efficiency point of view, it may be wiser to produce beef exports and import grains for local consumption. The problem is that earnings from large ranches are not equitably distributed to allow the landless to buy imported grain.

4. Whereas land reform dramatically reduced the number of large holdings in the sierra, policy has not discouraged land concentration in the east. Large land grants were made in the 1 '60s and 1970s, with the result that in 1981,

the largest 3 percent of holdings in the Santa Cruz area accounted for over half of the titled land. The fragile ecology of the jungle makes it difficult to sustain farming in one location without fertilizers. As a consequence, peasants entering the frontier tended to clear one plot, sell it—usually to a larger landowner—and clear another plot.

5. See A. Riding, *Distant Neighbors* (New York: Vintage Press, 1984).

6. The other lasting example of reorganization into collective farming is the Cuban land reform.

7. The eastern jungle, which has developed recently along the lines of modern commercial estates producing coffee, cocoa, and fruit, was not significantly affected by reform.

8. See Michael Carter and Elena Alvarez, "Changing Paths: The Decollectivization of Agrarian Reform Agriculture in Coastal Peru," in W. Thiesenhusen ed., *Searching for Agrarian Reform in Latin America* (Winchester, Mass.: Unwin Hyman, 1989).

9. In addition, social benefits already accessible to urban workers should be extended to the rural labor force.

BIBLIOGRAPHY

Alberts, T. *Agrarian Reform and Rural Poverty: A Case Study of Peru* Boulder, Colo.: Westview Press, 1983.

Alexander, L. *Debt Conversions: Economic Issues for Heavily Indebted Developing Countries.* International Finance Discussion Papers, no. 315. Washington, D.C.: Board of Governors of the Federal Reserve, 1987.

Altimir, O. *The Extent of Poverty in Latin America.* World Bank Staff Working Paper, no. 522. Washington, D.C.: World Bank, 1982.

Altimir, O. "Income Distribution Statistics in Latin America and Their Reliability." *Review of Income and Wealth* 33, no. 2 (June 1987): 111–156.

Arco, J., E. Margain, and R. Cherol, eds. *The Economic Integration Process of Latin America in the 1980s.* Washington, D.C.: Inter-American Development Bank, 1982.

Aspe, P., and P. Sigmund, eds. *The Political Economy of Income Distribution in Mexico* New York: Holmes & Meier, 1984.

Baer, W. "Import Substitution Industrialization in Latin America" *Latin American Research Review* 7, no.1 (1972): 95–122.

Baer, W. *The Brazilian Economy, Growth and Development.* New York: Praeger, 1983.

Baer, W., and I. Kerstenetsky. *Inflation and Growth in Latin America.* New Haven: Yale University Press, 1969.

Behrman, J. and J. Hanson, eds. *Short-Term Macroeconomic Policy in Latin America.* Cambridge, Mass.: National Bureau of Economic Research, 1979.

Bernstein, M. *Foreign Investment in Latin America: Cases and Attitudes.* New York: Alfred Knopf, 1966.

Berry, A. "Agrarian Structure, Rural Labour Markets and Trends in Rural Incomes in Latin America." In V. Urquidi and S. Trejo, eds., *Human Resources and Development: Latin America* vol. 4., London: Macmillan, 1983.

Berry, A. "Poverty and Inequality in Latin America." *Latin American Research Review* 22, no. 2 (1987): 202–214.

Berry, A., and W. Cline. *Agrarian Structure and Productivity in Developing Countries*. Baltimore: Johns Hopkins University Press, 1979.

Berry, A., and R. Soligo. *Economic Policy and Income Distribution in Colombia*. Boulder, Colo.: Westview Press, 1980.

Bethel, L., ed. *Spanish America after Independence, 1820–1870*. New York: Cambridge University Press, 1987.

Bethel, L., ed. *Latin America Economy and Society: 1870–1930*. New York: Cambridge University Press, 1989.

Bourguignon, F., W. Branson, and J. de Melo. *Adjustment and Income Distribution: A Counterfactual Analysis*. National Bureau of Economic Research Working Paper, no. 2943. Cambridge, Mass.: NBER, 1989.

Brass, T. "Agrarian Reform and the Struggle for Labor Power: A Peruvian Case Study." *Journal of Development Studies* 19, no. 3 (April 1983): 368–389.

Bresser Pereira, L. *Development and Crisis in Brazil: 1930–1983*. Boulder, Colo.: Westview Press, 1984.

Brockett, C. *Land, Power, and Poverty*. Winchester, Mass.: Unwin Hyman, 1988.

Brown, M. "Radical Reformism in Chile: 1964–1973." In W. Thiesenhusen, ed., *Searching for Agrarian Reform in Latin America*. Winchester, Mass.: Unwin Hyman, 1989.

Bruno, M., et al., eds, *Inflation Stabilization: The Experience of Israel, Argentina, Brazil, Bolivia and Mexico*. Cambridge, Mass.: The MIT Press, 1988.

Bruno, M., and S. Fischer, *The Aftermath of Stabilization*. Cambridge, Mass.: The MIT Press, 1991.

Bulmer-Thomas, V. *The Political Economy of Central America since 1920*. New York: Cambridge University Press, 1987.

Bunker, S. "Policy Implementation in an Authoritarian State: Colonization along Brazil's Transamazon Highway." *Latin American Research Review*, 18 no. 1 (1983): 33–58.

Caballero, J. M. "Agriculture and the Peasantry under Industrialization Pressures: Lessons from the Peruvian Experience." *Latin American Research Review* 19, no. 2 (1984): 3–42.

Calvo, G. "Fractured Liberalism: Argentina under Martinez de Hoz," *Economic Development and Cultural Change* 34 (April 1986): 511–533.

Calvo, G., R. Findlay, P. Kouri, and J. Braga de Macedo, eds. *Debt, Stabilization, and Development: Essays in Honor of Carlos Díaz-Alejandro*. Oxford: Basil Blackwell, 1989.

Cardoso, E. "Celso Furtado Revisited: The Post-War Years" *Economic Development and Cultural Change* 29 (1981): 117–128.

Cardoso, E. "The Great Depression and Commodity Exporting LDC's: The Case of Brazil." *Journal of Political Economy* 88 (1981) 1239–1250.

Cardoso, E. "Nineteenth Century Exchange Rates in Brazil: An Econometric Model," *Journal of Development Studies*. 19 (1983): 170–178.

Cardoso, E. "Latin America: Debt, Inflation and Stagnation: Which Way Now?" *Challenge* (May–June 1987): 11–17.

Cardoso, E. "Hyperinflation in Latin America." *Challenge* (February 1989): 11–19.

Cardoso, E. "Debt Cycles in Brazil and Argentina." In D. Felix, ed., *Debt and Transfiguration? Prospects for Latin America's Economic Revival*. Armonk: Sharpe, 1990.

Cardoso, E. "From Inertia to Megainflation: Brazil in the 1980s." In Michael Bruno and Stanley Fischer, eds., *The Aftermath of Stabilization*. Cambridge, Mass.: The MIT Press, 1990.

Cardoso, E., and R. Dornbusch. "Brazilian Debt Crises: Past and Present." In B. Eichengreen and Lindert eds., *The International Debt Crisis in Historical Perspective*. Cambridge, Mass.: The MIT Press, 1990.

Cardoso, E., and A. Fishlow. "The Macroeconomics of the Brazilian External Debt." In J. Sachs, ed., *Developing Country Debt and Economic Performance*, vol. 2. Chicago: Chicago University Press, 1990.

Cardoso, E., and A. Helwege. "Below the Line: Poverty in Latin America." *World Development* (1991), forthcoming.

Cardoso, F. H., and E. Faletto. *Dependency and Development in Latin America*. Berkeley: University of California Press, 1979.

Carter, M., and E. Alvarez. "Changing Paths: The Decollectivization of Agrarian Reform Agriculture in Coastal Peru." In W. Thiesenhusen, ed., *Searching for Agrarian Reform in Latin America*, Winchester, Mass.: Unwin Hyman, 1989.

Cavallo, D. "Argentina: Longterm Growth in the Light of External Balance Policies." in R. Dornbusch and L. Helmers, ed., *The Open Economy: Tools for Policymakers in Developing Countries*. New York: Oxford University Press, 1988.

Cline, W. *Economic Consequences of a Land Reform in Brazil*. Amsterdam: North-Holland, 1970.

Cline, W., and E. Delgado. *Economic Integration in Central America: A Study*. Washington, D.C.: Brookings Institution, 1978.

Collier, D. *The New Authoritarianism in Latin America*. Princeton: Princeton University Press, 1979.

Comisión Económica Para America Latina Y El Caribe (CEPAL). "Magnitud de la Pobreza en Ocho Paises de America Latina en 1986." Document for the Proyeto Regional para la Superación de la Pobreza. Mimeo. June 1989.

Coniff, M., ed., *Latin American Populism in Comparative Perspective*. Albuquerque: University of New Mexico Press, 1982.

Connolly, M. "The Speculative Attack on the Peso and the Real Exchange Rate: Argentina 1981." *Journal of International Money and Finance* 5 supplement (March 1986): 117–130.

Corbo, V., "Reforms and Macroeconomic Adjustment in Chile during 1974–84." *World Development* 13, no. 8 (August 1985).

Corbo, V., and J. de Melo. "Lessons from the Southern Cone Policy Reforms." *World Bank Research Observer* 2, no. 2 (July 1987).

Correa, H. "Sources of Economic Growth in Latin America" *Southern Economic Journal* 37 (1970): 17–31.

Couriel, A. "Poverty and Underemployment in Latin America." *CEPAL Review*, no. 24 (1984): 39–62.

Cuddington, J. *Capital Flight: Estimates, Issues, and Explanations*. Princeton Studies in International Finance, no. 58. Princeton: Princeton University, 1986.

Deere, C. D., "Rural Women and State Policy: The Latin American Agrarian Reform Experience." *World Development* 13, no. 9 (1985).

De Janvry, A. *The Agrarian Question and Reformism in Latin America*. Baltimore: Johns Hopkins University Press, 1981.

Denslow, D., and T. William. "Perspectives on Poverty and Income Inequality in Brazil." *World Development* 12 (1984): 1019–1028.

De Soto, H. *The Other Path*. New York: Harper & Row, 1987.

Devlin, R. *Debt and Crisis in Latin America: The Supply Side of the Story*. Princeton: Princeton University Press, 1989.

Díaz-Alejandro, C. *Essays on the Economic History of Argentina*. New Haven: Yale University Press, 1970.

Díaz-Alejandro, C. "Some Aspects of the 1982-1983 Brazilian Payments Crisis," Brookings Papers in Economic Activity, no. 1. Washington, D.C.: Brookings Institution, 1983.

Díaz-Alejandro, C. "Good-Bye Financial Repression, Hello Financial Crash" *Journal of Development Economics* 19, no. 1 (1985).

Dietz, J., and J. Street, *Latin America's Economic Development: Institutionalist and Structuralist Perspectives*. Boulder, Colo.: Lynne Rienner, 1987.

DiTella, G., and R. Dornbusch, eds. *The Political Economy of Argentina, 1946–1983*. Oxford: St. Antony's/Macmillan, 1989.

Dornbusch, R. "Mexico." *Economic Policy* (October 1988): 231–284.

Dornbusch, R. "Peru on the Brink." *Challenge* 31 (November-December 1988): 31–37.

Dornbusch, R. *The Road to Economic Recovery*. New York: Twentieth Century, 1989.

Dornbusch, R., and S. Edwards, eds. *Economic Populism in Latin America*. Chicago: Chicago University Press, 1990.

Dornbusch, R., and M. Simonsen. *Inflation Stabilization with Incomes Policy Support*. New York: Group of Thirty, 1987.

Dornbusch, R., F. Sturzenegger, and H. Wolf. *Extreme Inflation: Dynamics and Stabilization*. Brookings Papers in Economic Activity, no. 2. Washington, D.C.: Brookings Institution, 1990.

Eckstein, S., G. Donald, D. Horton, and T. Carroll. *Land Reform in Latin America: Bolivia, Chile, Mexico, Peru and Venezuela*. Staff Working Paper no. 275. Washington, D.C.: World Bank, 1978.

Economic Development and Cultural Change. Special Issue: Growth, Reform and Adjustment: Latin America's Trade and Macroeconomic Policies in the 1970s and 1980s. April 1986.

Edwards, S. "Stabilization with Liberalization: An Evaluation of Ten Years of Chile's Experience with Free Market Policies", *Economic Development and Cultural Change*. 33 (January 1985): 223–254.

Edwards, S. "Exchange Controls, Devaluations, and Real Exchange Rates: The Latin American Experience." *Economic Development and Cultural Change* (1989): 457–494.

Edwards, Sebastian, and Felipe Larrain. *Debt, Adjustment and Recovery: Latin America's Prospects for Growth and Development*. Oxford: Blackwell, 1989.

Eichengreen, B., and R. Portes. "Debt and Default in the 1930s: Causes and Consequences." *European Economic Review* 30 (June 1986): 599–640.

Enders, T., and R. Mattione. *Latin America: The Crisis of Debt and Growth*. Washington, D.C.: Brookings Institution, 1984.

Falcoff, M. *Modern Chile: 1970–1989, A Critical History*. New Brunswick, N.J.: Transaction Publishers, 1989.

Felix, D. "Alternative Outcomes of the Latin American Debt Crisis: Lessons from the Past" *Latin American Research Review*. 22, no. 2 (1987).

Fernandez, R. "An Empirical Inquiry on the Short-Run Dynamics of Output and Prices." *American Economic Review* 67 (1977): 595–609.

Feuerlein, W., and E. Hannan. *Dollars in Latin America: An Old Problem in a New Setting*. New York: Council on Foreign Relations, 1941.

Ffrench-Davis, R., "Debt-Equity Swaps in Chile." *Cambridge Journal of Economics* 14 (March 1990): 109–126.

Fields, G. "Who Benefits from Economic Development?" *American Economic Review* 67 (1977): 570–582.

Fields, G. "Employment and Growth in Costa Rica." *World Development* 16, 12 (1988).

Figueroa, A. *Capitalist Development and the Peasant Economy in Peru.* Cambridge: Cambridge University Press, 1984.

Fishlow, A. "Origins and Consequences of Import Substitution in Brazil" In L. diMarco, ed., *International Economics and Development.* New York: Academic Press, 1972.

Fishlow, A. "Brazilian Size Distribution of Income." *American Economic Review* 62 (May 1972): 391–402.

Fishlow, A. "Lessons from the Past: Capital Markets during the 19th Century and the Interwar Period." *International Organization* 39, no. 3 (1985).

Fishlow, A. "Lessons of the 1890s for the 1980s." In R. Findlay, ed., *Debt, Stabilization and Development.* New York: Basil Blackwell, 1988.

Fitzgerald, F. "The Reform of the Cuban Economy: 1976–86." *Journal of Latin American Studies* 21 (May 1989): 283–310.

Fodor, J. "Perón's Policies for Agricultural Exports, 1946–48: Dogmatism or Commonsense?" In D. Rock, ed., *Argentina in the Twentieth Century.* Pittsburgh: University of Pittsburgh Press, 1975.

Foxley, A., ed. *Income Distribution in Latin America.* Cambridge: Cambridge University Press, 1976.

Foxley, A. *Latin American Experiments in Neoconservative Economics.* Berkeley: University of California Press, 1983.

Furtado, C. *The Economic Growth of Brazil.* Berkeley: University of California Press, 1965.

Furtado, C. *Economic Development of Latin America.* Cambridge: Cambridge University Press, 1976.

Germani, G. *Authoritarianism, Facism, and National Populism.* New Brunswick, N.J.: Transaction Books, 1978.

Glewwe, P. *The Distribution of Welfare in Peru in 1985–86.* LSMS Working Paper no.42. Washington, D.C.: World Bank, 1988.

Goldsmith, R. *Desenvolvimento Financeiro Sob Um Século de Inflação.* São Paulo: Harper & Row do Brasil, 1986.

Goodman, D. "Rural Economy and Society." In E. Bacha and H. Klein, eds., *Social Change in Brazil, The Incomplete Transition.* Albuquerque: University of New Mexico Press, 1989.

Grilli, E., and M. C. Yang. "Primary Commodity Prices, Manufactured Goods Prices, and the Terms of Trade of Developing Countries: What the Long Run Shows." *World Bank Economic Review* 1 (January 1988): 1–48.

Hanson, J. "The Short-Run Relation between Growth and Inflation in Latin America" *American Economic Review* 70 (1980): 972–989.

Hanson, J. "Growth and Distribution in Colombia" *Latin American Research Review* 22 no. 1 (1987): 255–264.

Harberger, A. "Economic Policy Problems in Latin America" *Journal of Political Economy* 78 (1970): 1007–1016.

Harberger, A. "The Chilean Economy in the 1970s: Crisis, Stabilization, Liberalization, Reform." in K. Brunner and A. Meltzer, eds., *Economic Policy in a World of Change.* Amsterdam: North-Holland, 1982.

Hartlyn, J., and S. Morley. *Latin American Political Economy: Financial Crisis and Political Change.* Boulder, Colo.: Westview Press, 1986.

Helwege, A. "Latin American Agricultural Performance in the Debt Crisis: Salvation or Stagnation?" *Latin American Perspectives* 17 (Fall 1990): 57–75.

Helwege, A. "Is There Any Hope for Nicaragua?" *Challenge* 32 (November-December 1989): 22–28.

Helwege, A. "Three Socialist Experiences in Latin America: Surviving U.S. Economic Pressure." *Bulletin of Latin American Research* 8, no. 2 (Winter 1990): 211–234.

Hirschman, A. "The Political Economy of Import Substituting Industrialization in Latin America" *Quarterly Journal of Economics* 82 (1968): 1–32.

Hirschman, A. *How to Divest in Latin America, and Why.* International Finance Section. Princeton: Princeton University Press, 1969.

Hirschman, A. *Journeys toward Progress.* New York: Norton, 1973.

Hirschman, A. *A Bias for Hope.* Boulder, Colo.: Westview, 1985.

Hirschman, A. "The Political Economy of Latin American Development: Seven Exercises in Retrospection." *Latin American Research Review* 22 no. 3 (1987): 7–36.

Hoffmann, H. "Poverty and Prosperity: What Is Changing?" In E. Bacha and H. Klein, eds., *Social Change in Brazil: The Incomplete Transition.* Albuquerque: University of New Mexico Press, 1989.

Inter-American Development Bank, *Our Own Agenda.* Washington, D.C.: Inter-American Development Bank, 1990.

International Monetary Fund. *Fund-Supported Programs, Fiscal Policy and Income Distribution.* Occasional Paper, no. 46 Washington D.C.: International Monetary Fund, 1986.

Ireson, W. R. "Landholding, Agricultural Modernization, and Income Concentration: A Mexican Example." *Economic Development and Cultural Change* 35 (January 1987): 351–366.

Jarvis, L. *Chilean Agriculture under Military Rule.* Berkeley: University of California, 1985.

Jarvis, L. "The Unraveling of Chile's Agrarian Reform, 1973–1986." In W. Thiesenhusen, ed., *Searching for Agrarian Reform in Latin America.* Winchester, Mass.: Unwin Hyman, 1989.

Kakwani, M. *Income Inequality and Poverty: Methods of Estimation and Policy Implications.* New York: Oxford University Press, 1980.

Kay, C. "Achievements and Contradictions of the Peruvian Agrarian Reform," *Journal of Development Studies* 18 (January 1982): 141–170.

Khashayar, K., and D. Clark. "A Case Study of Effects of Developing Country Integration on Trade Flows: The Andean Pact." *Journal of Latin American Studies* 22 (May 1990): 331–352.

Klaren, P., and T. Bossert, *Promises of Development: Theories of Change in Latin America*. Boulder, Colo.: Westview Press, 1986.

Kuczynski, P. *The Peruvian Democracy under Economic Stress: An Account of the Belaunde Administration, 1963–68*. Princeton: Princeton University Press, 1977.

Lall, S. "Is Dependency a Useful Concept in Understanding Development?" *World Development* 3 (1975): 799–810.

Larrain, F., and M. Selowski, eds. *The Public Sector and the Latin American Crisis*. San Francisco: ICS Press, 1991.

Larrain F., and A. Velasco. *Can Swaps Solve the Debt Crisis? Lessons from the Chilean Experience*. Princeton Studies in International Finance, no. 69. Princeton: Princeton University, November 1990.

Lastarria-Cornhiel, S. "Agrarian Reforms of the 1960s and 1970s in Peru." In W. Thiesenhusen, ed., *Searching for Agrarian Reform in Latin America*. Winchester, Mass.: Unwin Hyman, 1989.

Lecaillon, J., et al. *Income Distribution and Economic Development: An Analytical Survey*. Geneva: International Labour Office, 1984.

Leonard, H. J. *Natural Resources and Economic Development in Central America*. New Brunswick: Transaction Books, 1987.

Levinson, J., and J. Onis, *The Alliance That Lost Its Way: A Critical Report on the Alliance for Progress*. New York: Quadrangle Books, 1970.

Londono, J. L. "Income Distribution in Colombia: Turning Points, Catching Up and Other Kuznetsian Ideas." Mimeo. Havard University, 1989.

Looney, R. *Economic Policy Making in Mexico: Factors underlying the 1982 Crisis*. Durham, N.C.: Duke University Press, 1985.

Love, J. "Raul Prebisch and the Origins of the Doctrine of Unequal Exchange." In J. Dietz and J. Street, eds., *Latin America's Economic Development*. Boulder, Colo.: Lynne Rienner, 1987.

Lustig, N. "The Impact of the Economic Crisis on Living Standards in Mexico: 1982–1985." *World Development* (1991), forthcoming.

McClintock C., and A. Lowenthal, eds. *The Peruvian Experiment Reconsidered*. Princeton: Princeton University Press, 1983.

Maddison, Angus. *Two Crises: Latin America and Asia, 1929–38 and 1973–83*. Paris: OECD, 1985.

Mahar. D., *Frontier Development Policy in Brazil: A Study of Amazonia*. New York: Praeger Press, 1979.

Mallon,, R. and J. Sourrouille. *Economic Policy Making in a Conflict Society*. Cambridge: Harvard University Press, 1975.

Malloy, J., ed. *Authoritarianism and Corporatism in Latin America*. Pittsburgh: University of Pittsburgh Press, 1977.

Malloy, J., and R. Thorn. *Beyond the Revolution: Bolivia since 1952*. Pittsburgh: University of Pittsburgh, 1971.

Manzetti, L. "Argentine-Brazilian Economic Integration: An Early Appraisal" *Latin American Research Review* 21, no. 3 (1990).

Marichal, C. *A Century of Debt Crises in Latin America: From Independence to the Great Depression*. Princeton: Princeton University Press, 1989.

May, H. *Problems and Prospects of the Alliance for Progress*. New York: Praeger, 1968.

Melvin, M. "The Dollarization of Latin America as a Market forced Monetary Reform: Evidence and Implications." *Economic Development and Cultural Change* 36 (April 1988): 543–558.

Mendelberg, U. "The Impact of the Bolivan Agrarian Reform on Class Formation." *Latin American Perspectives* (Summer 1985).

Merrick, T. "Population since 1945." In E. Bacha and H. Klein, eds., *Social Change in Brazil: The Incomplete Transition*. Albuquerque: University of New Mexico Press, 1989.

Mesa-Lago, C. "Social Security and Development in Latin America." *CEPAL Review*, no. 28 (April 1986): 135–150.

Middlebrook, K., and C. Rico, eds., *The United States and Latin America in the 1980s*. Pittsburgh: University of Press, 1986.

Molina, S. "Poverty: Description and Analysis of Policies for Overcoming It" *CEPAL Review* no. 18 (December 1982): 87–110.

Montiel, P. *Empirical Analysis of High-Inflation Episodes in Argentina, Brazil and Israel*. IMF Staff Papers. Washington, D.C.: International Monetary Fund, 1989.

Morley, S. *Labor Markets and Inequitable Growth* Cambridge: Cambridge University Press, 1982.

Morris, F., et al. *Latin America's Banking System in the 1980s*. World Bank Discussion Paper, no. 81. Washington, D.C.: World Bank, 1990.

Mosley,, P. "Achievements and Contradiction of the Peruvian Agrarain Reform: A Regional Perspective." *Journal of Development Studies* 21 (April 1985): 440–448.

Musgrove, P. "Food Needs and Absolute Poverty in Urban South America." *Review of Income and Wealth* 31 (March 1985): 63–84.

Newfarmer, R. *Profits, Progress and Poverty: Case Studies of International Industries in Latin America*. Notre Dame: University of Notre Dame Press, 1985.

Ocampo, J. A. "Recurrent Hyperinflation and Stabilization in Nicaragua." Mimeo. 1990.

Ocampo, J. A. "Investment Determinants and Financing in Colombia." Paper delivered at the World Bank Conference on "Latin America: Facing the Challenges of Adjustment and Growth," Caracas, 1990. Mimeo.

O'Donnell, G. *Modernization and Bureaucratic-Authoritarianism: Studies in South American Politics*. Berkeley: University of California, 1973.

O'Donnell, G., Schmitter, and L. Whitehead, eds., *Transitions from Authoritarian Rule: Latin America*. Baltimore: Johns Hopkins University Press, 1986.

Otero, G. "Agrarian Reform in Mexico: Capitalism and the State" In W. Thiesenhusen, ed., *Searching for Agrarian Reform in Latin America*. Winchester, Mass.: Unwin Hyman, 1989.

Pacini, D., and C. Franquemont, eds., *Coca and Cocaine*. Cambridge, Mass.: Cultural Survival, 1986.

Palma, G., "Dependency and Development: A Critical Overview." in D. Seers, ed., *Dependency Theory: A Critical Reassessment*. London: Frances Pinter Publishers, 1981.

Palmer, D. S., "Rebellion in Rural Peru: The Origins and Evolution of Sendero Luminoso." *Comparative Politics*. 18 (1986): 127–146.

Pastor, M. "The Effects of IMF Programs in the Third World: Debate and Evidence from Latin America." *World Development* 15 (February 1987): 249–262.

Pastor, M. "Capital Flight from Latin America." *World Development* 18, 1 (1990).

Pazos, F. "Have Import Substitution Policies Precipitated the Debt Crisis?" *Journal of Interamerican Studies and World Affairs* 27 (Winter, 1985–1986): 57–74.

Pfeffermann, G. P., and R. Webb. *The Distribution of Income in Brazil*. World Bank Staff Working Paper, no. 356. Washington, D.C.: World Bank, September 1979.

PREALC. *Mercado de Trabajo en Cifras, 1950–1980*. Santiago: Oficina Internacional del Trabajo, 1982.

Prebisch, R. "Peripheral Capitalism." *CEPAL Review*, no. 1 (1976).

Prosterman, R., and J. Riedinger. *Land Reform and Democratic Development*. Baltimore: Johns Hopkins University Press, 1987.

Ramos, J. *Neo-Conservative Economics in the Southern Cone of Latin America*. Baltimore: Johns Hopkins University Press, 1986.

Randall, L. *The Political Economy of Venezuelan Oil*. New York: Praeger, 1987.

Remmer, K. "The Politics of Economic Stabilization: IMF Standby Programs in Latin America, 1954–1984." *Comparative Politics* 19 (October 1986): 1–24.

Riding, A. *Distant Neighbors*. New York: Vintage, 1986.

Rippy, J. F. *British Investment in Latin America. 1822-1949*, New York: Arno Press, 1977.

Rock, D. "The Survival and Restoration of Perónism." In D. Rock, ed., *Argentina in the Twentieth Century*. Pittsburgh: University of Pittsburgh Press, 1975.

Rock, D. *Argentina: 1516–1982*. Berkeley: University of California Press, 1985.

Rodriguez, C. "The Argentine Stabilization Plan of December 20th." *World Development* 10 no. 10 (1982): 801–812.

Rodriguez, M. A. "Consequences of Capital Flight for Latin America." In D. Lessard and J. Williamson, eds., *Capital Flight and Third World Debt*. Washington, D.C.: Institute for International Economics, 1987.

Sachs, J. "Comprehensive Debt Retirement: The Bolivian Example." Brookings Papers on Economic Activity, no. 2 Washington, D.C.: Brookings Institution, 1988.

Sachs, J., *Social Conflict and Populist Policies in Latin America*. Working Paper, no. 2897. Cambridge, Mass: National Bureau of Economic Research, 1989.

Sachs, J., ed. *Developing Country Debt and Economic Performance*. vol. 2 Chicago: Chicago University Press, 1990.

Sampaio, Y. de S. B. "A Questão Agrária no Brasil e o Plano de Reforma Agrária do MIRAD." In A. S. Brandão, ed., *Os Principais Problemas da Agricultura Brasileira: Análise e Sugestões*. Rio de Janeiro: Instituto de Pesquisa Econômica e Social, 1988.

Sanderson, S. *The Transformation of Mexican Agriculture*. Princeton: Princeton University Press, 1986.

Scheetz, T. *Peru and the International Monetary Fund*. Pittsburgh: University of Pittsburgh Press, 1986.

Scott, C. "Rural Poverty in Latin America and the Caribbean." Mimeo. Prepared for the Special FAO Study on Potential and Perspectives for Food and Rural Development. London: London School, 1987.

Schramm G., and J. Warford. *Environment Management and Economic Development*. Baltimore: Johns Hopkins Universtiy Press, 1989.

Sedlacek, G. L., and R. Paes de Barros, ed., *Mercado de Trabalho e Distribuição de Renda: Uma Coletânea*. Rio de Janeiro: IPEA, Série Monográfica, 1989.

Selowsky, M. *Balancing Trickle Down and Basic Needs Strategies*. World Bank Staff Working Papers, no. 335. Washington, D.C.: World Bank, 1985.

Serven L., and A. Solimano. "Private Investment and Macroeconomic Adjustment in LDCs: Theory, Country Experiences and Policy Implications." Mimeo. Washington, D.C.: World Bank, August 1990.

Sheahan, J., *Patterns of Development in Latin America: Poverty, Repression, and Economic Strategy*, Princeton: Princeton University Press, 1987.

Sheahan, J. "Peru: Economic Policies and Structural Change, 1968–1978," *Journal of Development Studies*. 7, 1 (1980).

Sideri, S. *Chile, 1970–73: Economic Development and Its International Setting*. The Hague: Martinus-Nijhoff, 1979.

Simonsen, M. "The Developing Country Debt Problem." in G. Smith and J. Cuddington, eds., *International Debt and the Developing Countries*. Washington, D.C.: World Bank, 1985.

Singer, H. W. "The Distribution of Gains between Investing and Borrowing Countries." *American Economic Review* 40 (May 1950): 473–480.

Skidmore, T. *Politics in Brazil, 1930–1964: An Experiment in Democracy*. Oxford: Oxford University Press, 1967.

Skidmore, T. *The Politics of Military Rule in Brazil: 1964–1985*. New York: Oxford University Press, 1988.

Skidmore, T., and P. Smith. *Modern Latin America*. Oxford: Oxford University Press, 1984.

Solimano, A. *How Private Investment Reacts to Changing Macroeconomic Conditions: The Case of Chile in the 1980s*. World Bank Working Paper no. 212. Washington, D.C.: World Bank, 1989.

Stahler-Sholk, R. "Stabilization, Destabilization and the Popular Classes in Nicaragua, 1979–1988." *Latin American Research Review* 25 (1990): 55–88.

Stallings, B. *Banker to the Third World*. Berkeley: University of California Press, 1987.

Stein, S. *Populism in Peru*. Madison: University of Wisconsin Press, 1980.

Stepan, A., ed., *Authoritarian Brazil*. New Haven: Yale University Press, 1973.

Summers, R., and A. Heston. "Improved International Comparisons of Real Product and Its Composition: 1950–1980." *Review of Income and Wealth* 30 (June 1984): 207–262.

Swett, F. *The Political Economy of Development and Liberalization in Ecuador, 1948–88*. Occasional Papers, no. 20. San Francisco: International Center for Economic Growth, 1989.

Taylor, L. *Structuralist Macroeconomics*. New York: Basic Books, 1981.

Taylor, L., E. Bacha, and E. Cardoso. *Models of Growth and Distribution in Brazil*. New York: Oxford University Press, 1980.

Thiesenhusen, W. "Rural Development Questions in Latin America." *Latin America Research Review* 22 no. 1 (1987): 171–203.

Thiesenhusen, W. ed., *Searching for Agrarian Reform in Latin America*. Winchester, Mass.: Unwin Hyman, 1989.

Thomas, V. "Differences in Income and Poverty within Brazil." *World Development* 15, 2 (1987).

Thome, J. "Law, Conflict and Change: Frei's Law and Allende's Agrarian Reform" In W. Thiesenhusen, ed., *Searching for Agrarian Reform in Latin America*. Winchester, Mass.: Unwin Hyman, 1989.

Thorp, R., ed., *Latin America in the 1930's*. Oxford: St. Anthony/ MacMillan, 1984.

Thorp, R., and G. Bertram. *Peru 1890–1977: Growth and Policy in an Open Economy*. London: Macmillan, 1978.

Thorp, R., and L. Whitehead. *Latin American Debt and the Adjustment Crisis*. Pittsburgh: University of Pittsburgh Press, 1987.

Tokman, V. "Growth, Underemployment, and Income Distribution." In M. Syrquin and S. Teitel, eds., *Trade, Stability, Technology and Equity in Latin America*. New York: Academic Press, 1982.

Twomey, M., and A. Helwege, eds., *Modernization and Stagnation: Latin American Agriculture into the 1990's*. Westport, Conn.: Greenwood Press, forthcoming.

United Nations. *Foreign Direct Investment in Latin America: Recent Trends, Prospects and Policy Issues*. UNCTC Current Studies, ser. A, no.3. August 1986.

Urrutia, M. *Winners and Losers in Colombia's Economic Growth of the 1970s*. New York: Oxford University Press, 1985.

Walker, T., ed., *Nicaragua: The First Five Years*. New York: Praeger, 1985.

Weeks, J. *Limits to Capitalist Development: The Industrialization of Peru, 1950–1980*. Boulder, Colo.: Westview, 1985.

Wiarda, H. "Misreading Latin America Again." *Foreign Policy* 65 (1987): 135–153.

Wiarda, H., and H. Kline, eds., *Latin American Politics and Development*. 2 ed. Boulder, Colo.: Westview Press, 1985.

Williamson, J. *Latin American Adjustment: How Much Has Happened?* Washington, D.C.: Institute for International Economics, 1990.

Williamson, J. *The Progress of Policy Reform in Latin America*. Washington D.C.: Institute for International Economics, 1990.

Williamson, J., ed. *Inflation and Indexation*. Washington, D.C.: Institute for International Economics, 1985.

Wionczek, M., ed. *Politics and Economics of the External Debt Crisis: The Latin American Experience*. Boulder, Colo.: Westview Press, 1985.

World Bank. *Chile: An Economy in Transition*. Washington D.C.: World Bank Country Study, 1979.

World Bank. *Colombia, Social Programs for Poverty Alleviation*. Washington, D.C.: World Bank, 1990.

World Development. Special Issue: Latin America in the Post Import Substitution Era. 1977.

World Development. Special Issue: Liberalization with Stabilization in the Southern Cone of Latin America. August 1985.

World Development. Special Issue: The Resurgence of Inflation in Latin America. August 1987.

World Resources Institute. *World Resources 1990–91: Special Section on Latin America.* Washington, D.C.: World Resources Institute, 1990.

Wynia, G. *Argentina in the Post-War Era: Politics and Economic Policy Making in a Divided Society.* Albuquerque: University of New Mexico Press, 1978.

Zevallos, F. O. *The Peruvian Puzzle.* New York: Priority Press Publications, 1989.

Zimbalist, A., ed. *Cuba's Socialist Economy toward the 1990s.* Boulder, Colo.: Lynne Rienner Publishers, 1987.

Zimbalist, A., ed. *The Cuban Political Economy.* Boulder, Colo.: Westview Press, 1988.

INDEX

Accommodation, 147–148
Aeromexico, 175
Agrarian reform, 71, 205, 213, 220, 261(table). *See also* Land reform
Agricultural sector, 3, 11, 17, 20, 34, 94, 147, 205, 206, 242, 243, 252, 264, 274, 277
  colonial, 26, 27, 29–30, 31, 34–37, 289n.2
  exports, 13–14, 16, 33, 42, 52
  and import substitution, 96–97
  labor force in, 6, 85, 91
  land reform in, 255–256
  in Mexico, 269–271
  in Nicaragua, 214, 215
  in Peru, 272–276
  productivity in, 125–126, 253–254, 265, 275 technology in, 258–259
  trade competition, 39–40
Aid, foreign, 63–64, 65(table), 70, 211, 223, 248, 290n.4
Airline industry, 16, 173
Alfonsín, Raúl, 172, 185, 190, 191, 203, 221 Allende, Salvador, 161, 205
  agrarian reform of, 220, 262
  macroeconomic policies of, 210–212, 221
Alliance for Progress, 63, 64, 262
Altimir, Oscar, 226, 227, 229
Amazon, 262–263, 264

Andean Pact, 105
Andes, 3, 27
Aprismo, 52
Argentina, 3, 6, 12, 27, 45, 50, 92, 95, 99, 100, 114, 117, 124, 129, 155, 159, 181, 183(table), 187, 195, 197, 236, 294n.12
  agriculture in, 39, 91(table)
  austral plan of, 189, 190–191
  capital flight in, 119, 121, 122, 139
  debt in, 110, 112, 113
  economy of, 24, 42, 44(figs.), 94, 123, 186
  hide production in, 28, 32
  inflation in, 18, 145(fig.), 146, 153, 161
  investment in, 62, 73, 115
  populism in, 204, 206–207
  poverty in, 19, 229, 231, 296nn.3, 7, 8
  real exchange rates in, 77, 78(fig.), 119, 120(fig.)
  stabilization programs in, 169, 171, 177, 184–185
  trade with, 33, 40, 49, 102
Arreglo Romero, 113
Aspe, Pedro, 130–131
Austerity programs, 81, 178–179. *See also* Stabilization programs; International Monetary Fund